FURTHER DOCUMENTS FROM
F. TAYLOR OSTRANDER

RESEARCH IN THE HISTORY OF ECONOMIC THOUGHT AND METHODOLOGY

Series Editors: Warren J. Samuels, Jeff E. Biddle
and Ross B. Emmett

Recent Volumes:

RESEARCH IN THE HISTORY OF ECONOMIC THOUGHT AND
METHODOLOGY   VOLUME 24-B

FURTHER DOCUMENTS FROM F. TAYLOR OSTRANDER

EDITED BY

WARREN J. SAMUELS

*Department of Economics, Michigan State University,
East Lansing, MI 48824, USA.*

ELSEVIER
JAI

Amsterdam – Boston – Heidelberg – London – New York – Oxford
Paris – San Diego – San Francisco – Singapore – Sydney – Tokyo
JAI Press is an imprint of Elsevier

JAI Press is an imprint of Elsevier
The Boulevard, Langford Lane, Kidlington, Oxford OX5 1GB, UK
Radarweg 29, PO Box 211, 1000 AE Amsterdam, The Netherlands
525 B Street, Suite 1900, San Diego, CA 92101-4495, USA

First edition 2006

British Library Cataloguing in Publication Data
A catalogue record for this book is available from the British Library

ISBN-13: 978-0-7623-1354-9
ISBN-10: 0-7623-1354-4
ISSN: 0743-4154 (Series)

> For information on all JAI Press publications
> visit our website at books.elsevier.com

Printed and bound in The Netherlands

06 07 08 09 10 10 9 8 7 6 5 4 3 2 1

Working together to grow
libraries in developing countries

www.elsevier.com | www.bookaid.org | www.sabre.org

ELSEVIER   BOOK AID
             International   Sabre Foundation

CONTENTS

OTHER MATERIALS

LIST OF CONTRIBUTORS

Kirk D. Johnson	Department of Economics, Goldey-Beacom College, Wilmington, DE, USA
F. Taylor Ostrander	112 Ide Road, Williamstown, MA, USA
Warren J. Samuels	8476 SW 10th Road, Gainesville, FL 32607, USA

F. TAYLOR OSTRANDER:
UNDERGRADUATE COURSES
AT WILLIAMS COLLEGE

MATERIAL FROM ECONOMICS 1, TAUGHT BY WALTER B. SMITH, WILLIAMS COLLEGE, FALL 1929

Kirk D. Johnson (Editor) and
Warren J. Samuels (Editor)

INTRODUCTION

Taylor Ostrander's notes from Economics 1-2, taken during the 1929–30 academic year, provide insight into how the Principles of Economics course was taught at a prestigious liberal arts college at that time. Ostrander took Economics 1 at a momentous point not only in history but also as an environmental factor having great impact on his personal career. He worked on Wall Street during the stock market crash of October 1929. This was nothing if not momentous and through the Great Depression and the New Deal, starting in 1935, and World War II and beyond Ostrander found himself working in government agencies.

Ostrander's biography is given in Volume 22B, 2004.

Walter Buckingham Smith received his B.A. degree from Oberlin College in 1917, and his M.A. and Ph.D. from Harvard, in 1924 and 1928, respectively, also studying at the University of Chicago. He taught at the University of Minnesota (1922–23) and Wellesley College (1924–29) prior to moving to Williams in 1929 where he was Professor of Economics until 1950, at which time he moves to Claremont College. He published *Fluctuations in American Business, 1790–1860*, with Arthur Cole, in 1935 and *Economic Aspects of the*

Further Documents From F. Taylor Ostrander
Research in the History of Economic Thought and Methodology, Volume 24-B, 3–54
Copyright © 2006 by Elsevier Ltd.
All rights of reproduction in any form reserved
ISSN: 0743-4154/doi:10.1016/S0743-4154(06)24021-5

Second Bank of the United States, both with Harvard University Press in 1953. He also published a number of journal articles. Smith was born in 1895 and died in 1971.

Smith had a serious impact on Ostrander. Largely because of his Economics 1-2, Ostrander became an economics major. Smith, Ostrander considers, was largely responsible for his being invited to return to Williams to teach, after only two years of graduate work, on a one-year appointment as Instructor in Economics for 1934–35. During that year, Smith, breaking with custom, asked Ostrander to supervise a Senior student in his Honors Work in economics. The student was Herbert Stein, whom Ostrander considers brilliant.

Turning to the lectures, after a discussion of speculation, Smith provided, *inter alia*, a list of the amounts of currency in circulation in the U.S. as of November 1, 1929. The data was up-to-date but the nature of the ensuing decade and the respective roles of speculation and monetary and banking factors in creating depression were unimaginable. John Maynard Keynes was a monetary theorist, prominent enough but not the magisterial figure who emerged in mid-decade. The "Black" days – Black Thursday, 24 October; Black Monday, 28 October; and Black Tuesday, 29 October – pass undesignated. Still, business cycles are examined, with a narrow notion of "depression" as one phase; so also are business cycle theories examined and critiqued.

Minor corrections have been made. Ostrander numbered his sheets of notepaper 1, 2, 3, et seq with 1-A designating the back of the first page. The contents of -A pages – some of which are continuations of the lecture notes – are so designated and placed within square brackets. Most non-A pages continue the material of the previous non-A page. And unlike the transcriptions of other of Ostrander's notes, we have chosen not to begin each line with a capital letter, instead retaining the practice of the original not to do so. Significant punctuation changes from the original are intended to improve the clarity of these notes.

The sequence of materials is as follows: Assignments for Economics 1 and Ostrander's notes from Economics 1, followed by the assignments and notes from Economics 2.

Included with the Economics 1 materials kept by Ostrander is a newspaper clipping, as such unidentified as to paper name and date, but from the New York Times, April 13, 1931, p. 32. (Ostrander, noting that the date of publication was one year later than this course, thinks he must have misfiled the clipping and doubled the error (when he did not know its exact date) by guessing in his handwritten line at the top of the page that the clipping was from "Late 1929–Early 1930"). The radio talk described therein received considerable attention – even though Keynes's middle name was wrongly given. The article follows:

KEYNES SAYS SLUMP MAY LAST FIVE YEARS
British Financial Expert in Radio Talk Decries Prediction of an Early Recovery

It will be from two to five years before the present economic slump is entirely overcome, according to John Murray [sic!] Keynes, English economist and principal representative of the British Treasury at the Paris peace conference, who spoke over the radio yesterday from London over WABC and the Columbia network.

Characterizing the slump as "one of the most violent which has occurred in economic history," Mr. Keynes said that the problem of recovery would be correspondingly severe. Of those experts who predict a speedy return to world prosperity he said:

"The spokesmen of the business world, though they are not so gay and foolish as they were a year ago, still, it seems to me, are far too optimistic and have no sound bases for their optimistic talk. They predict a business recovery six months hence and a year hence for no better reason, so far as I can discover, than that so many months are surely long enough for something to happen."

Mr. Keynes observed that the science of economics, banking and finance was in a backward state, and declared that those who represented themselves as the experts "talk much greater rubbish than an ordinary man can ever be capable of."

(1) Class Notes of F. Taylor Ostrander

Economics 1.

Fall 1929

Assignments for Economics 1

I. INTRODUCTION

1. The subject matter of economics
   Read: Taussig, F. W., Principles of Economics. (1924) Chapter 1.
2. Fundamental characteristics of the present economic order
   Read: Garver, F. B. and Hansen, A. H., Principles of Economics. (1928) Chapter 3.
   Taylor, F. M., Principles of Economics. (1918) Chapter 2.

II. PRODUCTION

1. Labor in Production
   Read: Taussig, Principles. Chapters 2 and 3.
   Taylor, F. W., Scientific Management (1919)
   Smith, Adam, The Wealth of Nations. Edited by Cannan. Book I, Chapters 1, 2, and 3.
2. Capital
   Read: Taussig, Principles. Chapter 5.
   Garver and Hansen, Principles. pp. 464–468.
   Mill, J. S., Principles of Political Economy. Edited by Ashley. Chapter 4.
3. Management.
   Read: Garver and Hansen, Principles. Chapter 4.

Taussig, Principles. Chapter 6.

Lough, W. H., Business Finance (1917) Chapters 2, 3, and 4.

4. The combination of the factors of production

Garver and Hansen, Principles. Chapter 5.

Taussig, Principles. Chapter 4.

Federated American Engineering Societies. Waste in Industry. (1921) Chapters 2 and 3.

III. VALUE AND THE EXCHANGE OF GOODS

1. Value

a. Introduction

Read: Garver and Hansen, Principles. Chapter 6. pp. 98, 99

Taussig, Principles. Chapter 8.

b. Market Price (Competitive)

Taussig, Principles. Chapter 10.

Garver and Hansen, Principles. Chapters 7, 8, and 9.

[Handwritten, in margin: hour test, Nov 18, 4 pm, 1 Stetson Hall]

c. Costs and normal price (Competitive)

(a) The meaning of costs

Read: Davenport, H. J., The Economics of Enterprise. (1913) Chapter 11.

Garver and Hansen, Principles. Chapters 10, 11, and 12.

(b) Value under conditions of constant cost

Read: Taussig, Principles. Chapter 12.

Garver and Hansen, Principles. Chapter 13.

(c) Value under conditions of increasing cost

Read: Taussig, Principles. Chapter 13.

Garver and Hansen, Principles. Chapter 14.

(d) Value under conditions of decreasing cost

Read: Taussig, Principles. Chapter 14.

Garver and Hansen, Principles. Chapter 15.

d. Value under conditions of monopoly

Read: Taussig, Principles. Chapter 15.

Garver and Hansen, Principles. Chapter 16.

e. Speculation and prices

Read: Taussig, Principles. Chapter 11.

Garver and Hansen, Principles. Chapter 19.

Minneapolis Board of Trade, Handling the Farmers Grain.

Ibid, Modern Grain Exchanges.

Hardy, C. O., Risk and Risk Bearing. (1923) Chapters 11 and 12.

2. Money and banking
   a. Metallic money and government paper money.
      Read: Taussig, Principles. Chapters 17 and 23.
   b. Commercial banking
      (a) Banking operations
          Read: Taussig, Principles. Chapters 24 and 25.
             Fisher, I., Elementary Principles of Economics (1926)
             Chapter 9.
             Dunbar, C. F., History and Theory of Banking (4th
             edition) Chapters 1 and 2. [Handwritten: "Chapters
             11 and 12 in original"]
[Handwritten in margin: Hour Test, Dec 16]
      (b) Commercial banking in the United States
          Read: Taussig, Principles. Chapters 27 and 26 [Latter
             handwritten]
             Dunbar, History and Theory of Banking. Chapters 11
             and 12.
      (c) Changes in prices
          Read: Taussig, Principles. Chapter 22.
             Garver and Hansen, Principles. Chapter 21.
      (d) The theory of money and prices
          Read: Taussig, Principles. Chapters 18 and 30.
             Garver and Hansen, Principles. Chapter 22.
             Fisher, I., Elementary Principles of Economics. Chapter 8.
      (e) The business cycle
          Read: Taussig, Principles. Chapters 28 and 29.
             Garver and Hansen, Principles. Chapter 23.
             Mitchell, W. C., and others, Business Cycles and
             Unemployment. pp. 5–18.
3. International trade and exchange
   a. The foreign exchanges
      Read: Taussig, Principles. Chapter 32.
         Garver and Hansen, Principles. Chapter 34.
   b. The balance of trade and the balance of payments
      Read: Taussig, Principles. Chapter 33. [Handwritten between lines: or]
         Garver and Hansen, Principles. Chapter 35.
[Handwritten in margin: Midyear – Fri, Jan 30. NB: There is an error in either the
date or the day of the week. January 30, 1930 was a Thursday]
   c. The theory of international trade
      Read: Taussig, Principles. Chapters 34 and 35.

Garver and Hansen, Principles. Chapter 36.
    d. Protection and free trade
[Handwritten notation that this section would be eliminated]
        Read: Taussig, Principles. Chapters 36 and 37.
            Garver and Hansen, Principles. Chapter 37.
            Bastiat, F., Economic Schisms. (1922) Chapter 7.
            List, F., The National System of Political Economy. (1922)
            Chapter 26.
[Handwritten notation that following topics will be covered in the next semester]
    IV. THE DISTRIBUTION OF WEALTH
    V. MODERN ECONOMIC PROBLEMS

BIBLIOGRAPHIC FORMS FOR USE
IN ECONOMICS 1-2

Every paper submitted in course Economics 1-2, ought to contain a bibliography. The forms given below should be followed by the student for they have the sanction of current usage; they are the forms followed by publishers and scholars. It should be remembered: (1) that it is sometimes desirable to group titles in broad classes, (2) that items should be arranged alphabetically within each class, and, (3) that the name of the author should stand at the left of the page, and that additional information, if it runs beyond the length of one line, should be indented.

MODEL FOR ENTERING A SINGLE BOOK
Taussig, F. W., Principles of Economics. New York, The Macmillan Co., 1924.

MODEL FOR ENTERING AN ESSAY IN A COLLECTION OF ESSAYS
Knight, F. H., The Limitations of Scientific Method in Economics. In The Trend of Economics. Edited by Tugwell, R. G., New York, Knopf, 1924. pp. 229–267.

MODEL FOR ENTERING A SIGNED ARTICLE IN A MAGAZINE
Orton, W., Wages and the Collective Wage Bargain. The American Economic Review. June, 1929. Vol. 29, pp. 251–254.

MODEL FOR ENTERING A GOVERNMENT PUBLICATION
United States. Bureau of Labor Statistics., Index Numbers of Wholesale Prices in the United States and Foreign Countries. By Mitchell, W. C. (Bulletin 284). Washington, Government Printing Office, 1921.

(2) F. Taylor Ostrander Class Notes

ECONOMICS I
Fall 1929

A subject which defines phenomena in terms of price
　　wealth = economic goods　　　{scarcity
　　　　　　　　　　　　　　　　{expenditure of labor (application of
　　　　　　　　　　　　　　　　{utility – satisfying wants
　　　　　　　　　　　　　　　　{appropriability
　　　　　　　　　　　　　　　　{not free
　　free goods　　　{air
　　　　　　　　　　{sunlight
　　　　　　　present in such an abundance that they are equal to fill the desire of
　　　　　　　everyone freely to a point of satiety.
Economics–is the science of wealth (economic goods) – Taussig
　　　　　　　– is the wealth of nations – A. Smith
　　　　　　　–is the science of production, exchange, and distribution of wealth –
　　　　　　　Mill
　　　　　　　–examines individual and social action – closely connected with attain-
　　　　　　　ment and use of material requisites of well-being – A. Marshall
("Distribution of wealth" – "per capita" distribution
　　　　　　　　　　　　　– as among different social classes.)
　　　　　　　–is science which treats of phenomena from/in standpoint/terms of
　　　　　　　price.
　　　　　　　– Davenport
Utility–satisfaction of wants
　　　　　–ability to satisfy wants
Property–(property rights) – is liberty or permit – under sanctity or with protec-
　　　　　　　tion of custom and law – to enjoy benefits of wealth while assuming the
　　　　　　　cost which those benefits entail
　　　　　　　–exchangeable control (Garver and Hansen)
Value–power of exchange
　　　　　–ratio in which goods exchange in market
Price–value in terms of money
Wants–satisfied by　　{economic goods　　{Land – Material Resources
　　　　　　　　　　　　　　　　　　　　　{Labor
　　　　　　　　　　　　　　　　　　　　　{Capital
　　　　　　　　　　　　　　　　　　　　　{Management
　　　　　　　　　　　　{free goods

"Primary Concern of Economics is, the most {economic/efficient} way of satisfying human wants"
                              – Garver and Hansen
[Page 1-A – Miscellaneous comments on page one. See introductory remarks
regarding pagination.

The Wealth of Nations (1776) – Adam Smith
Mercantilists–wealth is money,
              garner money in country to make it wealthy
Utilitarian–economics is science of production, exchange, and distribution of
   wealth. – Mill
(History of change from carriage works to automobile factories)
         Studebaker – Buick

Economics studies the buying and selling of goods or services
   1. What is laissez-faire
      start
      tenets
      Mr. Hoover's opinion
   2. What is production & productivity
      is a middle man a producer
   3. kinds of division of labor – what is it
      condition leading to this division
      advantages and disadvantages

–Standard of deferred payment

Individual Exchange Co-operation
   –not autonomous
     Specialization
     Competition

         Co-operation → Exchange → Specialization (End of page 1-A)]

Present Order – (Garver and Hansen)
   1. Freedom of Enterprise
      production – occupation – trade – contract – exchange
      A. Limitations
         –governmental rules and regulations
         a. act to make production more efficient
      B. Modern Freedom Comparative
         –old Manor system exceedingly strict

      a. little freedom – serfdom – independence
2. Competition
  –production – sale
  –<u>usually</u> protects interests of consumers
3. Private Property
  –rights protected by law
4. Price as a regulator (money demand) – <u>Poor</u>
    is it a good regulator of production?
      Socialists say No.
     –governmental control
     –but, rich can divert production to follow their wishes, many people
       have little taste – or regard for final results, individual can make
       money at expense of others.

Present Order (F. M. Taylor)
  1. Individual
  2. Exchange
  3. Co-operation

Laissez-faire

  A minimum of governmental regulation
  In early times – medieval – all sorts of restrictions
    – Guilds – Laws – Colbert
  In middle of 18th Century came new philosophy
    began in France – a reaction
  They believed in certain "natural rights" of freedom
  Thought that self-interest would be automatic to good of community

[Page 2-A

Production – making wealth available for human wants.
  –by human activity
 –has making of <u>Utilities</u> for an aim.
 –satisfying of human wants
 except – predatory
  1. Economic advantages and disadvantages of division of labor.
    –some limitations on it.

"As the power of exchange is the source of the division of labor, so that division
is dependant – restricted – by the extent of that power, namely, the extent of the
market" – Adam Smith (Chapter III)

Labor – any human activity – mental or manual – leading to or assisting in – production of economic goods, or rendering of economic services.]

Adam Smith said that the government ought: to maintain army; dispense justice; maintain public works; maintain a sovereign.

But – all sorts of poor – or worse – social condition for workers – shocked public opinion
        – monopolistic combination – vs – free competition

Production

A. Smith says that only makers of <u>material</u> things are productive.
   but – no one "makes" anything
     – energy and atoms always the same.
     – artists, lawyers, etc. – produce something.

Producers   {place – transportation
(utilities)   {time – storage
           {form – transforming new materials
           {possession – selling

Factors of Production
           Labor – Capital – (Market)
           Management   Natural Resources
           <u>Labor</u>

Division of Labor = specialization

Division of Labor   {1. Geographical
                  {   –natural advantages
                  {   –specialization – concentration of organized skill}
                  {2. Individual

                    a. simple
                       Division <u>into</u> crafts
                    b. complex
                     Division <u>within</u> crafts

Advantages of Division of Labor
   specialization leads to skill (dexterity)
   saves time, labor (continuity)
   substitution of machines for human agencies
   adaptation of intellect to job

[Page 3-A

direct cost – outlays
overhead cost

prime requisites of production
    labor, natural agents – capital   (J. S. Mill)
    unemployed capital
    Saving makes possible the indirect method of production
Creation of Capital
    –saving – investment – surplus
    –application of labor
    – maintenance of it –
Interest on Capital – cause of its creation
    1. Process of Capital Formation?
        a. individual saving
        b. banking and investment machinery
    2. Significance of capital
        a. volume of production
        b. rate of interest
    3. What is Socialist's "Capitalistic System"
        [incomplete passage – F.T.O. note]
          is not paid capital

Business usage of [the] word Capital
    –amount of the investment in the productive enterprise
Economists' usage – capital consists of physical objects
    –Man-made agents of production
    Capital is specialized
    –or Free
    –or has industrial mobilit
    Capital Goods <u>vs</u> Capital Value]

<u>Disadvantages of Division of Labor</u>.
    factory system inevitable
    despoilation of nature
    monotony of labor
    occupational diseases

F. W. Taylor's System – Scientific Management
    analyze the job – set up efficient procedure

fit tools to job and man
set up standard task
carried division of labor to its extreme
–manual and managerial division
–office division

failure
  men rebelled
  trade unions fought it
    introduced non-skilled labor
    introduced supervision
    lowered some costs – efficiency
  raised costs of overhead – foremen, etc.,
    piecework   }
    task & bonus   } method of payment
    differential lease }

Capital –"produced good used in further production of goods." Taussig
    – previously accumulated stock of the products of former labor (J. S. Mill)
    – any durable source of income (Davenport)
  distinction between capital and capital value
    Capital production
    saving by individuals
  –capital – any physical agent of production other than man and natural resources.
  –is produced by man
  –is said to be saved. (surplus)
  producers capital – produces a money income
  consumers capital – gratifies a personal want
               – yields direct utilities
  –non-durable not usually called capital.

[Page 4-A

A liability – a debt to someone
An asset – a credit from someone

Entrepreneurship involves the assumption of the responsibility for carrying on and controlling individual business enterprise.]

Management
  entrepreneur → policy controls

→ the risk taker in production
= one who undertakes to do something.

placement of plant:
nearness to market, heavy raw materials, fuel supply, labor supply; adminis
tration: marketing, advertisement, salaries.

shifting risks
legal organization

Entrepreneurial Organization

–individual firm
–for all things not forbidden by law
–no differentiation between public and private accounts
–very little legal control
–no outside advice to be consulted
–close connection between effort and reward
–a partnership
–result of a contract between two or more competent persons
  for the lawful pursuit of business
–to combine their property and money
–draw up a partnership agreement
–states division of earnings
–optional
–what they shall undertake
–easily terminated – at death – or free will
–unlimited liability
–each partner responsible wholly for others doings
–each is agent for the other
–not practical in large industries
–an air of suspicion
–little credit {external
             {internal
–but greater freedom from law than a corporation

[Page 5-A

par value – one's proportional investment in the total capital investment of
a company]

A corporation – is an artificial person created by the law for some particular
                purpose.
–authorized by the State
Federal charter – National Bank.
(promoter – one who leads in initial stages of formation)

–after a petition has been presented
Some States are more liberal than others
  New Jersey especially – allowed a New Jersey Corporation to own stock in
    another company
general powers: is granted a charter
–may sue and be sued
–may buy and sell property
  –to follow out purpose it was formed for.
  –to condemn property if it "affects the interest of the general public"
–have powers to appoint officers and agents to act for the corporation.
  –may make all necessary contracts to follow set purpose.
special powers
    –have all sorts of varying powers
      limitations on favors

limited liability
    –in most cases, loss or liability is limited to par value of the stock
    –in National Banks a double liability
permanent life
    –does not depend on personal [life] of stockholders.
issues stocks and certificates
    stock {common   {gets dividends (after preferred and bonds)
                        {right to vote and to assets
          {preferred   {first right to dividend (after bonds)
                        {participating and non-participating
                        {accumulative and non-accumulative
                        {convertibility
                        {1st–2nd orders of preference
      [In original, lines drawn through the remaining topics on page. These
appear to be topics that were intended to be covered, but were omitted during the
delivery of the course:]
  ~~Bonds – rights of fixed interest contract – repayment of principal~~
  ~~Short Term Notes~~
  ~~Shorter Bank Loans~~

[In margin, bracketed: Earnings, Assets, Control]

Problems of [a] Corporate entrepreneur
  how to get long term loans
  how to get short term loans
  Common Stock – a right to one's fraction of assets if Corporation is dissolved

-a right to profits in proportion
-a right to vote or control
Preferred Stock – a preference to the assets in case of dissolution, of bankruptcy
-a preference to undivided dividends.

Bonds – security – payable at face value
a. mortgage bonds
   right of foreclosure
   right of fixed interest income
   a contract with company to loan it money
   repayment of principal in fixed limit of time
b. collateral trust bond
      in railroad consolidation
   bond holders put up money to buy large block of stock. The voting rights of
      the stock are in hands of the persons to whom the bondholders loan.
c. debenture bond
   no mortgage on a special piece of property.
d. gold bond
   payable in gold dollars
   -for insurance against paper currency which is below par
   -useful in unstable times or countries
e. income bond
   interest paid if earned
   -like preferred stock
issued by railroads – public utilities
   governments (state, county, city, nation)

Short Term Notes
   very like bonds – shorter term
   higher rate of interest – sold at a low [shorter] period

[Page 7-A:

   Are holding companies vertical combinations legal, horizontal combinations
      illegal?
   Management – W.I.N. – Entrepreneur?]
What form of financing should a company undertake
   an entrepreneurial decision – after company is given charter
   if sure of stable income – bonds are safe
   if not sure of stable income – bonds are not good guarantee against insolvency

Assets (Capitalization 1,500,000)		Liabilities	
Cash	$200,000	Common Stock	$400,000
Buildings	700,000	Preferred Stock	$100,000
Materials and Supplies	200,000	Bonds	$1,000,000
Goods unsold	200,000	Undivided Profits	$60,000
Notes Receivable	100,000		
Accounts Receivable	100,000		
Earnings	60,000		
	$1,560,000		$1,560,000

Liability – a claim of someone else on you
Asset – your claim on someone else

In modern business it is exceedingly hard to find the entrepreneur.
    –he is one who controls business policy
        –how to finance – how much and in what way

Combination of factors of production
Marginal Productivity
Ricardo saw – during time of wheat scarcity in England (Napoleonic War) –
that the produce of a fixed amount of land would not increase in exact proportion as the labor and capital, used on it, increased.

[Page 8-A:
(Garver and Hansen)
    Two primary means of Production
        A. Man   B. Nature
        –Labor}
        –Entrepreneurship}
        –Saving}
            when applied to [arrow pointing] Nature, result in; – Capital

Factors of Production
    Labor – Entrepreneurship – Capital – Natural Resources.
    {Population always increasing {labor   }
                                  {entrepreneurship   } variable factors
    {Capital rapidly accumulating   }

[Arrow from above set pointing to:]
    Must be applied to Natural Resources – relatively scarce constant
factor

Thus:
"At any certain stage in the progress of (agriculture), by increasing the
   labor, the produce is not increased in equal degree." – J. S. Mill
Agents of Production]

At any given state of technique of agricultural application of increased capital
and labor to land, will add a less than proportionate amount to the produce
raised – Marshall

If attempts are made to increase indefinitely the output of any factor of production by increasing the quantity of auxiliary factors used, a time will come, before
the absolute limit is reached, when, though there continues to be an increase in
output, that increase is less than proportionate to the quantity of assisting factors
added. – F. W. Taylor
   a change in state of arts – a change in amount of available land, – do not have
   bearing on Law [of Diminishing Returns].

Proportion in which Marginal Entrepreneurs combine the agents of production
   [Arrow from marginal entrepreneurs pointing lower on the page to: Just
   covers expenses]

1 unit @ $1.00 in $1,000 units

Variable Agents	Output	Fixed Agents charge	Variable Agents Charge	Total cost per unit of output
10	1000	1.00	1.00	2.00
20	2200	0.45	0.91	1.36

   Marginal Product   – 1200   Just covers expenses.
   Proportion in which Superior Entrepreneurs Combine the agents of
      Production
   Variable agents employed beyond the point of lowest total-unit-cost.

[Page 9-A:
What is market – what kinds
Difference in Market Price and long run
   The size of firm
   The size of plant
   Size of fixed equipment depends on
      extent of market
      advance of costs
      supply of available capital
   Amount of variables (labor and materials) able to be employed:
   – that amount which will yield the lowest total cost per unit of output.
      – diminishing returns.

"As the power of exchange is the source of the division of labor, so that division is dependant on – restricted – by the extent of that power. – that is, the extent of the market." – Adam Smith]

{Editor's Note: Two column note taking, table with comment arrowed into the table}

10	Total Product	Marginal Product	Value of Marginal Product	
20	2420	1320	1452	←Superior Entrepreneur
30	3713	1293	1422	
40	4884	1171	1288	
50	5962	1078	1186	
60	6875	913	1004	←
70	7480	605	666	

Law of Diminishing Returns – very important in agriculture
fertilizing – feeding
–so many other details enter into this in <u>great industry</u> – we cannot evaluate importance
–is important in mining
–drilling

<u>Large Scale Production</u>
   –<u>large scale management</u> possible without large scale production – as chain stores
   –but ordinarily closely connected.
   Size of equipment –
      limited by extent of market.
      –nearness to source of supply
      –state of arts
      –capital
   Number of plants and size of organization
      limited by natural ability of entrepreneur.
   –lack of centralization of management
   –lack of standardization
   Trust – a combination of industries for monopoly

   <u>Advantages</u> of large scale production
      saving in freight

saving in selling expenses
saving in buying expenses
no competitive costs
use of by-products
experimentation and research
increased use of machinery and power

SUMMARY OF COURSE SO FAR

Definition of Economics
A study of way in which the price system affects the utilization of our natural resources in gratification of our wants. [Double vertical line alongside this definition]
–involves a legal system
–technique of business practice [arrow from this line to section header below]

I. Production
    Factors
        Natural Resources
        Entrepreneur – management, methods
        Capital – material agents of production
        Labor – division
    Combination
        Law of Diminishing Returns
        Large Scale Production
            (Waste in Production)
II. Value, Price, Exchange

[Line drawn across page, separating above from below]
Value – Exchange is an inevitable result of large scale production
        Value and Price are resultants of Exchange [Arrows from "Value" and
            "Price" to first use "Exchange"]
    Value – is power in exchange
        – ratio between goods and goods quantitatively expressed
    Price – Value expressed in medium of exchange
Markets
    geographic – a place where buyers and sellers meet
    structural – interrelation and integration of whole business organization
    market forces – demand and supply

[Page 11-A:

"ceteris paribus" – other things being equal.]
Markets
   a. Wholesale
      Retail
   b. Competitive
      Monopolistic
   c. Producers
      Consumers
   d. Organized
      Unorganized
Functions of Marketing
   Functions of Value
      Demand Creation
      Assembly (Buying)
   Function of Physical Agents
      Transportation
      Storage
   Auxiliary Functions
      Financing
      Risk
      Standardization

Correlation
   –between relatively widely spread markets of same commodity – is very
      close.
   –between some markets of factor and finished product – is present, but not
      identical
  –a co-variation
   –monopolistic control prevents wide variation by controlling price
   –when price of a factor goes up, production of the finished product goes
      down (cranberries – sugar)
   –inverse relation of production and price
Demand – quantity desired, ability and willingness to pay
   –individual
      quantity an individual stands ready to buy at a particular price, at a given
      time, at given place.

[Page 12-A:

Monopolistic endeavors are toward inelastic demand.
Long-run and Short-run forces are always at work

relation to production [Arrow from "Long-run" to "relation to production"]
We shall study now the short-run forces affecting market price
[Scissors diagram with each blade labeled supply and demand, respectively.]

Division of Labor
   –Exchange
   –value, money, price, sale]
Market Price
   short-run circumstances – typical
Normal Price
   Long-run forces – average
Demand Schedule – Individual
   a <u>statement</u> of the amount and price the individual stands ready to take
Demand Schedule – Collective
   a statement of <u>sum</u> of individual schedules
   Change in demand, change in quantity available
                         change in <u>size</u> of demand.
   Elasticity – refers to ratio between amount buyers stand ready to take, with
      a drop in price.
         Price drop of 1%, amount rises 10%
         sensitivity of buyers to a price change
   Inelastic – when buyers are not sensitive
   Elasticity of One – ratio of drop to rise is always the same.
   <u>Luxuries</u> are elastic, <u>Necessities</u> are inelastic
   Existence of <u>Substitutes</u> has great bearing on elasticity

<u>VARIETY OF USES</u> AFFECTS ELASTICITY

Supply
   – an amount of goods a seller stands ready to sell at a particular price,
      at a given time and place.
   Individual supply schedule
      need for ready cash
      alternative uses for which good can be used
   Market Supply Schedule
      a summary of several Individual schedules
   <u>Equilibrium price</u>
   towards which forces of market are driving the price
   rate at which quantity sellers stand ready to sell <u>equals</u> quantity buyers
      stand ready to buy

[Page 13-A:

Cost
 distinction between expenses and real costs
  direct costs and overhead costs
   what constitutes overhead costs
   basis of opinion that costs have relations to long run prices
   constant, uniform, increasing, decreasing costs –
   internal and external economies
    and their relations to costs.
   Relation of diminishing returns to cost
Hour Test

 Ability to read the question
  read it 3 or 4 times
  don't include irrelevant material
  Plan answers – answer in outline form
      A –
        1 –
        2 –
        3 –
          a –
          b –
          c –
            1) –
 Cite examples]
Two types of Buyers – Consumer –   {Derived Demand
               {Business Man (Producer)

 Consumers Demand
  Utility – wants – desire
  Ability to pay
 Utility
  explained on many lines
  psychology, history, religion, vanity, superiority
  capability to satisfy human wants
 Diminishing Utility
  –increase of stimulus – does not result in an increase of response of
   equal proportion
  only applies when dealing with homogeneous things
  Utility
   –a capacity for satisfying wants

Marginal Utility

–utility of last unit, – or of any one unit if lost (from series).

Joint Demand

Derived Demands

  Labor Supply

  Raw Materials, etc.

  depend on ability to sell.

  depend on monetary banking conditions

[Page 14-A:

Marketing; a process of exchanging goods.

We are concerned with a study of institutions already set up, their influences, organization, etc.

  social institutions

Economics is way the price and business systems affect the national resources and their ability to satisfy our wants.

  Price phenomenon]

REVIEW OF COURSE, THUS FAR

Statement of Problems

  a) fundamental problems of economics definition

  b) institutional approach

  c) [incomplete]

Production

  a. Land   }

  b. Labor   }   Factors of Production

  c. Capital   }

  d. Management   }

  Diminishing Returns [In margin: "Important," with arrow pointing to Diminishing Returns]

Exchange of Goods

  a. examination of markets and marketing

  b. value

  Introduction

  Market Price

  Demand and Supply

    short-run considerations affecting price

[Horizontal line separating above from below]

Costs
    long-run or normal considerations affecting price
[Horizontal line separating above from below]
Value
    I. Competitive
      a. Market (short-run) – Demand, Supply
      b. Normal (long-run)
        Constant
        Increasing
        Decreasing
        Joint
        Example
   II. Monopoly

[Page 15-A:

Where demand for a product and the amount of that product produced are in stable equilibrium
    –the price accompanying this is normal price
    –and normal price is cost price]

I. Cost
   Money cost equivalent of money expenses
   Real costs
      sacrifice of human labor – human exertion
      (using up of equipment)
   Opportunity costs   –   waiting
                    –   competitive costs
   in labor field
      – to induce laborers to work for you – instead of someone else
      – to keep them busy and interested
   in interest field
      – make your capital earn as much as other firms

MONEY COSTS

1st	{Constant	{Fixed =	{Prime =	{Indirect
	{	{	{– direct	{
2nd	{Variable	{Variable =	{Supplementary =	{Direct
			– overhead	

      ~~Fixed Cost~~
      Taxes
      Executive Organization

A certain form of labor (skeleton organization)
Interest on Bonds
Maintenance

<u>Example</u> – a Railroad

	Constant (%)	Variable (%)
Fixed charges	28	
Maintenance of Way	10	5
Maintenance of Equipment	7½	7½
Conduct of transportation	19½	19½
General	3	
	68	32

Joint Cost – outlay made for two or more commodities which are produced
   jointly
wheat – bran
hide – meat
cotton – cotton seed

[Page 16-A:

Bounty is a payment per unit of output
  –paid by the government.
[Two demand and supply diagrams, unlabelled, showing result of shift to right of
  supply curve]
Do decreasing costs apply to a plant or industry?
  external and internal economies
[Assignment]
<u>WEDNESDAY</u>
  What is effect of speculation on prices
  Increase or even cut prices?
  Topic e
  Brace – <<organized speculation>>
  Federal Grain Commission "Methods and Operations of Grain" pp. 4–48
    Vol. [blank]
  (3) Orderly Marketing ~ Publicity Committee
    Num. Chamber of Commerce
  [Hand-drawn illustration depicting wheat with a flat
    price line, and onions resembling a sine wave]

Differential Cost Graphs [Diagrams, incompletely labeled, in margin illustrating
most terms.]

Normal price – average long-run, equilibrium price
–Has a close relation to cost of production
Constant cost
  with increased scale of production, the marginal cost remains nearly the
  same
Costs are root of economic problems.
Marginal producer
            –the highest cost man – who first goes out of business with a drop
              in price
            –or sometimes, the lowest cost man who first changes his aim
              of production into other channels.
            → a price sensitive man who will cease to produce with unfavor-
              able change in prices.
  II. CONSTANT COST
    with expansion of quantity on market due to rising demand marginal price
    (cost) remains nearly the same.
    –complete reorganization within the industry
    –tax or bounty change Price by their own amount
    unimportant – but a logical cost.
    Prerequisites for Constant Cost.
    –cannot encounter diminishing returns unless offset by increasing returns
    –variable agents obtained in increasing amounts without change in prices.
  III. INCREASING COST
    as quantity on market increases due to a rising demand the marginal cost
    slowly rises. tax does not increase the price by its own amount
    –a result of diminishing returns of production
    –a result of competitive bidding for factors of production (higher
      opportunity costs)
  IV. DECREASING COST
    as quantity in the market increases, the marginal cost slowly drops.

[Page 17-A:

In writing a paper
  Make an outline – follow it – attach it
    Introduction
      Problem Stated
    Body
    Conclusions
  Indicate Sources.
    (Taussig, F. W., Principles of Economics. New York, 1926, pp. 176 [ff.])

[Possible subjects for a term paper:]
What is a monopolist
    What is the device for monopolist to control prices.
    What is fundamental theory of monopoly price.
    Why do they discriminate.
Price is an indication of the way production will tend.
[Double margin lines alongside the following:]

Costs affect price only because they have some effect on supply

<u>Price</u>
  1. Competitive
      Short time analyses (market price)
      Long time analyses (normal price)
  2. Monopoly
      Buyers
      Sellers]
  due to
  a. Internal economies
    –using more thoroughly a machine
    –better combination of the agents of production
    –increased efficiency of management
      [In brackets to the left margin]
    –use of by products
    –new <u>invention,</u> etc.
    –expansion
  b. External economies
    –improvement of transportation
    –concentration of industries
  (A bounty decreases cost more than by its own amount.)
V. <u>MONOPOLY COST</u>
  Sellers monopoly
    <u>one who controls supply</u> – affects price
    Special examples – granted by the government
      Post Office – government business franchises
  Capitalistic monopoly
    control of scarce natural resources.
    –raw materials
      no substitutes
      control by patents

control by unfair practices
    –not permanent
    –tying clause
Monopolist wants to make maximum profit

[Diagram in left margin of notes showing total profit as two rectangular areas contained within two axes and two points on the demand curve, the text below the diagram: AB + BC = total profit, GH + HK = total profit, if AB + BC is greater than GH + HK, then the monopolist would restrict the price.]
    –as do all business men
    –but he can restrict supply without fear of competitors
Can restrict supply with an inelastic demand schedule
    –but not very well with an elastic demand schedule
    Often discriminates
        Amount that he can restrict prices is determined by the elasticity of demand
        –elastic – small chance of restriction
        –inelastic – large chance of restriction
    Ford has a monopoly – yet does not restrict price
        –elastic demand

[Page 18-A:

(1) Speculation
    Speculation is the risk which the owner of grain assumes of a loss through a fall in price, or the possibility he has of a gain through a rise in price

"charge what the load will bear"

[Diagram with U-shaped cost curve tangent to horizontal price line at a point labeled: cost]
[Statement accompanying diagram:]
    elastic demand gives monopolist complete control of supply but little control of price
Speculation
    in what fields is speculation located[?]
        hedge, future, margin
Bear – pessimistic
Bull – optimistic]
    Commodities which have difficulty of resale can be sold at discrimination.
    –geographical discrimination
    –personal discrimination
    Subsequent adjustment price

theatres – doctors – booksellers
getting in on both ends of the demand schedule.
[Unlabeled diagram showing three varying cost curves.]
Railroads <u>were</u> great discriminators
    Place discrimination
    led to Interstate Commerce Commission
   –"long and short haul" laws
VI. <u>SPECULATION</u> – IN GRAIN
    assumption of business risks
    hedge – passing of responsibility
            – either a purchase or a sale of a futures contract – to protect
                yourself from loss
  future – a contract calling for future delivery
            – a contract for future sale or buying.
  1. <u>Trading in common</u>
    –representations of all companies – all dealers – all buyers in one place
  2. <u>Broker</u> is a middleman
    –Informal Record – a binding contract
  3. Trading on Margin
    –the same for farmers as for Wall Street
    –trading partly on one's own money, partly on borrowed money
    –has <u>magnifying</u> effect on possibility of profit or loss. [Single vertical
    line alongside in margin]
  4. Speculative buying and selling
    –immediate great fluctuation
    –in long run – uniformity and lessened fluctuations
[Page 19-A:

  a "lamb" – one who gets sheared
            – operate on bull side.]
Speculation   → socially necessary risk
           <u>vs</u> gambling → a <u>created risk</u>
Speculation's effects on price (produce) in an organized market
–general consensus of opinion is that speculation evens out prices
 –lessens fluctuations
–often <u>Special</u> fluctuations
 –ignorant trader
 –corner (monopoly of supply)
Speculation in Stocks
  Stock – a share in the profits (dividends)
  –a right to control

–a right to proportional share in the total assets
Dealing through brokers
–informal methods
Marginal buying – long
Selling short –

Points of likeness and difference in stock and commodity speculation
[Single vertical line alongside in margin]
A. Likenesses
  1. large exchanges in each – similar
  2. well organized
  3. trading in common
  4. trading in large debts
  5. margin trading
  6. rapid adjustment of price.
B. Differences (mostly social results)
  1. Futures – only on commodity exchange
    (Short selling – delivery immediately
    –though one must buy back)
    –both selling something which one hasn't got
    –ultimate result the same
    –a technical and legal differences
  2. [Physical] demand and supply affects the commodity exchange only
    –immediately
    –causes ironing out of price fluctuations

[Page 20-A:

Currency in circulations in U.S. – Nov. 1, 1929

Gold Coin and Bullion	$363,051,117
Gold Certificates	845,907,509
Standard Silver Dollars	42,572,520
Silver Certificates	414,951,880
Treasury Notes of 1890	1,277,500
Subsidiary Silver	291,200,091
Minor Coins	117,555,669
U.S. Notes (Greenbacks)	266,504,063
Federal Reserve Notes	1,869,172,974
Federal Reserve Bank Notes	3,466,000
National Bank Notes	622,000
Total	$4,838,184,799]

3. Hedges in commodity exchange only
   –though collateral loan is somewhat similar
4. Stock market provides a place for marketing of <u>new</u> corporate shares
   –place where banks can get rid of surplus stock.

———————————

EXCHANGE, VALUE AND PRICES – A <u>SUMMARY</u>

definition of Value, and Price
I. a) Market price – short run analysis.
   b) Normal price – long run analysis.
      –an equality between price and cost must exist
         Costs under free competition
      1. definition
      2. kinds of costs
      3. cost circumstances
         constant, increasing, decreasing
      4. monopoly value
      5. speculation
II. Money and Banking
   a. Money
      –metallic and paper
   b. Banking
      –commerical
      –Federal Reserve System
      –investment banking

———————————

Money – a medium of exchange, in legal settlement of debt.
         –backed by approval of government, or custom.
Gold taken because of universal acceptance.
   –relative, constant scarcity
   –stability of value
   –easily divisible
Bimetalism – gold and silver both legal
   –and were linked together by an arbitrary <u>ratio of value</u>.
Monometalism $1 = 23.22 grains pure [gold]

[Page 21-A:

Does gold provide type of money which is a good standard for deferred payments [?]
Why has gold been adopted [?]
Silver is coined on government account
[Along the lower right margin are the symbols for money: M, FF, $ and the British Pound.]]

(Functions of) Money: is a medium of exchange
                    –for legal settlement of debts
                    : is a standard measure of value.
                    –relative exchange value
                    –a middle?
                    : is a standard for deferred payments.
                    –obligations are paid in money
                    : is a store of value.
          Advantages of gold.
             1. universally, commonly known and accepted
             2. easily divisible
             3. durable – little deterioration
             4. great value in small bulk
             5. relative scarcity, – constant demand,
             6. century-old tradition
          Kinds of Money [Single vertical line in margin alongside Government and Bank sections]
             1. Government
                    Metallic (Specie) – Gold, Silver (Sub.), Token (Copper–Nickel)
                    Government Paper
                       Greenbacks (U.S. Notes)
                       Gold Certificates
                       Silver Certificates
                       Treasury Notes of 1890
             2. Bank
                    National Bank Notes
                    Federal Reserve Notes
                    Federal Reserve Bank Notes
          Why not private money?
          –uniformity [lack of]
          –instability
          –adulteration

What is the <u>Gold Standard</u>?
–government or central bank stands ready to convert gold into coin/money, or money into gold at any time at a fixed standard; free
  23.22 grains = $1.00
–the price of gold never changes
–the gold must be eligible for all kinds of international debts

[Page 22-A:

  Pennies are legal tender up to 25¢.
  England abolished bimetallism in 1816.
  $16 ------- 1 ounce of gold
  $16 ------- 16 ounces of silver

[A cyclical flow diagram of prices with the following troughs and peaks,]

Troughs:
  1789, 1834, 1854, 1879, 1900
Peaks:
  1812
Inflexion points:
  1864, 1873
Demarcation of Periods:
  Silver period   1789 to 1830s trough
  Gold period   from 1830s to 1864 inflexion point
  Paper period   from 1864 to 1879
  Gold   post 1879
Label above the 1879 trough point – Bland–Allison Sherman Silver Purchase
$4.8665   =   £ 1.30]

Legal Tender (stop payment of interest on presentation)
  –a power of exchange confirmed by government in settlement of debts.
  –a law laid down by the courts.
What is <u>fiat</u> money
  –inconvertible paper money
  –given legal tender power (as Greenbacks when issued)
  –not convertible for gold.
Depreciating currency.
  –given unit of paper money commands less and less of the same unit of metallic money.
  –purchasing power of a unit of money over gold
Gold: – has unlimited legal tender power

: – <u>freely</u> coined at a given ratio
: – gratuitously minted
Bimetallism – a system which attempts to set up two metals as standard money
    –freely convertible at a fixed ratio
    U.S. adopted Monometalism in 1900
    History of Silver
        up to 1873 – bimetallism
                    – begun by Alexander Hamilton
        1873 – demonetization of silver (Coinage Act)
        1878 – Bland–Allison Act
        1890 – Sherman Silver Purchase Act
        1890 – Treasury Notes of 1890
        since 1900, government buys silver at the market price and stamps the
            dollar sign on a small portion –
                    –taking it on government account
                    –making money at present.
    Bimetallism a failure, because the fixed ratio was not in accord with
        market ratio, at all times.

[Page 23-A:

A Note a promise to pay
Gold Certificate   –substitute for bullion
                        –claim checks on coin.

As soon as irredeemable paper money was issued, prices rose greatly, premium
    of gold rose, paper depreciated
Promise of redemption led to fall of prices.
    – issuance of Greenbacks
    1. had an adverse affect on <u>fixed-income</u> holders
        –salaried classes
        –endowed institutions
        –people living on bonds, etc.
    2. affects debtors and creditors
        –hard on creditors, easy on debtors.
    3. increased total output of money.
Assignats – French]

Government Paper Money – convertible substitute for metallic money – up to
    1860, we had none. Then the Greenbacks – issued during Civil War, 1862
    –<u>inconvertible</u>, but not good for duties on imports – or taxes
    –legal tender – limited

–about $400,000,000

–redemption date, intended, but not specified. after 1879

–$346,000,000

–but convertible for gold

–$150,000,000 in a fund for their redemption.

Gold Certificates

–backed, dollar for dollar, by gold in Treasury

　–saves loss by abrasion.

Silver Certificates

–backed, dollar for dollar, by silver in Treasury

–but easily converted into gold.

Treasury Notes of 1890 (1893) – silver bought with paper money – exchangeable
　　for gold.

Ways and Means of Payment [Single vertical line in margin alongside this
　　subsection]

　　– Government

　　　a. Metallic money

　　　　–Bimetallism

　　　　　–didn't work – fixed ratio did not correspond with the market ratio

　　　b. Paper money

　　　– Banking

　　　　a. bank money

Banking

　　Commercial

　　Saving {Mutual

　　{Stocks

　　Trust

　　Investment Bankers and Bond Houses

　　Building and Loan

　　Commercial Banks

　　–National

　　–State – 2/3 of number, do ½ of business

[Page 24-A:

　　　Note – a promise to pay.

　　　Discount (taken off first) and interest (added afterwards) are fundamen-
　　　　tally the same

　　　Double entry bookkeeping

　　　National Bank Notes

　　　　created by

　　　a – buying circulating stock

b – depositing it with Treasury as collateral
Undivided Profits are differences between claims on the Bank and
    Resources available]
National Bank – to organize one:
    –group of people pledge their money in form of stock
    –application for charter made to Controller of Currency – a national charter
    –charter issued – a grant of legal power.
        –double liability
    –stock officially issued

	Assets		Liabilities	
	Cash	$70,000	Capital Stock	$100,000
7%	Loans and Discount	1,000	Notes outstanding	1,000
2%	U.S. Bonds	20,000		
	Building	10,000		
	[Total	$101,000	Total	$101,000]

Requirements–   in small town – $25,000
                     more in larger towns
                     even more in cities
National Bank Law – passed during the Civil War
–if a National Bank wants to put out Notes it must buy circulating
    U.S. Bonds [and] deposit them with U.S. Treasury
National Bank Note
–secured by bonds deposited with U.S. Treasury
–5% cash reserve also in Treasury
–a bond-secured note
–demand notes.
Merits – perfectly secure
–backed by Bonds and Government of U.S.
Demerits – inelastic
    can't increase or decrease readily to needs of trade

Deposits and Checking

Assets		Liabilities	
Cash	$100,000	Capital Stock	$100,000
Cash	100,000	Deposits	100,000
Loans & Discounts	10,000	Deposits	9,900
		Undivided Profits	100
[Total	$210,000	Total	$210,000]

[Page 25-A:

By what <u>processes</u> do bank deposits rise?
Suppose all banks are doubling deposits and checks   – any difference?
Primary deposit is a deposit of actual money.
Define a bank in terms of its functions
    –discounting, deposits, and note issue
National Bank Note is not Legal Tender.
Reserves – cash able to be paid out immediately]

A <u>deposit</u> – <u>a right to draw money</u>.
    –(a safe place to put money)
    –time, – must be given notice
    –demand, payable at call
Commercial loans
    –a loan to enable a commercial firm to buy, market, sell some goods.
    –short time loans for business purposes for quick buying and selling
Cash Reserve – actual money which a bank keeps on hand to meet demands of
    depositors – usually 5%
Clearing House
    –settlement of differences between banks
    –cancellations – <u>offsets</u>
Deposits created in two ways
    –by actual presentation of cash (Primary)
    –by discount
    –then <u>creating</u> deposits

If at one period – <u>every</u> bank is increasing loans and discounts, the cash
    reserves of all will <u>remain</u> about <u>stationary</u>
        –a Bank can increase its loans and deposits – only in relation to the increases
        of other banks

<u>National Banking System</u>
    –was founded during Civil War – 1863
    –a result of rather insecure currency
    1. thus it was to give a secure, standard currency
        –backed by collateral
        –to tax unstandardized "State Money" out of existence
    2. was to help finance the Civil War.
    3. Set up new requirements as to Bank Reserves.
        –set up Reserve Cities, Central Reserve Cities, Country Districts
        a. certain minimum bank reserves

[Page 26-A:

Later developments
1907 – Panic – under Theodore Roosevelt
        – dissatisfaction with National Banking System
        – National Monetary Commission started to investigate
1908 – under Taft more agitation
        – Aldrich Bill
1912 – Wilson had great control over Congress
1913 – Owen–Glass Bill

Index Numbers – various kinds
    simple arithmatic average
    weighted average
    median average
    simple geometric average]
        b. some held in banks own vaults
        c. rest held in reserve banks of cities
    Defects of this third point:
    –decentralized reserves
    –no central bank to which member banks could go for help – in time
        of runs
    –straining of cash reserves at periods (seasonal)
    –pyramiding of reserves
    –rigid reserve requirement
    Defects of old National Bank System
        1. No central system to affect credit conditions – control
           –decentralized reserves
        2. Inelastic Note issue
        3. did not supply the U.S. Government with a proper fiscal system
           –which suited its needs
        4. poor method of clearing checks
        5. the method of [handling] foreign exchange
        6. "The Banks did not behave in any way, but for their own good."

Federal Reserve System
    –a system of Regional Banker's Banks.
    –begun in 1914 (Owen–Glass Bill)
    –a product of
    –realization of defects of old System
    –observations of England's System
    Anatomy of the System.

12 Regions – each with one Central bank:
   Boston – New York – Philadelphia – Richmond – Atlanta – Cleveland – Chicago – St. Louis – Kansas City – Minneapolis – San Francisco – Dallas.
Federal Reserve Board – eight men
   –in Washington
   –Treasurer of U.S. and Comptroller of the U.S. – ex officio
   –Six other members appointed by the President (one a "dirt former")
   –Power of supervision and regulation
      –over Federal Reserve Notes
      –approve or adisapprove of changes in the discount rate
      –permit or require one [continued below]

[Page 27-A

[Hand-drawn organizational chart for the Federal Reserve System and those with whom it directly or indirectly deals.]
System serves to centralize our gold holdings.
Trust   ompany –
   –really means the managing of estates
   –also saving, selling bonds, and commercial banking]
   member bank to make loans – discount rate of another
   –change and suspend Reserve requirements of member banks
   –general bank examination
a. Federal Reserve Advisory Council
   –meets 4 times a year
   –one representative from each member Bank
b. Meeting of the Chairmen of Board of Directors of the Member Banks
   –one a year.
Reserve Banks deal with
a. member banks
b. the U.S. Government
c. certain ones with foreign banks
Reserve Banks are controlled by Board of Directors (9 men)
   –Three appointed by Federal Reserve Board
      –one of these is Chairman
      –connecting link with Washington
   –Six men elected by the member banks
   –they appoint a Governor – to manage the bank
Member Banks (big, middle-sized, little)
   –every National Bank must be a member of the Federal Reserve System
   –State Banks may be members

–unclear qualifications
–Savings Banks may <u>not</u> be members.
–nor Private Banks
→ –these banks <u>own</u> the Federal Reserve Banks – through <u>Stock</u>
   –to an amount of 6% of their paid-up Capital
   [In left-margin: compulsory – half paid-in by custom]
   –entitles them to stock rights
   → –share in Profits – <u>6%</u> [continued]

[Page 28-A:

[Ostrander has the summary tables on this page in two-column format: T-accounts down the left-hand side and arrowed remarks on the right. Here, each table is presented and below it the relevant remarks for that table.]

<u>Federal Reserve Banks</u>

I.	Cash	$3,000		Stock	$3,000
		8,000		Deposits	8,000

Stock to 6% of Capital Stock of Member Banks – ½ paid-up
Deposit to 7% (10–13%) of demand liabilities
Sum of all member banks

II.	Cash			Stock	
	Loans and Discounts	$80,000		Deposits	$80,000

Rediscounting
to credit of member bank

<u>Member Banks</u>

I.	Cash	89,000	Capital Stock	100,000	10%
	Federal Reserve Stock	3,000			
	Loans and Discounts	80,000	Deposits	80,000	
	Deposits in Federal Reserve System	8,000			

Any disaster of main system would affect the whole country, instead of one locality.

<u>Member Bank</u>

II.	Cash	19,000	Cap Stock	100,000
	Federal Reserve Stock	3,000		
	Deposits in Federal Reserve System	8,000	Deposits	10,000
	Loans and Discounts	80,000		100,000
		100,000		–80,000

[Arrow to Deposits line from:] drawn down by checks on other banks.
[Arrow to –80,000 from:] possible liabilities far in excess of cash

<u>Federal Reserve Bank</u>
Cash   —   Stock   —

<u>Member Bank</u>
Cash   —   Stock   —]

    –rest to U.S. Government
–proportional share in assets
–vote, etc.

    Member Banks can get Federal Reserve Notes
       1. must have Reserves against Demand Liabilities
       Central Reserve Cities 13%
       Middle Sized Cities   10%
       Country Banks   7%
    Federal Reserve Banks serve as Clearing Houses for member banks
  A. <u>Rediscounting</u> – many loans and discounts already out, but desire to
     loan more
     –thus it resells the new notes to the Federal Reserve Bank in return
     getting cash or a deposit account
  B. Member banks may <u>borrow</u> directly – with deposits of collateral.

General Points of the Federal Reserve System
  –Reserve bank can virtually force the member bank to raise its discount rate
  – by raising its own
  C. Federal Reserve Notes
     –in control of a <u>Federal Reserve Agent</u>
     –who is a <u>government</u> official
     –authorized by Federal Reserve Board
     –issued on two conditions
     a. deposit of collateral security
     b. ~~Member bank must have at least 40% of note issue in gold in~~
       ~~Federal Reserve Bank's vaults~~

[Page 29-A:

Who issues Federal Reserve Notes
  –by what collateral
  –are they elastic?
  –how retired

What are open market operations.]
   –makes an <u>elastic</u> currency
   –most collateral is in form of commercial paper
   –making currency issue vary with trade
   –are backed to <u>face value</u> by collateral in hands of Federal Reserve Agent
      <u>and</u> by 40% of face value in gold in vaults of Federal Reserve Bank
   Contraction –
      –as soon as a Federal Reserve Note gets out of its district and is turned in,
         it is returned
      –deposited by Member bank with the Reserve bank in return for credit.
   D. Federal Reserve Bank Note
         –is <u>designed</u> to take place of National Bank Notes
         –differing in one respect –
         –collateral is deposited by Reserve bank instead of National bank
         –otherwise the issue is the same as National Bank Note.

Open Market Operations
   –when money is scarce in open market, and Federal Reserve Bank has too
      much spare cash.
   –it can buy certain bonds in open market
   –thus alleviating the credit situation
   –while earning interest on the bonds
   Buying bankers acceptances
   –another way of making money.
   Another reason for Federal Reserve System
   –to create a central bank which could control interest rates
      –steadying them
      they do this by –
      1. issuing Federal Reserve Notes in time of money scarcity
      2. by putting on the brakes when panic signs are shown
         (outflow of gold large stocks of goods high interest)
         –putting up rediscount rate
         –slowing up gold outflows
         –slowing up speculative borrowing.
[Page 30-A:

[Hand drawn Index Number time-line chart from 1860 to 1930. Lows at 1860,
1896, 1921, and sharp drop in the mid-twenties; highs at 1865, 1920.]
   Populists – and greenbackers – all came from Middle West, – the great farm
   belt – mostly debtors.

Opposition came from New England   – Manufacturers – the creditor class.]

Price Changes
A. measured by index numbers
   –a series of numbers designed to show the variations in price of a large group of goods
   –must take one year as a base
    –a period of time with reference to which the index number reflects a change
B. what are the consequences of a price change
   –with rising price, the bond holder loses
   –with falling price the bond holder gains in purchasing power
    –real income drops with rising price
   –with rising price, the debtor (mortgaged) farmer gains.
    –loses with declining prices (1896)
   –Salaried and wage-earning classes lose by rising prices
    –salaries and wages follow prices but slowly; skilled workers slower than common laborers
   –Entrepreneurs gain by rising prices
    –wider margin of profit between selling price and cost
     –due to slow wage-rise [as wages lag]
    –market increases and number of profits-per-unit increases

[Page 31-A:

Price change – effect on Railroads]

C. Causes of Price Changes
   1. Period from 1860 to 1896
      –opening up of new West, with efficient output
      –period of railroad development, efficient transportation
      –manufacturing given impetus by the Civil War increasing goods
      –America began to take on its modern form.
      –gold supply increasing but slowly, – especially with respect to stock of goods exchanged.
      –Substitutes for gold
        –Greenbacks did not increase
        –National Bank Notes increasing but slowly
        –Silver losing
        –Expansion in credit banks – but not sufficient

–<u>Summary</u> – greatly increased goods and exchange, with little
  increase in means of exchange – thus falling prices
2. Period from 1896 to World War.
  –greatly increased supply of gold
    –opening of African mines
    –new processes of smelting
    –thus greatly increased bank reserves
    –giving rise to increased loans and discounts.
  –thus <u>shortage</u> of means of payment was <u>alleviated</u>

[Non-numbered page (hand-out, no source) inserted depicts a chart titled
"ENGLISH PRICES AND WORLD GOLD PRODUCTION" covers period
1800–1925, showing generally inverse relationship between prices and gold production, especially after Great War.]

3. Period from 1914 to 1920
  –World War
  –<u>greatly</u> increased supply of gold in the <u>U.S.</u>
    –exporting abroad
    –payment by gold
    –fancy prices
  –Federal Reserve System inaugurated
    –enlarged deposits and discounts
    –<u>greatly</u> increasing <u>business production</u>
      –besides <u>war</u> income of production
  –Liberty bonds bought with <u>borrowed</u> money credit
    especially created by the government for this purpose.
  –leading to increased prices

THEORY OF MONEY AND PRICES

[Page 32-A [Definitions]

P = prices (general average)
T = volume of trade (Q)

M = money – gold [and other currency]
M^1 = Bank deposits

V = velocity of circulation of money – rate of turnover
V^1 = velocity of circulation of bank deposits

M acts as a reserve for M^1

PT = MV]

–many opposing and dissenting theories (138 – Polish authors)

–we use the Fisher theory

$$P = (MV + M^1V^1)/T$$

Price level varies directly in proportion to quantity of money,

Price level varies directly in proportion to velocity of circulation,

Price level varies inversely in proportion to volume of trade.

There is some variation (long-run and seasonal) in velocity of circulation

Big influx of M – more money – low interest rates – stimulate borrowing thus evening up M^1.

–Old theory of prices said that prices varied directly as the nominal quantity of money.

–This did not take enough into consideration, enough of the dynamic forces which were acting on prices.

–Fisher's theory

  –Value of money exchanges received equals value of money exchanges made

  –This theory takes into consideration the rate of circulation, amount of goods sold

  –Also takes into consideration bank payments – loans and deposits, and rate of circulation of them

[Page 33-A:

  Keynes – A "Managed" Currency

  –international difficulty

  –tendency to inflate

  –Constant flux,

  –Some degree of correlation between the various parts of the business world.

  Period when margin of profit between costs and prices becomes [incomplete]]

THE BUSINESS CYCLE

[Page 34-A: Introduces discussion of the business cycle with a list of sixteen important business crises in the U.S., a chart of fluctuations between 1902 and 1914, and a comment "disposing of two erroneous causes" as follows:]

Important Business Crises in the U.S.

  1802

  1808

  1816

1818–19
1825
* 1837 –
1847
1857
* 1873 – Republican (Grant)
1883–84 – Republican (Garfield–Arthur)
* 1893–95 – Democratic (Cleveland)
1903 – Republican (T. Roosevelt)
1907 – Republican (Progressive)–(T. Roosevelt)
1914 (?) – Democratic (Wilson)
* 1920 – Democratic (Wilson)
* 1929 – Republican (Hoover)

[Graph with three hand-drawn time lines depicts cycles of Speculative Prices, General Trend of Business, and Interest Rates, from 1903 to 1914.]

period of peace [characterization of period from 1903 on]
institution of Federal Reserve System not yet accomplished [as of 1914]
We have disposed of two erroneous causes of Business Cycles
    –that Political Parties are their cause
    –that they came in inevitably ten year cycles
–used to refer to fact that business conditions change in more or less
    rhythmic waves.
Periods of Prosperity, Crisis, Depression, Revival

[Diagram of business cycle with the timing of speculation, trade and interest labeled]
–certain amount of order between various correlated parts of business world
    Crisis – stock prices low – going down
            commodity prices – falling
            interest high
            bank reserves low
    Depression – stock prices low – starting to rise
            commodity prices – low
            interest rates fallen
    Depression leads to revival
    –low interest
    –have gotten rid of accumulated stock

–beginning of reemployment

–large financing

Prosperity –

[In margin alongside the following, with single vertical line alongside to left, and curly bracket to right of statement: watch these five elements:

–speculative prices high

–commodity prices high

–physical volume of production high

–interest rates going up and bank reserves decreasing

–employment full]

Why do we have fluctuations?

Many theories:

[Page 35-A:

Thompson's Theory of <u>Overproduction</u> and <u>Underconsumption</u>

    a. Wide division of wealth between rich and poor – the rich are the saving people.

    b. Rising prices brings increased profits which accrue to the rich, this capital is further spent on increased profits.

    c. But the mass production this makes possible, is too much for the poor consumers to buy – thus the market becomes glutted.

    d. Then the rich's profits are cut, has capital to be invested, and decreased production, thus a period of depression.

Criticism of this theory

    –rate of interest in business cycles does not follow out this theory

(1) Banking and Monetary theories

    a. Hawtrey – everything inherent

      –any of a number of causes may start the rise of prices, and all that goes with it

      –increased borrowing

      –increased wages

      –increased demand

      –smaller pro[portion] of bank reserves

      –borrowing, increased demand for circulation

      –increased interest rates

      –forced sales

–mob psychology brings more sales – they drop
–each step an inevitable result of one preceeding it.
–criticisms [of Hawtrey]
   –"increased demand for circulation" not important
   –applicable to America?
   –it does not take account of enough factors
   b. Fisher
      –lagging adjustment of the interest rate
      –fluctuations of volume of trade a result of change of price level
      –extraneous forces.
(2) Physical nature theories
   a. Moore and Jevons – Rainfall Theory
      –allege a variation in rainfall, in set cycles.
      –more rain, more crops, more manufactured goods bought.
      –that a boom may be started by rainfall, is the only advantageous
         contribution of this theory.
(3) Psychological theories
   a. –General state of optimism
      –results in enough stimulation to justify itself.
   b. –General state of pessimism
      –results in enough depression to justify itself
   c. –Is in back of Herbert Hoover's mind at the present
(4) Changing technique of production theories
   a. –Cassel – Schumpeter
      –improved technique, increased invention, improved methods of
         business
      –all this [is] an inevitable result of Progressive Society
      –exploitation of each new invention
      –increased borrowing, and employment
      –increased production
      –falling prices
      –decreased employment
      –return to [a] normal
      –after a collapse.

[Page 36-A:

This is the real way to   →
attack the problem.
[Arrow points to opposite page, point (1) a, below]]

Some Proposed Remedies [for business cycle]

(1) Banking and Monetary
   a. attempt to control the amount of <u>bank credit</u> – through central banks
      –raising rediscount rate
      –open market operation
      –[and/or] keep the supply of money in circulation somewhere near
         an average level
      –rediscounting
      –open market operations
      sale and purchase of securities by central banks (Federal Reserve
      [System]), purchase by member banks, tightens up supply of
      money, thus slows up loaning.
      purchase of securities by central (Federal Reserve System) banks
      from member banks in a time of depression, to make available more
      'cheap' money.
   b. Compensated Dollar
(2) More complete information on business trends
      –Research work
      –Analyzing
      –Constant reports – as are now published by the government, etc.
      –Hoover's great argument
(3) Have Building of Public Works during times of Depression
      –to stop further depression
      –to start the <u>up</u> movement again
      –this does not go to the root of things, at all – is a "perils pill"

[Page 37-A: [Miscellaneous notes on foreign exchange.]
   Foreign exchange
      –under gold standard
      –under purchasing power ratio
      –under speculative ratio
   Par Rates [to U.S. Dollar]
      [English Pound]   £ 4.8665
      [French Franc]   F 0.039175
      [Italian Lira]   £ 0.052631
   France has gone through a period of devaluation
   4.86 will buy 113 grains of gold
      –must be packed, labeled, insured, shipped at considerable cost
      –loss of interest for duration of transport

–about 0.02 cents to ship 4.86 dollars.
quoted rates are the same in London and New York.]

International Exchange
  –Bill of Exchange
    –a draft, one bank calls on another to pay money to a third party
    –a banker's checks
    –in several types
      –Banker's bills – a bank draft – between banks
      –Commercial bills – a draft between two individuals
    –Time – an Acceptance – payable (blank) days after acceptance
    –Sight – payable on presentation
    –Domestic Bills of Exchange
    –called a "Trade Acceptance"
    –International Bills of Exchange
    –called a "Commercial Bill."
  –Foreign Exchange – refers to various phenomena
    –sometimes to the rate alone
      –"mint power of exchange"
        1 dollar has 23.22 grain of gold
        1 £ has 113 grains of gold.
      –refers to the rate of exchange in the ratio to the gold content.
      –par ratio, give a clue to the amount of gold, in grains, each unit of currency
        contains
    –what makes the rate fluctuate:
    –gold export, gold import rate.
    –what gives rise to demand for foreign exchange
    1. Commodity importations
    2. Interest payment on foreign bond holdings
    3. Travelers expenses
    4. Immigrants remittances
    5. –Backwash; payment on old, retired stocks
    6. New U.S. investments [abroad]
    –an increase in demand, leads to increase in [exchange] rate.

[Page 38-A:

Drafts – an order by A to B, calling on B to pay
  –time
  –sight

Acceptance

Around 1893 – we had a hard time keeping the gold standard –
–money was flowing out of U.S. Treasury
–being shipped abroad, a result of selling of American investments held abroad.

Niederlandische Maatjopy Handelsbanken
Direction der Disconto Gessellschaft
Svenska Handelsbanken, Aktieballoget]

Means of payment – international
  –shipment of goods made
  –Savannah to Liverpool
  –Savannah draws a draft on Liverpool, calling for payment of money in 60 days.
  –amount of £1,000, rate at par.
  –Savannah sells draft to G.T. Co., they credit him with a deposit
  –G.T. Co. sends draft to its London office which presents it to Liverpool for acceptance
How does a bank get funds with which to pay, or buy, foreign exchange?
  –importing
  –export of goods, builds up foreign balances on deposit.
  –international investments
  –travel
  –international loaning, due to interest rates
In Foreign Exchange
  –Exports pay for Imports
  –Movements of Securities important
  –Short Time interest rates also important

[In the left hand margin, alongside following two terms: left over from Mercantilism]
  "Favorable Balance of Trade" means a larger amount of exports than imports, measured in money value.
  "Unfavorable Balance of Trade"
  larger amount of imports than exports.
  Balance of Payments is far more important
    –it takes into consideration all Payments, invisible as well
    Creditor Nation – we receive interest

With an unfavorable balance of payments,
  –an outflow of gold is imminent
  –rate goes up,
  export of goods, securities

[Page 39-A:

1928

	Due from abroad	Due to foreigners
Merchandise	5,334,000,000	4,497,000,000
Freight	143,	227,
Tourists	168,	693,
Interest	882,	359,
War Debt Receipts	210,	—
Immigrant Remittances	28,	217,
Charity, Missions	—	52,
Net Increase in American		
Long Term Investment [Abroad]		1,339,
Foreign Investments in U.S.	481,	
	7,384,	7,246,]

Review

  –Economics – the price system with its effect on the utilization of our resources
    for the satisfaction of human wants.
  –the science of exchange values.
  –Value – ratio in exchange, power of a commodity to command other
    commodities in exchange.
  Production is taken care of in response to money demand.

Questions

Prime and Supplementary Costs ↔ (overhead – ? Garver and Hansen)
  –overhead costs – direct (right)
Opportunity Costs
  –Free Capital – industrial mobility
Consumers – Producers, Markets
  –Retail   –Wholesale Markets
Prime (Cost) → Direct   Supplementary (Cost)   → Overhead
Opportunity – alternative uses – competing
Wealth – economic goods
          { –scarcity
          { –utility
              –not free
              –expenditure of labor

MATERIALS FROM ECONOMICS 2, TAUGHT BY WALTER B. SMITH, WILLIAMS COLLEGE, SPRING 1930

Kirk D. Johnson (Editor) and
Warren J. Samuels (Editor)

(1) ASSIGNMENTS FOR ECONOMICS 2

I. INTRODUCTION [added by hand: – Existing Order]
II. PRODUCTION [added by hand: – Labor, Capital, Entrepreneurship – Combination]
III. EXCHANGE
  1. Value
  2. Money and Banking
  3. International trade and exchange.
    a. The foreign exchange
      Read: Taussig, Principles, Chapter 32
      Garver and Hansen: Principles, Chapter 34
    b. The balance of trade and the balance of payments
      Read: Taussig, Principles, Chapter 33
      Garver and Hansen: Principles, Chapter 35
    c. The theory of international trade
[In margin: second semester]
      Read: Taussig, Principles, Chapters 34 and 35
      Garver and Hansen, Principles, Chapter 36

Further Documents From F. Taylor Ostrander
Research in the History of Economic Thought and Methodology, Volume 24-B, 55–108
Copyright © 2006 by Elsevier Ltd.
ISSN: 0743-4154/doi:10.1016/S0743-4154(06)24022-7

    d. Protection and free trade
       Read: Taussig, Principles, Chapters 36 and 37
          Garver and Hansen, Principles, Chapter 37
          Bastiat, F., Economic Sophisms (1922), Chapter 7
          List, F., The National System of Political Economy (1922),
            Chapter 26
          Taussig's "Readings in International Trade" [added by hand]

IV. DISTRIBUTION
    1. Functional Distribution
      a. Wages, Productivity theory of
         Read: Taussig, Principles, Chapter 52
            Garver and Hansen, Principles, Chapter 24
      b. Wages, Relation of the Supply of Labor to
         Read: Taussig, Principles, Chapters 53 and 54
            Bullock, C. J., Selected Readings in Economics, pp. 275–286
            Pearl, Raymond, The Biology of Population Growth, Chapter 7
            Fairchild, F. B., Furness, E. S. and Buck, N. S., Elementary
              Economics, Vol. II, Chapter 43
      c. Wages, Differences in
         Read: Taussig, Principles, Chapter 47
            Garver and Hansen, Principles, Chapter 25
      d. Rent
         Read: Taussig, Principles, Chapters 42, 43, and 44
            Garver and Hansen, Principles, Chapter 26
      e. Interest
         Read: Garver and Hansen, Principles, Chapter 27
            Fisher, I., Elementary Principles of Economics, Chapters 19, 20,
              21, 22, and 6
      f. Business Profits
         Read: Taussig, Principles, Chapters 49 and 50
            Garver and Hansen, Principles, Chapter 28
            Foster, W. T. and Catchings, W., Profits, Chapters 2, 5, 6, 7, 8,
              and 9

[In margin: hour test, March 20]

    2. Personal Distribution
       Read: Taussig, Principles, Chapters 55 and 51
          Garver and Hansen, Principles, Chapter 31
          National Bureau of Economic Research, Bulletin

V. THE CONSUMPTION OF WEALTH
   1. The American Standard of Living
      Read: Hoyt, E. E., The Consumption of Wealth, Chapters 26 and 27
   2. The Psychology of Consumer's Choices
      Read: Bullock, C. J., Selected Readings in Economics, pp. 236–254
         Hoyt, E. E., The Consumption of Wealth, Chapters 3, 4, and 5
         Veblen, T., Theory of the Leisure Class, Chapters 1–7.
         Mitchell, W. C., The Backward Art of Spending Money" –
         American Economic Review, Vol. II, pp. 269 ff.
   3. The Consumer's Guidance of Economic Activity
      Read: Cannan, E., Wealth (1928), Chapter 6
         Chase, S., Your Money's Worth (1927), Chapters 1, 2, and 3
         Civilization in the United States, Edited by H. Stearns, pp. 381–
         395
VI. SOME CURRENT ECONOMIC PROBLEMS
   1. Labor Problems
      a. Trade Unionism
         Read: Garver and Hansen, Principles, Chapter 29 [added by hand]
            Taussig, Principles, Chapters 56 and 57
            Hoxie, R. F., Trade Unionism in the United States, Chapters 2, 3,
            and 4
            Marshall, L. C., Wright, C. W., and Field, J. A., Materials for the
            Study of Economics, pp. 668–709
      b. Methods of Adjustment of Labor Disputes
         Read: Taussig, Principles, Chapter 59
      c. The State in Relation to Labor
         Read: Taussig, Principles, Chapters 58 and 60
      d. Cooperation
         Read: Taussig, Principles, Chapter 61
   2. Industrial Combinations and Monopolies
      Read: Taussig, Principles, Chapter 65
         Garver and Hansen, Principles, Chapter 17
         Ripley, W. Z., Trusts, Pools and Corporations (1916), pp. xi–xxxiii,
         and pp. 484–505, 703–734

[In margin: Test, May 12]

   3. Railroads
      Read: Taussig, Principles, Chapters 62, 63, and 64
         Garver and Hansen, Principles, Chapter 18

4. Taxation
   Read: Taussig, Principles, Chapters 68, 69, 70, and 71
       Garver and Hansen, chap[ter] [added by hand]
5. A Critique of the Existing Economic Order
   Read: Taussig, Principles, Chapters 66 and 67
       Garver and Hansen, Principles, Chapter 32 [In margin: 26, 27, 29]
       Bullock, C. J., Selected Readings in Economics, pp. 668–681
       Marshall, Wright and Field, Materials for the Study of Economics, pp. 911–920
       Young, A. A., "Economics and War," Economic Problems, New and Old, pp. 1–20
       Carver, T. N., The Present Economic Revolution in the United States, Chapter 9
       Taylor, F. M., Principles of Economics, Chapters 46, 47, and 48
       Mill, J. S., Principles of Political Economy, Book V, Chapters 1, 8, 9, 10, and 11
       Communist Manifesto. Marx–Engels [added by hand]

[In margin: Final Exam]

(2)

[Ostrander's folder for Economics 1-2 also included the Syllabus for 1933–34. The principal textbook became Fairchild, Furniss and Buck. Other heavily relied-upon materials included H. D. Henderson, Supply and Demand; D. H. Robertson, Money; and S. Chase, The New Deal.]

ASSIGNMENTS FOR ECONOMIC 1-2
1933–34

I. INTRODUCTION: The subject matter of economics.
   Read: Fairchild, Furniss and Buck: Elementary Economics (1932)
       Chapter 1.
II. PRODUCTION
   1. Labor in production
     Read: Fairchild, Furniss and Buck, Elementary Economics, Chapters 2 and 5
         Smith, Adam, The Wealth of Nations, Edited by Cannan, Book I, Chapters 1, 2, and 3.

   2. Capital
      Read: Fairchild, Furniss and Buck, op. cit., pp. 32–40
         Mill, J. S., Principles of Political Economy, Edited by Ashley, Book
         I, Chapter 4.
   3. Management
      Read: Fairchild, Furniss and Buck, op. cit., Chapters 6, 7, and 8.
         Berle, A. A. and Means, G. C., The Modern Corporation and Private
         Property, Chapters 3–6.
III. PRICES
   1. Value
     a. Introduction
       Read: Fairchild, Furniss and Buck, op. cit., Chapter 11.
          Henderson, H. D., Supply and Demand, Chapter 2.
     b. Market Price (Competitive)
       Read: Fairchild, Furniss and Buck, op. cit., Chapter 12.
          Henderson, H. D., op. cit., Chapter 3.
     c. Costs and Normal Price (Competitive)
       (a) The Meaning of costs
          Read: Fairchild, Furniss and Buck, op. cit., Chapter 13.
            Henderson, Supply and Demand, Chapter 4.
       (b) Value under conditions of increasing cost
          Read: Fairchild, Furniss and Buck, op. cit., Chapter 14.
       (c) Value under conditions of decreasing cost
          Read: Fairchild, Furniss and Buck, op. cit., Chapter 15.
       (d) Value under conditions of monopoly
          Read: Fairchild, Furniss and Buck, op. cit., Chapter 16.
       (e) Related Prices; Joint Demand and Supply
          Read: Henderson, Supply and Demand, Chapter 5.
       (f) Speculation and prices
          Read: Fairchild, Furniss and Buck, op. cit., Chapter 30.
       (g) Critique of the Price System
          Read: Chase, S., The New Deal.
   2. Money and Banking
       (a) Metallic money and government paper money
          Read: Fairchild, Furniss and Buck, op. cit., Chapters 18 and 19.
       (b) Commercial banking
         a. Banking operations
            Read: Fairchild, Furniss and Buck, op. cit., Chapter 20.
               Dunbar, C. F., History and Theory of Banking (4th or 5th
               edition), Chapters 2, 3, and 4.

b. Central Banking
Read: Fairchild, Furniss and Buck, Chapter 21.
    Hardy, C. O., Credit Policies of the Federal Reserve
    System (1932), Chapters 2–4.
c. The Theory of money and prices
Read: Fairchild, Furniss and Buck, op. cit., Chapter 22.
    Robertson, D. H., Money (1929), Chapters 2, 3, and 7.
d. Fluctuations in Business
Read: Fairchild, Furniss and Buck, op. cit., Chapter 23.
    Robertson, D. H., Money (1929), Chapter 8.

3. International trade and exchange
  (a) The foreign exchanges
    Read: Fairchild, Furniss and Buck, op. cit., Chapter 25.
  (b) The balance of trade and the balance of payments
    Read: Fairchild, Furniss and Buck, op. cit., Chapter 26.
  (c) The Theory of international trade
    Read: Fairchild, Furniss and Buck, op. cit., Chapter 24.
  (d) Protection and free trade
    Read: Taussig: Principles of Economics, Chapters 36 and 37.
    Fairchild, Furniss and Buck, op. cit., Chapter 46.
  (e) World War Debt Settlements
    Read: Moulton, H. G., War Debts and World Prosperity.
    Hansen, A. H., Economic Stabilization in an Unbalanced
    World, Chapters 2 and 3.

IV. DISTRIBUTION
1. Functional Distribution
  a. Economic Rent
    Read: Fairchild, Furniss and Buck, op. cit., Chapters 31 and 32.
    George, Henry, Progress and Poverty (Schalkenbach ed.),
    Chapters 3–6.
  b. Interest
    Read: Fairchild, Furniss and Buck, op. cit., Chapters 33 and 34.
  c. Wages
    Fairchild, Furniss and Buck, op. cit., Chapters 35, 36, 39, 40, 48, 50.
  d. Business Profits
    Read: Fairchild, Furniss and Buck, op. cit., Chapter 37.
2. Personal Distribution
  Read: Fairchild, Furniss and Buck, Chapter 38.

V. CURRENT ECONOMIC PROBLEMS
1. Public Finance and Taxation
  Read: Fairchild, Furniss and Buck, op. cit., Chapters 41, 42, and 44.

2. Agriculture and Farm Relief
   Read: Black, J. D., <u>Agricultural Reform in the United States</u>, pp. 177–270; 480–490.
3. Railway Economics
   Read: Fairchild, Furniss and Buck, <u>op. cit.</u>, Chapters 27 and 28.
VI. A CRITIQUE OF THE EXISTING ECONOMIC ORDER
   Read: Fairchild, Furniss and Buck, <u>op. cit.</u>, Chapters 47 and 53.
   Marx, <u>Communist Manifesto</u>.
   Chase, S., <u>The New Deal</u>.

(3) ECONOMICS 2
SPRING 1930

[Due to water damage, the right side of the pages of notes, to an average of one-half inch or more, is often indecipherable.]

Theory of International Trade

Differences between Domestic and International Trade
   Tariff – peculiar taxation
   Wage Levels – Mobility (<u>less</u> over international barriers)
      –immigration and emigration
      –expense
      –lack of information
      –sentiment and custom
   Transportation
   Currency – Foreign Exchanges
   Lack of Mobility of Capital
      –sentiment
      –lower interest in old countries
      –higher in new countries

What do we import
   –we have least comparative advantage in their production
   –find it most economical to import
   1. Raw Silk
   2. Rubber   240,000,000
   3. Coffee   264,
   4. Cane Sugar   258,
   5. {Paper   149,

{Newsprint	138,
{Paper Base Stocks115,	
{Wood Pulp	
Furs	156,
Petroleum	115,
Hides & Skins	113,
Tins	108,
Copper	
Fruit	
Wool	83,

What do we export
  –certain Raw Materials
  Cotton
  Petroleum
  Meat and Meat Products
  –manufactures

[Page 1-A:

gold – convertible into money at a fixed ratio
        but not into commodities at any fixed ratio.
Exams – order and planning
                critical capacity (real criticism not grandiness).
          – value exported in 1928   5,500,000,000
                imported in 1928   4,500,000,000
          while Total National Income was 90,000,000,000
                –International Trade about 1/20th of Total Trade.
  Money incomes – money value
  Real Incomes – amount able to be purchased by the Money Income.
    –depend on Productivity.]

Manufactures
  Automobile
  Farm Machinery
Textiles
  –cheaper, not final or high grade.
  –to South America etc., not Europe.
1. Principle of Comparative Advantage
2. Reciprocal Demand – charges, – incomes

1. Comparative Advantage
  a. How explain the International Specialization?

England – textiles (wool and cotton)
   Coal – Iron and Steel
   Commerce
Germany – Steel – Coal
   Dyes
   Chemicals
   Nitrates

b. Case I – Absolute Advantage
U.S.
   1 man, 1 day = 10 units of copper
   1 man, 1 day = 5 units of cloth
      100,000 laborers
England
   1 man, 1 day = 5 units of copper
   1 man, 1 day = 10 units of cloth
      100,000 laborers
if specialization
   U.S. – 2 men, 1 day = 20 units of Copper
   England – 2 men, 1 day = 20 units of Cloth
   Effect of this on World's Total Production – will increase it
   Real Incomes increase with specialization
   Total World Production Increases with specialization

c. Case II – Comparative Advantage
U.S.

1 man, 1 day = 10 units of copper	2
1 man, 1 day = 5 units of cloth	1
England – 1 man, 1 day = 6 units of copper	3
1 man, 1 day = 4 units of cloth	2

If all 4 men moved to U.S. and worked on copper, the Total World's
   supply would greatly increase, from 16 to 40
–exhort them to move
If specialization,
   In U.S. 2 men = 20 units of copper
   In England 2 men = 8 units of cloth
Total Supply in world would then
   increase in Copper 16 → 20
   decrease in cloth 9 → 8
If two countries can each produce different commodities
   –each will specialize in that which they can <u>best</u> produce
   –rate of exchange will change

If each country specializes
–the total world production will be increased
–the average wage will be increased.
2. Reciprocal Demand
Stage 1
U.S. buys 1,000,000 yds cloth @ $10 yd.
= $100,000
U.S. exports 1,000,000 lbs copper @ $10 lb.
= $100,000
–a balance of payments
–equilibrium.

[Page 3-A:

"Hitherto you have always repelled foreign products, because they approximate more nearly than home products to the character of gratuitous gifts." – Bastiat
–if they exclude what is half-gratuitous (Lisbon orange) why not exclude what is altogether gratuitous (sun)
–as long as you exclude products in proportion as their price approximates to zero, what inconsistency it would be to admit the light of the sun – whose price is at zero.
–reciprocal obstacles could only be reciprocally hurtful.
–Road Makers and Obstructives working together.
Theory, is practice explained – Bastiat

"dumping" – where total supply is in hands of a monopolist, excess may be dumped abroad at a lower price than domestic]

Stage II
decrease in U.S. demand for Cloth, and increase in English demand for Copper.
Stage III
New Equilibrium
U.S. exports 1,500,000 lbs copper @ 0.11 lb.
$121,000 [sic]
U.S. imports 1,340,000 yds cloth @ 0.094 yd.
$121,000 [sic]
increase in American wage
decrease in English wage
Demand, as well as conditions of Supply, is very important
–affecting money income
–affecting purchasing power

Tariff
  –tax on commodity imports (or exports)
  –ad valorum
    –money value
  –specific
    levied, – so many cents per pound,
    –physical unit
[In margin alongside, with bracketing of three following points; to the left of bracket: almost the same]
  {Protective – to protect domestic concerns from foreign competition – <u>making up</u> differences in Price
  {Revenue – to furnish public moneys
  {Bounty – a payment by the government to a producer for some (service)
So long as a country is exporting a commodity
  –an import tariff on that commodity will have no effect on price.
  –tariff will not <u>always</u> raise the price
    –not when placed on exports

[Page 4-A:

[Rough supply/demand diagram with a reduced supply]
  Effects of Tariffs on Production (Protective)
    –of an agricultural import
    –a commodity made by a manufacturing process having room for technical improvement
    –where there is no room for technical improvement]
  Placing a tariff on imports will raise the price of the imported commodities by about the amount of the tariff
    –but a falling off of demand as a result of this tariff – and price rise, might lower costs, price
    –so that we could import it as a raised price – though not raised by the amount of the tariff – though the price, as compared with world price, will have been raised by the full amount of the tariff.
    When the tariff is placed on imports, which <u>could</u> be produced entirely in this country, the rise in price will not rise to the full value of the tariff, but this commodity will be produced at home – and no imports will be brought in.

Effects of Tariff
  –will not raise the price of an export
  –will cause some increase in prices on imports, which can be produced at home
  –(total) increase on imports not produced here

Effect of Tariff on Production
1. On an exported commodity (wheat)
   –tariff will have <u>no</u> effect
2. On an <u>imported</u> agricultural produce (coffee)
   –an immediate rise in price to the full amount of the tariff
   –with subsequent lowering of the total price
   –little effect on total production
3. On an imported commodity made by a manufacturing process
   –with room for technical improvement (sugar)
   –immediate effect is slight
   –but slowly a new group of marginal producers will arise in the country, and
       thus <u>cut down</u> foreign production by the amount of its production
   –by profiting by the raised price in competition with foreign producer
   –this is under conditions of increasing cost.
   –No room for improvement
   –This is encouraging a high-cost industry, in which we have <u>no</u> comparative
       advantage
   –thus a diversion of factors from our proper fields to this unnatural field.
   –This raises the price at which the consumer buys the commodity
   –This counteracts the advantages of geographical specialization
       –of which we make use to a <u>great</u> extent within our own country – National
           Specialization
       –then why not <u>international</u> specialization?

Bad Arguments for Protection
1. If we don't have Protection, we will have our markets flooded by the products
   of Pauper Labor
   –the temporary readjustment period, it is true, would be painful.
   But, we already export many goods which compete freely with goods made
   abroad.
   We already have a good many free goods – this would be disastrous to only
   a small group.
2. High wage argument.
   –tariff to maintain them
   and wages are high because of the high rate of productivity
[The following is on page 5-A; arrow on page 6 indicates intent for it to enter
here:
   Protective tariff an impediment to specialization
   –an impediment to high productivity – thus an impediment to high wages.
   Where highest wages in U.S. Agriculture! – no tariff there.]

3. Home Market argument.

Income Manufacture – urban population, lessen surplus of farm laborers – increase the size of the market in which agriculture sells

–But in reality, only one market has been substituted for another.

–no more foreign market

–It is not of benefit anyway, for it means high costs to agriculture (labor and supplies) and higher costs to manufacturers

4. Keep a favorable balance of trade

[In margin alongside: Mercantilism]

Money in country would increase

–but only money incomes would increase

–not real incomes

5. Equalize the <u>costs</u> of production

"<u>Scientific Theory</u>"

–Tariff duty just enough to make our costs of production equal the costs of production abroad

–Comparative Advantages are always changing

–equalized tariff would have always to change

–Leads to a complete loss of all advantages of international trade

–if carried to a logical conclusion.

–How equalize Costs of Production?

Whose costs shall be taken?

Differential Costs here and abroad

–protect the lower or higher producer.

[Page 7-A:

Free Trade Arguments
1. Tariff, raises price to consumer
2. Makes possible less efficient producers
3. Tariff keeps out goods made in more favorable climates

–Makes impossible the geographical Specialization of Labor.

–If carried to its logical conclusion, would result in ending of International Trade

4. Import Tariff here, make import tariffs abroad

–Slow down export industries in form of import

[In margin: opposite of U.S. mercantilism]

–Raise their costs of production

–as well as raising the costs to agriculture

5. Is only favorable to Import Industries

–is unfavorable to all export, as well as all domestic industries.]

–This policy – as well as all other tariff polices – is open to retaliating measures

–As soon as some producers are protected – and enabled to go against comparative advantage – other producers clamor for protection

6. It's often argued that a high Tariff is a good Revenue Agent.
   –but high tariff cuts the imports
   –a regressive tax –
   –more from poor than from rich
   –opposite from progressive Income Tax.
   –a larger fraction from income of poor than from income of rich
   –marginal utility

GOOD DEFENSE FOR PROTECTION

A. Economic arguments
   1. Infant Industry
      –a new firm is bound to make mistakes
      –gives them protection till they get on right track
      –gives a market, on which he can try out their advantages of large scale production
      –get started the utilization of good natural resources
      –Real Test of this argument
         –after a number of years can the tariff be removed and this industry exist
      –Will the industry ever be willing to admit maturity

[Page 8-A:

   2. Criticism
      –cities have their own evils that come with them →
      –poor living
      –change in normal standards
      –Is mill hand higher than farm hand
      –would not cities develop anyway – for trading and exchange
   3. But a Tariff Duty, accompanied by a Domestic Monopolist,
      –will enable him to entirely keep out competitors
      –and charge even higher prices]
B. Defense Argument – Military
   –if Defense is placed more important than Economy
   –if one expects to go to war regularly

–then it is advisable to put protective tariff on certain industries in order to
have them get by, in times of peace, so that in times of war, the Nation
might be self-sufficient.
–Chemicals
–<u>Foodstuffs</u>
C. Can be used as a Club in bringing down, or keeping down reciprocity tariffs
on the part of other countries
–<u>Diplomatic Argument</u>

More Bad Arguments
7. Lists' argument
–a Cultural life is all-important
–comes only when large numbers of people live together, as in a city
–so, in an agricultural country, a tariff is necessary to enable industries
– thus cities – to grow up.
8. Tariff to Combat a Foreign Monopolist
–forcing him to cut off the Monopoly Profit in order to shift the Demand
Curve (elastic) at a more fruitful place

[Page 9-A:

What is Distribution of Wealth
1, 2, 3.
How does Theory of Diminishing Returns apply
Relation between Distribution and Income
are Incomes from Prices
or Prices from Incomes
1928 – Total Production of U.S.
90 Billion
1922 – total Production had been
65 Billion]
Export Debenture Tariff
–Bounty, on exports
–Import Tariff necessary at the same time
–or Foreigners would buy wheat at the World Price, bring it here, and export
it, collecting bounty
–It does not make for <u>efficient</u> production,
–It will lower price in World Market
–Will Raise the Cost of living.
–Stimulate the growth of the High Cost Farm
–(same argument as is used, by Free Traders against Protective Tariffs

– was seen by all Republicans when a bounty is proposed – but not when Tariff)
Legislation on Tariffs
–must consider Political, Social and Psychological effects
–as well as Economic
IV. DISTRIBUTION
    –The proportion of National Dividend
   A. Functional Distribution
     –among the four factors of Production
     –return in form of Wealth or Income to these Factors

Land	– Rent
Capital	– Interest
Entrepreneur	– Profits
Workers	– Wages

   B. Personal Distribution
     –among the people – as social classes or groups.
     –a further subdivision of the above divisions,

[Page 10-A:

[At the top of this page are a few calculations:]

$$\begin{array}{ccc} 195 & 195 & 195 \\ \underline{3} & \underline{5} & \underline{4} \\ 585 & 975 & 780 \end{array}$$

$$100/1000 = x/2800$$

$$280000 = 1000x$$
$$x = 280\angle 4$$
$$70$$

No. of Men	Product in Bushels	Marginal Product	Wage for all Men
1	1000		1000
2	1800	800	700
3	2400	600	585
4	2800	400	390
5	3000	200	195

Marginal Product – product of the last worker added, whose marginal product just
pays for his cost at the prevailing rate.

Malthus – a Cambridge man – and a reverend.
   His first theory of Population published 1798
   Godwin (Shelley's father-in-law) – an anarchist
   Condorcet – a Frenchman

–had both taken up the theory first
–human misery and evils grow out of ineffective institutions
[An arrow is drawn from this point to the next page's discussion of Malthus]
–one high social class, church
Malthus wrote on 'Poverty of Nations'
–instead of "Wealth of Nations" – as Adam Smith]
A. Functional Distribution
Wages – per unit of Time
 –functional share in distribution received by human beings in return for services
1. Productivity Theory of Wages
Every one will get the same wage
–through force of competition
–any one worker is worth only the output of the last added.
Wages tend to equal discounted value of this Marginal Product.
Proofs –
Wages should be paid on basis of output
–said by Scientific Managers
–used in case where unit output is easily determined
One man, in a key position, able to speed up all Production, is paid more than an alternative, slower man
If wage more than Marginal Productivity is Paid – it is disastrous
Forces of Demand and Supply determine general level of wages
Demand, depends on Marginal Productivity
–thus on the supplies of other factors.
Improvements in technique, enable man to obtain a greater return for his labor – increased Marginal Productivity, lead to increased wage.
2. Malthusian theory of Population
–Human suffering not a result of institutions
–He opposed to that the pessimistic theory of Population
–human suffering an inevitable result of the tendency of population to surpass the subsistence available
a. was primarily interested in Quantitative Theory of Population
–food necessary for subsistence
–attraction between the sexes inevitable
–however – since contraceptions this does not necessarily result in children.

[Page 11-A:

Population of the U.S. almost 12,000,000 – 1928 [sic]
Increase in last decade (1918–1928) 14,300,000

At this rate it would take 80 years to double the population.]
–There is a tendency of population to increase beyond available means of subsistence.
–a potential ability, if not counteracted by other forces.
–by geometric progression.
  –while food increases only by arithmetic progression.
–Food Supply is a check on Population.
–This tendency is counteracted by other checks
  a. positive
     famine, war, pestilence, disease
  b. Preventive
     –from reason – moral restraint — voluntary
     –thought it would be accomplished through late marriage.

Criticisms
  –development of means of producing food.
  –increase in food supply has been faster than population
  –but sometime this must be slowed down.
  –he was making a long-run prediction
    –ahead of his time
  –he did not see that people might make a higher standard of living
  –thus, with increased ambition there will be less increase of population
  –the converse of Pearl's statement that in "harsh environment, a response of
     organisms in curtailing vegetative processes, and increasing reproduction."
     [the reading list contains the following: Raymond Pearl: The Biology of
     Population Growth, Chapter 7]
     –in an easy environment – curtailment of the reproductive process.
     –also a curtailment in dense Population.
  b. Qualitative Theory of Population
     Differential Birth Rate
     –Far more important to U.S. today than Malthusian Theory
     –High Birth Rate is more noticed as one goes down the scale of per capita
        wealth
     –But is it advisable to have the future population of the country recruited
        from the rich?
     Standard of Living
     –an ideal of living held up by the community – way they would like to live.
     –way people actually live, from statistics
     Relation to Wages
     –Wages and standard of living are interacting in raising each.

Relation of Standard of Living to Population
–limiting of population is a condition of the maintenance of a high
   Standard of Living.
–which will fall with an increase in population.
–but not necessarily the cause of the high Standard of Living
Motives for Immigration
–mainly Economic
   –although somewhat religious and political
–Restrictions on Immigration
–Exclusion
–Chinese, Japs, Indians – by treaty
–Insane, diseased, criminal
–Quota to any given country was 3% of 1910 population in this country
–Then changed to 2% of 1890 population
–Recently a set limit of 150,000 was fixed, and numbers apportioned to
   countries on basis that the population had numbered in 1890.

[Page 13-A:

1. Professionals and Entrepreneurs
2. White Collar Laborers – Clerks
3. Skilled Workers
4. Semi-Skilled Workers
5. Manual Laborers]

The more people seeking jobs, the lower the wages, the lower the marginal productivity, etc.

3. Difference in Wages – Why?
   –from one occupation to another
   –from one section of the country to another within the same occupation
   Compensating Differences   Adam Smith
      Expense of Education Time
      Risks (Physical Danger)
      Physical, Manual – rather than Intellectual
      Social Disesteem
      Seasonal Unemployment (vs [?] government)
   Willing to take a lower annual return on some other jobs, rather than
      undertake the above jobs.
J. S. Mill said that more disagreeable jobs got lower incomes, while agreeable
   jobs got higher wages.
   –disagreeing with Smith

–Morons in lower groups – more of them
–Intelligent People in higher groups, fewer.
1. Natural Ability
2. Environment
3. Self-Perpetuating stratification
4. Education (Training)
5. Connections, family, name, capital, etc.
    –opportunity
Democracy has effect on breaking down the barriers between the economic
groups.
    –we have idea that one man is as good as another
        –lower group man wants to rise – doesn't accept his position passively
        –some Democratic tradition at the top
        –Public School – State University

[Page 14-A:

Land–all natural resources
    –limited in amount
    –spatially immobile
    –non-reproducible

Rent –payment for naturally given resources and for permanent man-made
    improvements
[Hand-drawn illustration appears to be a depiction of Taussig's rent model in
which productivity, as measured by lower costs for a given level of output, yields'
higher rents]
Cost–payments for factors of production
    –payment for expenditure of human energy
    –reasonable return on investment]
Rent
    Economic Rent is distinguished from Commercial Rent
    –resulting in a simplified, unrealistic picture
        –but inevitable
    Differences in Rent from Fertility, Situation, Improvements.
    –Economic Rent
        –payment for the use of soil opposite from man-made improvements
        –Explicit –decided on beforehand-stated
            –derived from tenant
        –Implicit
            –rent derived by a landlord who is cultivating his own land.
            –not a definite statement of money

Cash Tenant – payment of cash at stated intervals
Share Tenant – payment by means of goods – in a fixed amount or in proportion
    to crop
Garver and Hansen go at the theory by <u>amount</u> of physical product and
    <u>market value</u> of product
    –marginal productivity of land
<u>Taussig</u> – calls Rent the producers surplus.
    –available only to producers who are producing below the marginal cost.
    –differential gain
Differences in Rent depend on
    –differences of fertility
    –cost of producing
If any particular piece of land should disappear, the loss to Society will be to
    the amount of the Rent – as Marginal Productivity or Producer's Surplus.
Rent is not a factor in Price } Taussig
    –but a result of Price } Taussig
    –does not help determine the Price – as true cost does –
    –the true cost of the <u>marginal producer</u> sets the price.
    –rent to superior producers is a consequence of this price
    (– but, all incomes are a result of price – wages, etc.)

[Page 15-A:

Taussig's view of the Marginal Producer is one that just meets the Demand Curve
    by his additions to supply
    –his cost includes money outlays for factors, and expenditure of labor
Most modern economists say the Marginal Producer is one that has to make
money outlays for factors and expenditures besides the <u>opportunity cost</u> of bid-
ding <u>land</u> away from other producers.
    –thus rent becomes a factor in Cost.]
    Rent is a factor in Price (Garver and Hansen)
    –land must be bid away from competing entrepreneurs
    –just as labor, and capital must be.
    –thus becomes a part of cost.
    (–even to Marginal Producer ←–)
    –Only time that Rent is not a factor in Price (cost), when Taussig's view
    holds – is when the land is suitable only for <u>one</u> sort of production, – very
    special case (as Royalties paid to mine-holders)

<u>'Single Tax'</u>
    –would bring in so much to the government that any other form of taxation
    would be unnecessary

–tax on economic rent.
–no tax on marginal producer
  –for it would put him out of business
–fundamentally – to abolish private ownership of natural resources.
–[Blank line]
–A Tax is needed that won't affect production or output
–Landowners take a share from producers, which share does not have an effect
  on the supply produced
  –if this were taken away, there would be no effect.
–Landlord can't add the amount of tax to rent, for the tenants could not pay.
  –and he cannot allow the land to be idle.
–Land belongs to all people – it is wrong for any <u>one</u> lucky person to appropriate
  the surplus value of land
  –that should belong to the State.

[Page 16-A:

Payment necessary to equalize the values of present and future goods.]
[But, how to figure out what is unearned increment
  –What to do if its purchasing power of money changes.

<u>Interest</u>
  Explicit – contract rate
              –call loan rate
  Implicit – expected return on investment
              –implied in a price
              –property values
Adding to the money supply does not have any permanent effect on the interest
rate.
  –prices will rise, and more money will be borrowed, more money will be paid
    over as interest, but the rate remains the same. [In margin: at any one time]
The Source of Interest is Impatience; Time Preference Influences on the Rate
  a. Psychological
      –certainty and uncertainty
      –foresight
      –self-control
      –love of posterity
      –habit.
  b. Character of Income
      –its distribution in time
      –if increasing – a high rate of impatience

–borrower
  –if decreasing – a low rate of impatience
  –lender
–its amount
  –marginal utility – low rate,
  –easy to save, if abundant
There is a relation between Implied and Explicit rates of interest
During a period of expansion, interest rises.
Productivity of Capitalistic Process is far more than that of direct Process.
  –control of some natural resources
  –men able to accomplish more

[Page 17-A

Usury Laws.   of no avail (service charges)
  –only way to stop usury is to increase the supply of funds.
Accounting – two sides
  Balance Sheet – Income – Profit and Loss – Sheet — double entry]
  Rate of Interest represents the premium of present over future money.
  Supply of Money is related to Psychological motives and character of Income.
Demand for Money
  Spendthrift loans – no production
    travel, munitions
    Business Borrowings
  –Bonds, Stocks, Short Time, etc.
  –owing to increased productivity of the delayed method of production
    –able to pay the premium for present over future, plus profit
  –development of new industries and lines of trade
Profits
  Business Profits
  –net incomes over all payments for running the business, and putting aside for
    depreciation – explicit expenses
  Pure Profits
  –income left after both explicit expenses and imputed costs have been taken off
    –which goes to the entrepreneur
  Imputed Costs
  –what the Entrepreneur could earn if he were working as a salaried manager
  –plus reasonable return on his original investment
  Entrepreneur
  –hard to define
  –in a private business the owner and manager is it

–in a corporation, the <u>theoretical</u> entrepreneurs are the stockholders, who have
  the vote
–but in actuality, it's the small group who <u>control</u> the <u>policy</u>. (Garver and
  Hansen)
–(the one's who actually take the risk) (Clark)
In a perfectly static world – no "risks," or changes, – there would be no profits.
–great fortunes made because of some change in this dynamic world.

[Page 18-A:

The answer seems to be that we must keep the profit motive, but restrict <u>and</u>
supervise the lines into which it could be turned.]
  The connection of Profits to uncertainty and Risks is very real.
    –changes in demand, costs, technique, etc.
    –tied up to ability to foresee.
    –two ways of passing on – dodging – risks
      –Insurance
        –fire, theft, loss, liability, war
        –replacing on total, but uncertain loss, but a partial, but certain loss.
      –Contracts for Futures Delivery
  Other conditions for Profit
  –Monopoly Gains
  –Fortuitous gains
  –Natural Ability
The Profits Motive
  –Is it a good plan to have Production determined by desire for Profits.
  –It is necessary to take a practical point of view
    –admitted that the quest for profits unrestricted – leads to waste and production
      of unnecessary items
    –but would any alternative plan, abolishing profits, do away with waste and
      deception?
  To say that the Profit motives make for a quick change of production, and better
    efficiency,
    –is to forget the experience of the U.S. during the War when to insure efficient
      production it cut out private profit.
  B. Personal Distribution
    –distribution of national income among the classes of Society,
      –instead of among the few factors of production.
        –which is functional
      a. Incomes Received
        –from side of person who receives it
      b. Incomes Produced

–from side of producers who turn it out
Information
a. Income Tax Bureau
  –Probate Courts
  –social workers (research)
b. From files of corporations, etc.
The two should agree in total amount
Distinction between Wealth and Income (Real [?])
  –Wealth is the Stock, already in existence
  –Income is the new flow, from year to year.
  –both are expressed in terms of money.
Corrections must be made for variation in the Purchasing Power of the dollar
  –by Index Numbers

National Income of the U.S.
  1909 –
  1920
  1928   89,000,000,000

Per Capita	Income	Index No.
1909	299	312
1910	307	315
1915	326	319
1918	537	340
1920	697	341
1922	597	369
1926	772	455
1928	790	

Change of the Purchasing Power of Money must be accounted for [Arrow from this statement to the column of Index Numbers]

Income Tax Reports 1924	No. of People
1,000–2,000	2,413,881
2–3,000	2,112,993
3–5,000	1,800,900
5–10,000	433,330
10–25,000	191,216
25–50,000	47,061
50–100,000	15,866
100–150,000	3,005
150–300,000	1,876
300–500,000	456
500,–1,000,000	241
1,000,000–	75

[In margin next to following table: Functional →]

Distribution between factors of production 1910

Wages & Salaries	67.5%
Interest	16.8%
Rent	8.8%
Profit	6.9%
	100.00%

Percentage of Income going to Producing Groups   1918

Mfgr.	31.47%
Agr.	21.01%
Govt.	8.87%
Transport	8.67%
Minerals	3.83%
Banking	1.27%
Misc.	25.38%
	100.00%

Total National Wealth today is about 1? [sic]
Average Per Capita Income 1914

U.S.	326
Amsterdam	263
United King.	243
Canada	195
France	185
Germany	148
Italy	112
Japan	29

[In right-hand margin: no corrections have been made for differentials in Purchasing Power of relative Monies.]

[Page 21-A:

Production has got to be taken into consideration
–even more than Distribution
[Diagram, similarly shaped to a chi-squared distribution with a narrow right-tail.]

Causes of Inequality
a. What are trades giving rise to great fortunes in the first generation.
b. What are the ways in which the later generations puts them to work.
a. What kind of means of gaining great fortunes do we find.
   –unfair practices   – Rockefeller, Gould
   –special abilities   – Morgan, Ford
   –a combination of lucky circumstances
Altruistic Hedonistic criticism of Inequality

–not working for greatest happiness of the greatest number,
Summary of the message of these statistics
–Historically there has been no great change in the social <u>distribution</u> of income
–Increase in the per capita Income for all classes
–also Per Capita Wealth increases
–due to increasing Production
–Real Incomes – in spite of the increase of prices – has increased

Modal Income.
–income received by the largest number of persons gainfully employed.
Altruistic Hedonistic criticism of Inequality
–based on marginal utility of money.

Disappearance of the Middle Class – and its Phil[osophy]
–larger lower class
–larger upper class.
–greater division
Suggestions of Change
–Inheritance Taxes

[Page 22-A:

Causes – Taussig – Differences of Inborn gifts.
            Maintenance of acquired advantages
            –through environment
            –through inheritance of property
    "Lessening of individual Capital – by inheritance Tax, lessens Social Capital"
– Does It? [Added in pencil: No]

% of Yearly Income

Income	Food	Clothes	Shelter	Fuel&Light & Fixtures	Furniture	Misc.
Under $900	44%	13%	14.5%	6.8%	3.6%	17%
900–1200	42	14	13.9	6	4.4	18
1200–1500	39	15	13.8	5.6	4.8	20
1500–1800	37	16	13.5	5.2	6.5	21
1800–2100	35	17	13.2	5	5.5	23
2100–2500	34	18	12.1	4.5	5.7	24
2500–	34	20	10.6	4.1	5.4	24.7]

F. M. Taylor said that inequality is inevitable
–some jobs have payments made for different agreeableness

–not true that today's rich are paid because of the disagreeableness of cutting
coupons
–but these payments would have to be made under any system.
–some jobs have a standard of living tacked on – equalities of salaries necessary
–Differences of wage necessary to show the relative importance of places for
labor – how to distribute the labor
Taussig's proposed systems of change
1. Taxes on Inheritances
–will it discourage saving?
–probably not.
–our high taxes today do not seem to have discouraged saving any.

Consumption
1. Way in which people actually do spend their income
2. Growth of Wants
3. Way choices of Consumers help to guide Production
1. Engel's Law:– As the size of income increases the proportion of the total
spent on necessities, such as food and shelter, decrease while the proportion of the total spent on Miscellaneous and Luxuries increases.
2. Explaining type and character of wants – Origin of demand
–old Instinct theory of explanation has gone out of vogue
–man was pugnacious – therefore, he bought fire-arms.
–Habit and Learned Traits
Custom – a long established wage – belonging to groups of people
–food.

[Page 23-A:

American Scales and Standards of Living
–Differences by Amount of Income
–slight – uniformity of American life
–Differences by Occupation
–slight – similarities are striking
–Differences by Country of Origin – and Race
a. usually wiped out in two generations
b. negro – very important
–Differences by Sections of the Country
–appreciable.

'congenital idiocy'

Veblen – we live in a world of traditional Emulation
{Conspicuous Expenditures

{Conspicuous Waste
    –asserting supremacy
Competitive Game of Money Making

Consume ostentatiously]
    –some grew up out of necessity.
    –some out of superstition, fear, ignorance, divinity
Customs are passed down by:
    –the Church, the school,
    –the Family, (environment)
    –Newspapers – radio,
    –<u>government</u> and the law
    –Society – group life
Customs are broken by:
    –Education
    –Advertiser
    –usually wasteful
        –buy from A, what B already [undecipherable word]
        –buy what you don't need
    –Scientific Discoveries
3. Choice between alternative Wants
    –Jevons and earlier Economists
    –Diminishing Utility – Comparative
        –Budgeting the expenditures so that the Dollar had the same Marginal use
        in any line.
    –But Humans are not as a whole rational and budgetary.
    –could they be if they wanted to be
    –Are all satisfactions reducible to a common denominator?
    –is there only quantitative pleasure?
        –or is true qualitative pleasure
    –Sidgwick says No. ([added in pencil:] R & V says Yes) [Not identified]
    –Are individuals free to choose? – No! Limitations
    –Sumptuary limitation by the State
    –Forced purchases – by State
    –Food Laws – cut out poor food
    –Patent Medicines
        –<u>must</u> be <u>labeled</u>
    –Marketing System

[In margin: lack of information – see Stuart Chase]
    –Standard Packages (not precise)

[Page 24-A:

What is the Labor Problem
   protection of labor market
   humanization of work
   [Preceding two lines added in pencil]
What is a Trade Union
–marketing organization, selling labor services – protection
   [Preceding line added in pencil]
–how significant in U.S. – workers
  –20,000,000 wage earners
  –4,000,000 Unionists
   [Preceding two lines added in margin in pencil]
What is reason for slight development in America
  –contrasts with abroad.]
Labor Problems
  –there is no <u>one</u> labor problem
  –but different problems, according to the point of view
  –Some Problems:

   <u>workers standpoint</u>
   –<u>hours</u>
   –<u>wages</u>
   –working conditions
   –accident insurance
   –women and children
   –strikers
   –<u>unemployment</u>
   –education
   –<u>discipline</u>

   Employers Standpoint
   –Hours
   –Wages
   –Productivity
   –Quality
   –Quantity
   –<u>Discipline</u>

   General Public's Standpoint
   –Product
   –Cost

–Regularity of Output
–Quality and Quantity
Garver and Hansen say – the main problem is the 'protection of the labor market.'
1. Trade Unions
    –group of organized workers
    –Garver and Hansen – Marketing organizations selling labor services
    a. Structural Grouping in Hoxie
        –<u>Craft</u> (or trade) <u>Union</u>
        –local and national organization
        –each member may perform <u>all</u> the tasks <u>in</u> the craft.
        –association of people doing <u>one</u>, very narrow job – skilled workers
        –bricklayers, engineers
<u>Industrial Union</u>
–industrial scope is coterminous with the capitalistic enterprise
–association of all workers in one particular industry

[Page 25-A:

Occupation	Percentage of Workers who were organized in 1920
Extraction of Minerals	41%
Mfgrs	23
Transportation	37
Building Trades	25
Stationary Engineer	12
Stationary Firemen	19
Trade	1
Professional Services	5
Clerical Occupation	8
Public Service	3
Domestic & Personal Services	7]

[Page 26 is a very complex set of columns, insertions, bracketed sets, and asides.]
local, district and national organization
    –territorial
    –industrial
    –skilled and unskilled
    –brewery — coal mine
<u>Unimportant</u>
    <u>Trade (or Crafts) Unions</u>

–city central bodies
–constituent unions retain their individual independence
–combination of several craft unions – federation
–as within a city, or country, or state or nation
–Chicago Group of trade unions.

General Labor Union
  –only local forms exist today
  –anyone who's a working Man
  –as old 'Knights of Labor'

Compound Craft or Crafts Unions
  –amalgamated
  –combination of two or more related crafts unions
    –carpenters and joiners
    –iron, tin and steel
  –industrially related craft unions → quasi-Industrial federations
      b. Functional Grouping–   Hoxie
          –by purpose, and philosophy
  –Business Unions
  –trade conscious, not class-conscious
  –regardless of workers outside its organic group
  –satisfied with things as they are
  –look at things as do business men
  –mainly craft unions
  –would cover the A. F. or L.
  –Uplift Unions
  –idealistic
  –improve conditions generally
  –old Knights of Labor
  –Revolutionary Unions
  –class-conscious
  –two forms:
    –Socialistic, accepts 'temporary' condition
    –Radical, no compromise
  –interested in a thorough-going overthrow of existing conditions
  –Syndicalist
  –I.W.W.
  –Predatory Unionism
  –aims at immediate ends
  –hold-up and guerrilla, forms

–willing to use violence
–selfish – absence of fixed principle
–<u>Dependent Unionism</u>
–There are Unions and Unions – no generalization can be made.
–Importance of Trade Unions in the U.S.
–There are great fields of work in which there is little or no organization

[Page 26-A:

[A chart of five groups below the heading of 'Labor']
Labor:
   Unorganized
   I.W.W.
   Amalgamated
      B. of L.E., B. of L.F., B. of L.C. [Brotherhoods of Locomotive Engineers,
      Locomotive Firemen, and Locomotive Conductors]
      A.F. of L
Hoxie – General Characteristic Types – The Essence of Unionism
Trade Unionism is not a simple, consistent entity, but a complex of the utmost
diversity
–an <u>opportunistic</u> phenomenon
  –arising in direct response to immediate need
  –by a trial and error method
  –theory slowly developed – on basis of experience.
–no fixed union norm.
–but there <u>are</u> distinct union types.
  (see previous page) – classified both structurally and functionally
  –essentially contradictory types
–Unionism – a consciousness of common interest apart from the rest of Society
–Trade – Unionism – The viewpoint of a particular group – the wage-workers
  –structured form is the agency of the group, in propogating its function
    –is dependent on and Secondary to the functional essence.
    –no correlation between the two types
  –a specific case of group psychology
    –subject to environmental and temperamental forces.
  →–is at the bottom <u>non-unitary</u>.
  –different functional types <u>do</u> exist
  –changes and grows functionally from within.
  –differing structural types and very likely to agree functionally
  –as agriculture, and clerical workers
[In margin: esoteric pragmatic interregnum]

Organized Workers
  –Amalgamated Clothing Workers of America
  –an industrial union
  –wide jurisdiction
National Organization – President – Executive Committee
National Convention – Amendments to Constitution
  –resolutions of policy – legislation
0.50 per month dues – Initiation fee $10.00
  –punctilious handling
  –have gone into banking – Amalgamated Banks
Have set up machinery for settling labor disputes
Made agreements with Employers to certain number of weeks of work per
  year – and furnishing [competent?] workers by the union.

Brotherhood of Locomotive Engineers
  –a limited craft union
  –District, R.R., Grand International organization
  –Grand Chief Engineer – and other National Officers
  –National Convention
  –Elaborate Benefits Funds and Pension Funds
  –Dues of $8.00 a year
  –have gone into banking business
  –Strict qualifications for membership.

American Federation of Labor
  –a union of unions
  –a true federation
  –over 100 craft unions in it
    –each a National or International union
    –with many locals
  –also – Departmental Trade Councils
    –Building Trades, metal Trades, Railway Workers, and Union label Workers.

[Page 27-A:

Historical review of trade unions – by periods
  I. Beginnings in the local craft union 1798–1827
  II. Predominance of trades unions 1827–1837
  III. Predominance of utopian, socialistic and social uplift unionism 1849–1853
  IV. Reorganization of local Unions, and beginning of national trade-unions
      1853–1860
  V. The revival of trades unions 1860–1866

VI. Attempted Amalgamation of National Craft Unions 1866–1874
VII. Predominance of its Universal Labor Union 1879–1890 – The Knights of Labor
VIII. Predominance of federation of National Craft Unions – 1840 – to present –The American Federation of Labor and national employer's associations
  IX. Beginnings of industrial unionism
      Two tendencies
      –harmonizing and unification of structural types
      –fanning out, separation, and distinction of functional types]

[A flow diagram whose structure is as follows:]
    Outer circle comprised of and connecting:
      A.F. of L. → Department → Trades Councils → Locals → State
    Internal lines comprising and connecting
      A.F. of L. → National and International → Locals
      A.F. of L. → State → Locals
      City Councils → Locals

    –National Departments
    –are National Trades Councils
    –Trade Councils
    –decide disputes between crafts.
    –to some extent a bargaining organization to enable all the workers in a particular line of industry to present a united front to the employers.
    –is only a partial answer to the charge that A.F. of L. is one craft – there is still no organization for non-skilled workers

    Closed Shop – entirely union, or entirely non-union (has become to mean only entirely union)
      –this is used as a part of demand for collective bargain – which would be unthought of in a non-union closed shop and ineffective in an open shop.
    Open Shop – open to either union or non-union men at the same time (–has come to mean only entirely non-union)

    Collective Bargaining – fundamental purpose of trade unions
      –workers presenting a united front to the employer in matters of wages
      –with threat of united strikes
      a. Carried on by local representatives of the workers
        –over whom the employer has the power of discharge
        –thus prefers

   b. Carried on by outside men from the Union National Headquarters – represents the local workers
   –much more effective
   –hated by the employers.
[Page 28-A

Lump of Labor Theory
   –just so much work to be done
   –increased efficiency is taking work away from someone]
   –How far can collective bargaining go toward raising wages?
      –it cannot surpass economic forces as represented by productivity
      –but a raise in productivity is followed by a raise in wages – only in the long run.

[In margin alongside preceding lines:
   a. Enable worker to obtain the real wages due to his productivity]
      –it is the duty of the Trade Union to make this wage raise occur in the
         shortest possible time
   –can do nothing if there is not open competition of labor
      –as in a small, one factory town
   –Trade Unions can help raise wages by increasing the productivity of its
      members – through increased efficiency
   –or by limiting the number of men in its union, insuring a higher wage to the
      few who are in it.
[In margin alongside preceding lines:
   b. increase productivity
      1. personal
      2. relation to other factors
      3. of industry as a whole]

Piece Work
   –payment of wage in accordance with the individual output
   –objected to by Trade Unions
   –Lump of Labor Theory
   –is usually based on the output of the most efficient worker
   –increases output, with a gradual lowering of wage – per unit of output
New Machinery
   –many trade unions have opposed introduction of new Machinery – on the
      lump of labor theory.
   –Molders Union
   –Printers (Typesetters) Union.
Hours of Labor
   –"A decrease in hours – increases the pay" – Ira Steward

–is true to a certain extent
–greater efficiency for shorter time
–especially in heavy manual jobs
–but it cannot be followed beyond a 7 or 8 h day.
–unless there is new invention to increase production
The Strike
–a concerted withdrawal of workers with the view to return to the <u>same</u>
employment under improved conditions
–Sympathetic Strike
–by a group of workers not directly concerned – with purpose of helping
some already on strike
–Pullman strike
–General Strike
–Strike of workers in all lines.
–mutually sympathetic
–also part of the program of certain radical groups
–Outlaw Strike
–contrary to orders of the National Union.
Lockout –
–employer takes away the chance of working.
Sabotage – usually means soldiering on the job – while drawing pay
–sometimes destruction of machinery
–Relation of Strikes to Law.
–May be called if object is lawful and means used are lawful.
–Lawful Strikes – object[ive]s
–changed stop rules, higher wages, shorter hours.
–Unlawful Strike Object[ive]s
–to bring about closed shop.
–against non-union materials

[In margin: Injunction → [pointing to unlawful strike objectives], indicating
application of injunction thereto]

–strikes with intent of injuring the employer – not benefiting workers
–thus sympathetic
Lawful Means –
–Picketing, if peaceful
Unlawful means –
–Picketing, if not peaceful
[Bracket enclosing both forms of picketing, plus: hard to judge between]
–Boycott

Enforcement – legal weapons of employers
  Bring Suit against Trade-Union
  –Danbury Hatters Case.
  –damages assessed against the individual workers
  –Coronado Coal Co.
  –against the union
Injunction – temporary restraining order – when unlawful results will come
  from evident procedure.
Strikes are spectacular – good news-items
  –actual amount of time lost is very small on the whole.
  –a fighting move – not to be commended
  –but a most effective way of enforcing collective bargaining in the state of
    things as they are
  –creates a certain amount of ill-feeling

Arrangements for Settling Industrial Disputes

  a. Private
     Preventative
     –welfare work – picnics – dances
     –personnel department
     –Profit-Sharing
       –putting the worker into an interest in the output
       –hard to get this idea into the workers head.
     Settling – arbitration machinery
     –Voluntary – Employer representative–Union representative–Impartial
     Arbiter
     –Sometimes Compulsory

[Page 31-A:

  Paper – Thursday May 1,
  United Shoe Machinery Co.
    1. Date and Time of Organization
    2. Forms of business organization
    3. Economies of large scale management or Production
    4. Monopolistic Power (279) & Profits (361-2) [numbers added in pencil,
       here and below]
    5. To what extent did it use unfair practices (505)
    6. Profits
    7. Experience with the law (431-4) – State & Federal (475-6)
  Jenks and Clark – The Trust Problem
  Elliot Jones – The Trust Problem

    Bureau of Corporations – Federal Trade Commission
      Outline
      Bibliography]
  b. Public
    –States send out industrial delegates to settle disputes
    –Some States require a report of all disputes to be made to the Department of Labor.
    –both the above have not been very effective

    –Kansas
      –set up compulsory courts to settle disputes
      –The Kansas Industrial Disputes Act – Court
      –some of its decisions were declared unconstitutional by the Kansas Supreme Court
      –was disregarded by Coal owners in a dispute
      –compulsory arbitration
      –was dropped in a short time

–Canadian scheme
    –disputes in the offing
    –application to Department of Labor
    –if no settlement, a complete investigation of both sides with 60 day period of probation
    –then publication of facts –
    –marshalling Public Opinion
    –only after investigation and 60 day period can there be lawful strikes
    –but the workers were not prone to abide by the 60 days

Legislation of Hours
    –For Men – little, except in respect to dangerous trades.
    –For Women – generally the 8 h day.
    –For Children – Prohibited usually
    –both come under 'Police Power' of the States, while Men are said to come under the 14th Amendment – Liberty to make contract.

Minimum Wage Legislation
    –Only for women.
    –an impartial group to set the very lowest wage consistent with health and good morals.
    –1st problem, the investigation and publication of offenders
    –2nd problem, certain workers weren't worth even the minimum rate
    –make applications to work below the minimum

–3rd problem – ultimate
–relation of the Minimum Wage to the amount able to be paid Labor in Distribution
Social Insurance
1. For loss of income due to industrial accident
2. For loss of income due to sickness
3. For loss of income due to old age
4. For loss of income due to unemployment

1. Prior to 1910 in U.S. (Workers Liability then Employers Liability)
   –had curious defenses for employers
     –assumption of risk of danger when taking a job
     –fellow-worker negligence not included
     –uncertainty of amount to be paid
     a. [bracket and arrow suggesting that defenses were to go here]
     b. amount had to be decided by Jury.
     c. large cost of trying the case
        –stood by U.S. government
     d. Ambulance Chasing
2. After 1910 – Workers Compensation Act.
   –little or no uncertainty as to how much shall be paid
   –set schedules, as $500 for loss of foot, $5000 for loss of life, etc.
   –handled by a State body or Commission
   –which decides on the validity – and the award
   –Employers are usually required to insure themselves
     –i.e., contributions on the part of all manufacturers to a general fund (casualty company) – from which payments are made

[Page 33-A:

[Two small diagrams; first indicated to be discarded; second apparently to illustrate relation of premiums and wages]
   The British Dole –
   –a fund formed in all years – Threefold Contribution
     –workers 1/3, employer 1/3, State 1/3
   –a device for finding jobs – employment agencies
     –registration necessary for insurance
   –since war – great unemployment
     –change in world demand
     –backward industrial organization
   –has made a great hole in the fund –

–made enlarged State grants necessary
–a certain difficulty of administration
–what to do with married women claiming dole?
–what to do with people who are willing to live on the small allowance of this dole?
Trade Unions in Britain are one cause of the poor condition there – not willing to accept reduced wage]
   –May insure with public or private companies – or with himself
   –are certain, the cost of procedure is small
   –although, the doctors bills being in some cases paid by the same Fund – they are apt to make frequent calls – charges higher
Theoretical discussion – on whom does the weight of the premium fall?
   1. On Consumer
   2. On Employer
   3. On Worker
As a general rule, in the end – the expense falls on the Worker
   –his marginal productivity remains the same
   –but his marginal cost to the employer is greater –
   –thus his wage should be lower
This scheme – through control of rates – the insurance Co. – leads the employers to put in further safeguards, and preventive devices
   –'Safety First!'

Unemployment
   –much more important to prevent unemployment, than give out doles
   –which are palliative, not remedial
  –Causes of Unemployment
    1. Drifter – <u>unemployable</u>
    2. Introduction of New Machinery
      [In margin, in pencil: transitional]
     –putting out old <u>permanent workers</u>
    3. Shifting Demand
     –domestic
     –world
    4. Seasonal Character of Industry
     –canning, fruit picking
     –change in Seasonal Demand
    5. Cyclical Works of Business
     –try to eliminate it, but make it easier to shift – from standpoint of workers
      –unemployment insurance

[Page 34-A:

Monopoly Profits
  [diagram: although unlabelled, shows profits as aggregated difference between
    cost and price for volume of output]
    –prevail where the good is incapable of resale – as sugar.
  Monopoly – (Ely) Substantial Unity of Action by one or more persons,
    Giving exchange control
    Especially in respect to price.
  Monopoly – word must be correlated to size of district involved
    –town, country, State, National, etc.]

Cooperation
  –Rockdale Stores in England – retail trading
  –owned by a large number of individuals who are the traders
  –only salaries paid – no profits
    –all are turned back to the owners
  –Is a scheme for enabling the consumer to save money – but has no great
    importance in the capital–labor struggle
  –Has not been very successful in production
    –a business executive is needed at the level of the business.
    –no way of supplying necessary [capital ?]
  –Cooperative marketing
    –has been very successful in the U.S.
  –Cooperative Granaries – farm machinery

INDUSTRIAL COMBINATION AND MONOPOLIES

  I. Simple Monopoly
      –charge the same price to everyone = uniformity
 II. Discriminating Monopoly
      1. Professional Men and Artists
      2. Different Prices in order to attack varying scales of Society
         –books, theaters
      3. Charging different prices on the same service – on basis of the difference
         of commodity
         –railroad rates
Effect of Monopolies
  –on small-scale economies
  –on large-scale economies

–on quality of the good
–on quantity of the output
–Relation of Monopolies to Industrial Progress.
Monopoly Sellers – complete control of Supply
       Buyers – complete control of Demand
          – Beef Trust
          – Public (Franchise)
Methods of bringing about Combinations
–purposes for Combination, always to increase prices, (thus profits) above the
    free competitive level.
–Pool
    –a voluntary unity of action
    –loose agreement, no unity of ownership or control.
    –common fund of profits, usually.
    –as Steel Rail Pool
    1887–1893
Patent Pool – "bath tub pool"
          – manager
          – control of one very essential tool
          – control of a fund of [indecipherable]
Market Pool
    –country divided into separate marketing districts
    –one producer for each district
    –Addyston Pipe Co. Case.
    –fictitious bidding.
    –always broke down, because of their very looseness
    –someone always broke out on his own
    –was not enforceable by law
Trust
    –form of organization, group of stockholders in various companies turned over
        controlling stock to Trustees, on receipt of Trust Certificate, which enabled
        them to share in profits. Voting rights given up.
    –not as loose as in pool.
    –no temptation to sneak out
    –Standard Oil Co.
Investment Trust – very much the same as above
    –purpose different
    –diversified investment to small buyers

(Trust Co. – professional trustees)

[Page 36-A:

Return to Competition after a Monopoly regime does not mean, inevitably, lower prices.
–as in American Tobacco Co.
[Chart showing highly variable pig iron prices and monopoly prices of steel rails]
    Pig Iron – a highly competitive market
    Steel Rails – cut in price doesn't increase sales (inelastic demand), but
        although 3 of 4 competitors cut to same place
–No Conspiracy – merely tacit]
Trust disappeared because of the intervention of the government
–minority stockholders were unrepresented
New New Jersey laws were very free – allowed the Holding Company
–form of business organization – for the purpose of combining other companies
    by a holding and controlling interest in the stocks of the small companies.
–New York Central – an operating and a holding company
In 1911 – The Supreme Court held that Holding Companies (Standard Oil and
    American Tobacco) were capable of dissolution – when formed for
    monopolistic [indecipherable]
Since 1911, either complete Consolidation or a loose organization, Open Price
    Association.

Sources of Power of Monopolistic Control – Unfair Practices

    –Railroad discrimination and pipeline controls
    –Price War
    –Buying up Competitors
    –Starting false (low-price) competition
    –Exchange Trade Agreements
    –Large Scale Management and Production
    –Tying Clauses
    –Patents
    –"Pittsburgh Plus" Price system
        –steel sent from nearest mill, but freight was collected as from Pittsburgh

Relation of State to Industry
    Common Law
    Sherman Anti-Trust Act 1890
    Clayton Act

[Page 37-A:

Income is a flow, Wealth is a stock.

Three periods in Government's attitude toward Industry
  1. Common Law – laissez faire
  2. Trust busting
  3. More modern move toward combination]
Federal Trade Commission Act – (Wilson) 1914
–five men – to take care of all industry but railroads and banks
–investigate, publicity
  –power to demand information
–recommend, help with dissolution plans of Trusts broken up
–investigate foreign conditions
–power to suppress unfair competition

Clayton Act 1914
–an omnibus bill – supplementary to above
–defined unfair practices
  –lessening competition
  –exclusive trade agreements
  –tying clauses
  –holding companies
  –interlocking directorates
    –no man on boards of two banks each with capital of $5,000,000
    –or two industries each with a capital of $1,000,000
Since these acts destined to enforce competition and broke [sic] up combination
have been passed, there has been a certain reversal of public sentiment towards
combinations
  –idea that open competition is often <u>very</u> wasteful.
Thus Webb Law 1918
  –combination allowed to promote foreign export trade
  –Also a motive – old <u>mercantilism</u> still existent in one place on the earth, the
    U.S. Congress.
Government benevolence toward farmers
  –authorizing marketing organizations
In 1921 – An act authorizing the combination of telephones and telegraphs
Transportation Act of 1920 – advocates unification into a <u>few</u>, big, competing
systems – rather than old free competition.
Every big Combination is not necessarily successful
  –some have been very much so
  –but a great majority have failed
    –change of demand
    –potential competition becoming actual competitors

Railroads
What is their relation to the Consuming Public
  –to the Producing Public
  –effect of railroad rates on geographic specialization
What is their relation to the government
  –rates and rate regulation
  –security and security issues
  –combination, consolidation, and merger
Internal Problems

  Cost
  a. many outlays for factors
  b. real costs – human efforts and exercise
a) Cost – overhead – fixed
            –direct – variable
  overhead – for outlays not attributable to any particular operation
  direct – for outlays which can be distributed to the exact operation
    [indecipherable]

	Overhead –if no trains run	Direct –for actual running of trains	Total
Fixed	28		28
Maintenance of W&S	10	5	15
Maintenance of Equipment	7 ½	7 ½	15
Conducting Transport	19 ½	19 ½	39
Taxes	3		3
	68%	32%	100%

Amount of wages paid varies directly with number of trains run
  –or fuel.
Every big industrial concern has overhead costs
But is especially important in connection with railroads.
  –necessity of meeting fixed costs – unattributable – gives rise to price discrim-
    ination.

History of Railroad Rates
1. Fluctuating
2. Discriminating
  a. place discriminations
    –got railroads into trouble
  b. personal discriminations
    –as Standard Oil Co.

c. Commodity discriminations
   –"what the traffic will <u>bear</u>"
   –Class rate
   –in order to pay <u>somehow</u> this one
Joint Cost – quantities of one inevitably produced along with quantity of
   another good – in invariable [proportion]
   –hides and beef
   –cotton and cotton seed
   –wheat and bran
   –total money income <u>must</u> cover costs of producing both
–does not enter into Railroad operation in its strictly literal meaning
   –except in case of "Back Haul"

$$A \rightarrow 0.50 \rightarrow B$$
$$A \leftarrow 0.45 \leftarrow B$$

Overhead cost in relation to Price Policy.
–average (per haul) cost of operation goes down with each additional haul
   made
   –railroads are thus very anxious to increase their operation – growth of traffic
   –decreasing costs a result of <u>very</u> heavy overhead.
Between main traffic centers a great deal of Competition – among 'trunk lines'
   –a town with a single railroad is in a helpless position.
Certain <u>Place</u> discrimination still exists as a result of competition

Valuation
   –necessary in order that "reasonable return" may be determined
   –'reasonable return' on a 'fair value'
   –5 ¾% has been determined as the 'reasonable' rate
   –But, on what to apply that rate?
   a. Market Value
      –means virtually accepting whatever rate has been charged, as suitable for
        the regulation-regime
      –great possibility of over-capitalization
      –assumes that all previous rate regulation has been O.K.
        –arguing in a circle
   b. Original Cost
      –valuation of right of way
      –Is replacement – paid for by monopoly profit – to be taken as original cost
        –easy to cover.
      –How to distinguish Original Cost from Later expenses
        –poor accounting – change of hands

–not able to be found by historical averages
–What to do with a Changing Purchasing Power of the Dollar.
–Should the profits derived from sale of former right of way be subtracted?
c. Replacement Cost
  –Replace it just the same as it is or in a different, more modern way
  –two different figures possible.
  –Continual revaluation necessary to keep up with Level of Prices.
  –boosting and lowering of rates
  –but this makes the income of the stockholders very speculative.
O'Fallon Case – 1929
  –I.C.C. had laid too much emphasis on Original Cost
  –lost its case and must use the principles of Replacement from now on.
Railroads during the War.
  –were taken over by Governments 1917–1920
  –that the government did not run them very well is largely private propaganda
  –There was an enormous dispute.
    –not because of poor management
    –but because of a steady rate,
      –kept so by commission
    –and because of changing level of Prices.
  –But they were operated with considerable efficiency, and the period cannot
      be taken as an example by either side because of the extreme conditions
      of War

Transportation Act of 1920

1. Consolidation – not more than 19 systems
   –Cost of Transportation about equal
   –Certain Competition retained
   –Consolidation must have approval of I.C.C. and private systems
2. An increased grant of power to I.C.C.
   –its approval necessary
     –for construction and abandonment
     –for security issue
3. A new proviso for rate regulation
   –5 ¾% for reasonable return
   –this is to be the average rate of return for each district
4. Recapture clause
   –often a Railroad makes over 6%, one-half of surplus goes to government,
      one-half to a special fund.

Public Expenditures and Taxation
1. Differences between government expenditures and private expense
   –government ones are for common good.
   –can direct expenditures into the more valuable line
   –away from <u>emulative</u> element of the private expenditures.
2. Various trends of Public expenditures.
   –have been greatly increasing
   –1800 – Federal expenditures $2.00 per capita
   –1900 – Federal expenditures $7.00 per capita
   –1919 – Federal expenditures $180.00 per capita
   –1923 – Federal expenditures $20.00 per capita
   –government doing more than before
   –rising price level
   –Municipal and State especially have been increasing even faster and
     more.

–U.S.	3,207,000,000	}	
–States	1,264,000,000	}	1926
–Cities	4,004,000,000	}	

–Proportion for War, 1920

Past Wars	
Pensions	5.8
Obligations unpaid	28.7
Interest	<u>16.3</u>
Reduction	19.0
	69.8%
Current, future wars	<u>23.8</u>
Total Military Expense	93.6%
Primary functions of government	3.9
Public Works	<u>1.5</u>
Research – education	1.0
	100%

somewhat exaggerated in that year—but at least 75% or 80% today

[Page 43-A:

[Two diagrams, each accompanied by commentary:
   (1) Downward sloping curve plus pairs of lines perpendicular to the axes,
showing increase in price and decrease in quantity due to tax (no labeling).
Comment:] If a flexible demand, the supply will be reduced and price raised –
whole tax passed on to consumers.

(2) Downward sloping curve intersecting two upward sloping curves, the [latter showing shift to left. Comment:]
  –Increasing cost – tax raises cost by an amount less than itself.
  –Decreasing cost – tax raises cost by an amount more than itself – although the fact of decreasing cost, and the extra means available counteracts this.]

3. Sources of Revenues
    –Industrial Earnings
      –when Government is a producer
    –Fees – special return to individual paying
    –Loans
    –Taxes
    –a compulsory payment by person or corporation to a government, destined to defray cost of government services, performed for the common benefit; paid without reference to individual benefit

  a. Federal and State Income Taxes
  b. Federal and State Inheritance Taxes
  c. Federal Customs and Tariffs
  d. Excises – indirect taxes
  –trend is away from c and d, toward a and b

  Direct tax – paid and borne by person on whom it is assessed.
  Indirect Taxes – can be shifted (intent of legislators)
    –tariffs – cost turned over to consumer, not importer
    –line between the two is somewhat in definite
  –Taxes on commodities will have different effects as they are laid on things produced under increasing or decreasing costs.
  –Single taxers say the Landlords are already charging all the tenants can pay.
    –Thus the tax could not be shifted
  –Income Tax – are not in general shifted

Socialism – Critique of Existing Order
  –studied to give contrast to the order we have, show what else we might have
  –as a point of 'Liberal' education – along with other ghosts, we should understand this modern bugbear.

[Page 44-A:

  old government functions
    protection of property – enforcement of contract –
    protection of peace and life.]

Definition of Socialism
–Skelton [not identified] – an indictment of the capitalist system – an analysis
  of it. – a substitute or panacea for the evils of capitalism, – a campaign
  against capitalism

Socialism	Present Economic Order
–Government ownership	–Private property – no longer unlimited [?]
–Abolition of inheritance	–Inheritance – though taxed
–Government management	–Free and private enterprise – Free contract
–Authoritarianism	–Voluntarism – with certain limitations
–Government Control	–Production and allocation of resources in response to market demand

Indictment of the Modern Capitalist Order
  1. Production for Profit – instead of for use
    –production of socially unnecessary things
    –production of what people want – no matter what the quality of that want
  2. Wastes of Modern Competition
    –advertising
    –competitive stealing [selling ?]
    –distribution
  3. Commercial Crises – cyclical
    –unemployment
  4. Unfair distribution
    –exploitation of workers
  5. Bourgeoisie temperament – Ben Franklin
    –investors – thrift
  6. Leisure Class
  7. Spiritual Evils – poor working conditions

Kinds of Socialism
  1. Utopian – ideal State – rationally planned
    – Fourier
      –small communities – limited numbers
      –self-sufficing

[Page 45-A:

Hegel – What is real
        What is natural
        What is the nature of the Cosmos

thesis	antithesis	synthesis
one proposition	another proposition	a unity

Iron Law of Wages –
  –always just at a minimum necessary to keep off starvation
Marx took a lot from Malthus
  –adopted his conclusion, but not his method]
2. Marxism – scientific socialism
    –Economic Interpretation of History
     Marx inverted the Dialectic of Hegel
    –accepted the continual flux and change
    –looked at the Social process as a thing of flux
    –Feudal order ↔ Trader in villages = Democratic state
    Democratic State ↔ growth of proletariat=Socialist state
    –Every social order contains the seeds of its own dissolution
    –Intellectual and Social history of any era depends on the Economic
       Organization of that era.
    –for people are understood in terms of the way they make their [money ?]
   –Class Struggle
    –all history is this
    –those who have ↔ those who have not
    –are economic classes
  –Marx's Theory of Value
    –took over in an erroneous form Ricardo's labor theory of value
    –labor is the only common element in all commodities
    –labor is the source of all value
     –especially socially necessary labor.
    –surplus value – not turned over to the rightful owners – but kept by the
       employers – who are in a position of power
    –gives rise to interest, profits, rents
    –workers create all value, but
    do not get all value
  –Practical Predictions
    –growth of reserve army of unemployed
    –growing misery of the proletariat
    –growth of trusts and combinations
     –large-scale operations
     –inevitable ending of free competition
    –Increasing Commercial Crises
    –Decreasing Quantity of Middle Class.

[Page 46-A:

Ely, Outline of Economics

Clay, H., Economics for the General Reader]
Criticism

   –Economic Interpretation – interesting worthwhile – used today – Tumer-
      Beard [Frederick Jackson Turner; Charles A. Beard]
   –but any <u>single</u> explanation is dogma,
   –should be used as <u>one</u> method, among many
   –Theory of Value – almost incomprehensible
   –things as they are – or as they ought to be?
   –what of Natural resources – no labor?
   –what of Capital – Interest
   –His predictions have not come true
   –except in the line of combination
 3. Guild Socialism
   –each industry operated as a unit – [indecipherable] the workers organized
      as guildsmen
   –the industry in hands of workers – rather than the government.
   –organization of consumers
   –a syndicalist organization
   –Political officials to handle jurisdictional disputes.

Criticism of Socialism
   –a Socialist State would have many of the same problems as the Capitalist State
   –what to produce?
   –how much to produce?
   –who to produce it?
   –in the Capitalist State these are left to the results of profit and demand
   –an extremely difficult task to answer these questions, without the play of profit
      and demand.
   1. will <u>political election</u> get men who can run industry better than the method
      of private capitalism
   2. [blank]

   –How to keep away from Red Tape
   –What of Malthusian principle
      –if income is assured, will not the family increase?

[Page 47-A:

"Moments of Astute Vacuity"
   –in the White House
      (Coolidge)]

Critique of Existing Order
  –instruments have to be valued with reference to the purpose involved
  –Wealth is one means, not an end.
  –an ideal of the <u>Good Life</u> for the greatest number
  1. How effective is the existing order in bringing about this sort of ideal?
     –Does private capitalism produce the <u>right</u> things? – not entirely
       –lunacy of demand
     –Are men producing things at a <u>maximum?</u>
     No – we increased by twice during war
     –Do we have proper Regularity and of Production? – No
     –our Seasonal and Cyclical periods
     –Are goods distributed rationally
       –are distributed so as to act as an incentive
       –but a certain amount of waste
  2. What is the effect of the existing order upon the type of the person?
     –Competition – gives a competitive ideal – carried over from business,
       into all forms of life
     –Private Property – its effect on human nature – timidity
  3. We have a state which is leaderless.

MATERIALS FROM ECONOMICS 5 AND 6, MONEY AND BANKING, AND PUBLIC FINANCE, TAUGHT BY WALTER B. SMITH AND WILLIAM H. WYNNE, WILLIAMS COLLEGE, 1930–31

Warren J. Samuels (Editor)

INTRODUCTION

Economics 5, offered in the Fall, and Economics 6, offered in the Spring, comprised a year course. The first part, covering U.S. money and banking including U.S. and foreign banking, finance and investment, extended into the second semester, and was followed by public finance. The monetary and finance material apparently was taught by Walter B. Smith and the public finance material by William H. Wynne. The Williams College Catalog indicated two semesters, each with its homogeneous content for money and banking and for public finance.

Walter Buckingham Smith received his B.A. degree from Oberlin College in 1917, and his M.A. and Ph.D. from Harvard, in 1924 and 1928, respectively, also studying at the University of Chicago. He taught at the University of Minnesota (1922–23) and Wellesley College (1924–29) prior to moving to Williams in 1929

Further Documents From F. Taylor Ostrander
Research in the History of Economic Thought and Methodology, Volume 24-B, 109–181
Copyright © 2006 by Elsevier Ltd.
All rights of reproduction in any form reserved
ISSN: 0743-4154/doi:10.1016/S0743-4154(06)24023-9

where he was Professor of Economics until 1950, at which time he moves to
Claremont College. He published *Fluctuations in American Business,
1790–1860*, with Arthur Cole, in 1935 and *Economic Aspects of the Second Bank
of the United States*, both with Harvard University Press in 1953. He also published a number of journal articles. Smith was born in 1895 and died in 1971.

William Harris Wynne received his B.A. and M.A. from Queens University,
Canada, in 1919 and 1920, respectively. He studied law at the University of
London and Inns of Court, 1920–21. After positions at Trinity College, Cambridge
(1921–24), and at Queens University (1924–25), he moved to Williams in 1925,
where he published *State Insolvency and Foreign Bondholders* in 1951 with Yale
University Press, and several journal articles.

I am indebted to Alan de Brauw, Holly Flynn and F. Taylor Ostrander for assistance.

MATERIALS FROM ECONOMICS 5, MONEY AND BANKING, TAUGHT BY WALTER B. SMITH, WILLIAMS COLLEGE, FALL 1930, EXTENDING INTO SPRING 1931

Introduction

F. Taylor Ostrander was an undergraduate student at Williams College during the
first years of the Great Depression. He took Walter B. Smith's course, Money and
Banking, Economics 5, during the Fall 1930 semester. The course outline (item 1,
below) indicates the comprehensive coverage given in the course. Three-quarters
of a century later, we know something of what subsequently transpired in the
areas of money and banking covered in the course. From Ostrander's notes we
learn something of how Smith treated these subjects. Much of the course was
devoted to the details of monetary and banking systems and instruments and their
history. Smith knew his material very well; his mind-set, based on his doctoral
study at Harvard, was that of the mainstream of money and banking thought at
the time. For example, his notion of the role of reserves was in terms of "hard
money," i.e., redemption into gold under a gold standard as the framework of
thought – not surprisingly given experience and thought up to that time, with its
emphasis on "backing," or security tied to reserves. Still, it may be surprising to
some how modern the course was – in terms of what was taught on comparable
topics in post-World War II money and banking courses. Remarkable is it, perhaps, that three and one-half pages of notes are devoted to business cycles.
Among the notes on the business cycle is the statement, "–Smith's guess – when
all facts are collected – no one thing will ever explain it all." Smith's treatment of

business cycles is also typical for its time. His emphasis is on prices rather than on spending and the causes of changes in spending. In retrospect, he gets certain relationships (between phases of the cycle and causes) reversed. The concluding lines of the notes, which deal with Hawtrey's theory, illustrates the weaknesses of the time.

One senses that this money and banking course was conducted at a high level. Money and banking was then and has been since a central course for majors in economics and business, perhaps slightly diminished in stature as macroeconomics came into its own after World War II. The Williams College undergraduate was an elite student academically. One suspects that many went on to successful careers in business, including banking and finance. This course helped them. Also, by the 1960s the corporate finance part of money and banking was taught in a separate course by that name.

Only corrections and minor stylistic changes have been made. Editorial remarks are contained in square brackets. Ostrander usually wrote his notes on one side of a sheet, marked 1, 2, 3,. . ., 28. On the back of a page, facing the next page, numbered 1-A, 2-A, etc., he occasionally continued his note taking; but also occasionally entered other notes. The former are treated as regular notes; the latter are marked within brackets.

Published below are (1) the outline for Econ. 5 (1930–31), (2) assignments for Econ. 5 (1930–31), (3) questions on the Federal Reserve System, (4) the mid-year examination for Economics 5, and (5) Ostrander's Notes taken in class.

(1) OUTLINE FOR ECON. 5 (1930–31)

I. INTRODUCTION
   1. Problems at issue
   2. Determining factors in monetary and banking policy
II. MONEY
   1. Functions of money
      a. A medium of exchange
      b. A standard of value
      c. Other functions
   2. The history of metallic currency
   3. Government paper money
III. COMMERCIAL BANKING
   1. The nature and functions of credit
   2. Credit instruments
   3. The nature and functions of a commercial bank

   a. Note issue
   b. Deposit banking, and the clearance principle
   4. History of commercial banking in the United States
   5. Commercial banking and capital formation
   6. Commercial banking and business fluctuations
      a. Secular, seasonal and cyclical variations
      b. Monetary theories of the business cycle
   7. Some related financial institutions
      a. Commercial Credit and discount companies
      b. Commercial paper houses
   IV. THE FEDERAL RESERVE SYSTEM
   1. Distinctive characteristics of central banks
   2. The movement for banking reform in the United States
   3. Structure of the Federal Reserve System
   4. Operations of the Federal Reserve Banks
      a. Note issue
      b. Rediscount
      c. Open market operations
      d. Other operations
   5. The Reserve Banks and the money market
   V. FOREIGN BANKING SYSTEMS
   1. English banking
   2. French banking
   3. German banking
   VI. INTERNATIONAL FINANCIAL RELATIONS
   1. Foreign exchange under the gold standard, a paper standard, and the
      gold exchange standard
   2. The Bank of International Settlements
   VII. INVESTMENT BANKING
   1. Underwriting
   2. Investment trusts
   3. Savings banks
   4. Trust companies
   VIII. AGRICULTURAL CREDIT IN THE UNITED STATES
   1. The Federal Farm Loan Board, the Federal Land Banks, and the Joint
      Stock Land Banks.
   2. The Federal Intermediate Credit System
   IX. SOME UNSETTLED PROBLEMS OF MONETARY THEORY AND
       POLICY
   1. The quantity of money and its relation to money and prices

2. The future of the gold standard
3. The relation between the internal and external depreciation of the currency
4. Reparations payments and their effect upon the currency
5. The bank rate and international movements of gold
6. The influence of central banks on the money market and on business
7. Commercial banking and capital formation
8. Banking concentration
9. International cooperation.

(2) ASSIGNMENTS FOR ECON. 5 (1930–31)
[Editor's note: additions to typed list made
in longhand are enclosed within braces.]

I. INTRODUCTION
II. MONEY
   a. The functions of Money
      Read: James, F. C., The Economics of Money, Credit and Banking (1930), Chapters 1, 2, 4, 5, 6, and 7.
      Foster, W. T. and Catchings, W., Money (1923), Chapters 1, 2, 3, 4, 6, 10, and 11.
      Robertson, D. H., Money (1929), Chapters 1, 3, and 6.
      Edie, L. D., Money, Bank Credit and Prices (1928), Chapters 1, 2, and 3.
   b. The History of Metallic Currency
      Read: James, F. C., The Economics of Money, Credit and Banking, Chapter 3.
      Holdsworth, J. T., Money and Banking (1920), Chapters 3 and 4 to page 46.
      White, Horace, Money and Banking (3rd ed.), Book I Chapter 5 and Book II Chapter 6.
   c. Government Paper Money
      Read: Dewey, D. R., Financial History of the United States (1918), Chapters 2, 12, and 15.
      White, H., Money and Banking, Book II, Chapters 1–5.
      Phillips, C. A., Readings on Money and Banking (1920), Chapter 5.
III. COMMERCIAL BANKING
   1. The Nature and Functions of Credit

Read: James, F. C., The Economics of Money, Credit and Banking,
Chapter 8.
Phillips, C. A., Bank Credit, Chapter 1.
2. Credit Instruments
Read: James, F. C., The Economics of Money, Credit and Banking,
Chapter 9.
3. The Nature and Functions of a Commercial Bank
Read: James, F. C., The Economics of Money, Credit and Banking,
Chapter 12.
Dunbar, C. F., The Theory and History of Banking (5th ed.),
Chapters 1 and 2.
Phillips, C. A., Bank Credit, Chapter 2.
a. Note Issue
Read: Edie, L. D., Money, Bank Credit and Prices, Chapters 5 and 6.
Dunbar, C. F., Theory and History of Banking, Chapter 5.
b. Deposit Banking
Read: Dunbar, C. F., The Theory and History of Banking, Chapter 4.
Phillips, C. A., Bank Credit, Chapters 3 and 4.
Robertson, D. H., Money, Chapter 3.
{Hawtrey, Currency and Credit, Chapter 1}
{Mill, J. S., Principles, Book 3, Chapters 11 and 12}
4. History of Commercial Banking in the United States
Read: James, F. C., The Economics of Money, Credit and Banking,
Chapter 11.
Holdsworth, J. T., Money and Banking (1920), Chapter 9.
{White, Horace} Money and Banking.
Dowrie, G. W., American Monetary and Banking Policies
(1930), Chapters 2, 3 and 4.
5. Commercial Banking and Capital Formation
Read: James, F. C., op. cit., Chapter 14.
Robertson, D. H., Money (1929), Chapter 5.
6. Financial Institutions Closely Allied with Commercial Banks
Read: James, F. C., op. cit., Chapters 16 and 17.
IV. THE FEDERAL RESERVE SYSTEM
1. Characteristics of Central Banks
Read: Dunbar, C. F., The Theory and History of Banking (1929),
Chapter 6.
Kisch, C. H., and Elkin, W. A., Central Banks, Chapter 6.
Young, A. A., Economic Problems New and Old, Chapter 5.

2. The Banking Reform Movement in the United States
  Read: James, F. C., op. cit., Chapter 18.
3 & 4. Structure and Operations of the Federal Reserve System
  Read: James, F. C., op. cit., Chapter 19.
      Dunbar, C. F., The Theory and History of Banking (1929),
      Chapter 12.
      Burgess, W. R., The Reserve Banks and the Money Market,
      Chapters 1–15.
      Read, H. L., Federal Reserve Policy (1930), Chapters 1–5.
      United States. The Federal Reserve Board. Digest of Rulings of
      the Federal Reserve Board. (1928), pp. 201–290.
      {Governor Strong – Collected Papers, Testimony, etc. of the Late
      Governor Strong, edited by Burgess}
5. The Reserve Banks and the money market
  Read: James, F. C., op. cit., Chapter 20.
      Fisher, I., The Stock Market Crash and After (1930), Chapters
      1–16.
      Dowrie, G. W., American Monetary and Banking Policies,
      Chapters 6 and 9.
      Riefler, W. W., Money Rates and Money Markets in the United
      States, Chapters 1–10.

V. THE BUSINESS CYCLE
  1. A review of current theories
  2. A survey of some of the facts of the business cycle
  3. Banking and the business cycle
  Read: James, F. C., The Economics of Money, Credit and Banking,
      Chapter 13.
  Hansen, A. H., Business Cycle Theory.
  Mitchell, W. C., The Business Cycle, the Problem and its Setting,
      Chapter 1.
  Hawtrey, R. G., Trade and Credit, Chapter 5.
  Hawtrey, R. G., "Monetary Theory of the Trade Cycle and its Statistical
      Test," in the Quarterly Journal of Economics, vol. 41, pp. 471–486
      (1926).
  Robertson, D. H., Money, Chapter 8.
  Aftalion, A., "The Theory of Economic Cycles based on a Capitalistic
      Technique of Production," Review of Economics and Statistics, vol. 9,
      pp. 165–170 (October 1927). (Smith also gives pagination, without
      other identification, for: Walter Buckingham Smith, "Wholesale

Commodity Prices in the United States, 1795–1824," *idem*, vol.
9:171–183 (October 1927)).
Mitchell, W. C., Business Cycles, pp. 570–598.

QUESTIONS:

(1) What basic factor or factors explain the business cycle according to Hawtrey?
Aftalion? Mitchell?

(2) What does the term business cycle mean? Does it imply regularity of recur-
rence of business changes in time? Does it refer to price phenomena or to all
sorts of economic phenomena? Does it involve a consideration of agricultural
prices and output?

(3) Do you think that there is such a thing as a standard cycle?

(4) Do you think that if the central banks of the world were able to control the
money market that they could eliminate the business cycle?

[Editor's note: On the back of the second page of assignments is a handwritten
schedule of dates of reading for the last two months of the course, not included
here. Those making reference to new authors of writings are:

A. E. R. – Whitaker – volume 20, p. 93
Cassel – Theory of Social Economy, pp. 473–485
Sprague – A.E.R., volume 19, p. 61
Report of the Federal Reserve Board, 1923, pp. 1–39
Anderson, B. M., "Commodity Price Stabilization: False Goal of Central Bank
Policy"]
Dowrie, Mortgages and Business Policies, Chapter 9.

(3) QUESTIONS ON THE FEDERAL
RESERVE SYSTEM

1. "The Federal Reserve Act linked banking and politics together in a manner
and to an extent that many careful observers at the time the law was passed
pointed out as being highly undesirable. This view has been sustained by experience." Bankers Magazine. April, 1929, p. 541.

(a) How is the Federal Reserve System linked to politics?

(b) Do you agree with the conclusion set for in the above quotation? Illustrate
by the years 1919–20, and 1929–29 [sic]

2. "Governor Strong. The Federal Reserve System is not run today – that is,
credit extended and investments made by the system – with a view to earning

money to pay expenses and to earn dividends." Stabilization Hearings, 1927, p. 372.

Do you think that this is good policy? Why?

3. "It is the business of a central bank to protect the paper money of the country by converting it into gold on demand. This is its first and most essential function, and everything else must be subordinated to this." B. M. Anderson. The Chase Economic Bulletin. Vol. IX, p. 4.

Do you agree? Why?

4. "The immediate problem then becomes, to a large extent, one of so economizing the available supply of gold that there will always be an ample margin above the needs of business, and, by means of central banking policies, of so controlling the use of this gold, as a basis for notes and deposit currency, that neither inflation nor deflation can ensue. E. W. Kemmerer. Bankers Magazine. Vol. 118, pp. 359–362.

(a) Why economize gold so as to have the ample margin referred above?

(b) How may the economy in the use of gold be secured?

5. "In the writer's opinion, the goal in view should be a stabilization of the purchasing power of the dollar which would be expressed by the general level of commodity prices being maintained as constant as possible. This price level is satisfactorily indicated by the Bureau of Labor index for wholesale prices. . . . It is sometimes asserted that the general level of commodity prices is not a sufficiently comprehensive measure of the purchasing power of money. Attempts have accordingly been made to compile a still more general index, which is to include also wages and the value of capital assets as expressed for example, in the prices of shares. Such attempts which are obviously based on statistical points of view rather than on considerations of practical economy, must be sternly repudiated." G. Cassel. Bankers Magazine. March, 1929, pp. 416–417.

(a) What is the meaning of "the general level of prices"? a change in the "general level of prices"?

(b) Is the Bureau of Labor Statistics Index Number an adequate indicator of movements in the general level of prices?

(c) What objection can you see to including wages in your index number?

6. "In general, central bank policy has a very limited control of the general average of commodity prices in a gold standard country. The relation between goods and gold is an international matter." B. M. Anderson. The Chase Economic Bulletin. Vol. ix, p. 8.

(a) Do you agree? Why? or why not?

(b) Is this true in the short run, or in the long run?

7. "Many have traced this disease (stock speculation in 1928–29) to lack of proper control of credit – just as they traced the business inflation of 1920 to the same source. In so far as credit was a contributing cause, the chief agency of control was of course, the Federal Reserve authorities. They have been criticized by conservatives, and perhaps justly, for keeping the rediscount rate artificially low until the upward movement of the past three years was well under way. But if they were at fault for this reason, their choice was a forced one. They made it in order to keep the New York rate below the London rate. If they had not done so, gold would have continued to flow into this country in large amounts, and would in itself have permitted credit inflation. Also, the Bank of England would have been seriously embarrassed in maintaining its gold reserve." New Republic. November 13, 1929, p. 337.

(a) What is business inflation?
(b) Do the factors mentioned in this quotation weaken the claim that the Federal Reserve System may control the volume of bank credit in the United States? Would you describe the factors mentioned above as economic or political?

8. "If the Federal Reserve banks can control the volume of bank credit, they can control the volume of credit available for security speculation." B. M. Anderson. Bankers Magazine. May, 1921, p. 733.

(a) Do you think that the Federal Reserve System can control the amount of bank credit in the United States?
(b) Do you think that they could restrict the credit available for use in stock speculation without raising interest rates generally?

9. "Governor Strong. Just to give the committee an idea of the great variety of factors that are considered as bearing upon changes in discount rates, I have made a list of some of the current information that is being studied at the bank . . . indices of money, rates, employment, production, prices. . . sales of retail stores, sales and stocks of wholesale dealers, savings bank deposits, changes in rents, changes in wages, movements of funds about the country, foreign exchange rates, business profits, volume of building, failure statistics, the reports of car loadings, the consumption of electrical energy, all the crop statistics, all the foreign trade reports, such information as we can get on stocks of goods on hand-inventories, speculation, bank clearings, what the bank reports show as to changes in the deposit and loan account." Stabilization Hearings, 1927, pp. 357–358.

Explain the relevance of each of these sorts of information to determination of the rediscount rate.

10. "Governor Strong. There was what appeared to be a speculative or unhealthy development under way in 1922 and 1923. The reserve banks then sold all of their Government securities down to only $73,000,000, as I recall, and the result of those sales was not to reduce the volume of credit materially, but it drove the member banks to borrow from the reserve banks and what had been an investment account was converted into a borrowing account. . . . The influence exerted by the reserve system upon credit as a result of sales was really to make the increases of the discount rate more effective." Stabilization Hearings, 1927, p. 330.

(a) What is the term usually used to describe the action of the Federal Reserve bank mentioned above?

(b) How does this make the rate "effective". Illustrate by means of a series of balance sheets of member banks and the Federal Reserve Bank.

11. "The National City Bank, without attempting to pass upon the justice of permitting non-member acceptance dealers to borrow from the Reserve Banks at rates lower than member banks can demand on most of their eligible paper, questions the effectiveness of the dual action of the Federal Reserve Bank of New York in raising its rediscount rate and at the same time lowering its rate for buying acceptances." The New York World. September 3, 1929.

(a) Do you agree with the National City Bank? Why?

(b) Do you think that such an action would deprive member banks of profitable business?

12. "Governor Strong. The development of the bill market in New York is the outgrowth of the need of the rest of the world to draw on the surplus credit of this country to finance the movement of goods, and especially of trade taking place between this country and foreign countries." Stabilization Hearings. 1927, p. 314.

(a) What is the "bill market"?

(b) What is the relation of the Federal Reserve System to it?

(c) Do you agree that there is "surplus credit" in the United States which the rest of the world needs?

13. "Central banking carries the 'clearance principle' one stage further than it has ever been carried before. . . . Having solved the problem of supply of bank credit in this way, we are now confronted with the problem of control."

(a) Does the existence of a central bank enable the banking system to "multiply the volume of bank credit" to an extent which would not be possible without a central bank?

(b) Do you think that the problem of control is more important in the United States at present (1930) than the problem of supply?

(4) ECONOMICS 5

Mid-year Examination   January 23, 1931

PART I: Required

1. "The quantity theory has been severely criticized from a great many stand-points." Present and comment upon as many of these specific criticisms as you can.

2. On the basis of the financial and banking history of the past four years, Mr. Warburg advanced five lessons to be learned:
   1. "The independence and cohesion of the Federal Reserve System should be strengthened so that its preventive powers may be exercised in a timely manner."
   2. "Cooperation between central banks is of the highest importance, not upon the assumption that discount policies as such can regulate prices, but on account of the assistance these banks can give to one another and because of the psychological effect which, as leaders of public opinion, they may exercise when excessive optimism or excessive pessimism threaten the economic safety of the world."
   3. "We should beware of high prices. It is safer for all industries – includ-ing agriculture – to build on the lowest level of prices on which they can prosper, than to try to make the largest possible gains by exacting the highest possible prices."
   4. "We should not shun cooperation with other countries, but seek it."
   5. "And finally, banking and finance involve not only a sacred trusteeship toward depositors and investors. They carry, in addition, the weighty responsibility of safeguarding stability by exercising care in limiting the use of bank credit as far as practicable to finance the productive processes of industry and commerce." New York Times, January 9, 1931.
   (a) Precisely what is the meaning of each of Mr. Warburg's statements?
   (b) Do you agree or disagree? Why?
   (c) Are there any other lessons which you would suggest?

3. (a) To what precise causes do you attribute day to day changes in the call money rate?
   (b) Why was the regional plan adopted under the Federal Reserve System instead of a single central bank?
   (c) Explain clearly what is meant by eligible paper.
   (d) Discuss open market operations under the following headings: (1) their nature and how carried out; (2) the purpose for which they are

employed; and (3) their probable effects on the amount of Reserve Bank credit in use.

4. Answer either (a) or (b).
   (a) Outline the history of the adoption of the gold standard in Europe and the United States in the 19th century. Be as detailed and specific as you can. Among other things consider: (1) the reasons for the adoption of the gold standard; and (2) some of the effects of its adoption.
   (b) Discuss the economic consequences of variations in the price of silver and illustrate by reference to the history of (1) Franc, (2) the United States, and also by reference to the present position of China and Mexico.

PART II: Answer 2 questions

5. "It is important to insist upon the fact that the banker's business is founded on his deposits, and limited by them, because a fashion has grown up lately of regarding the bankers as 'creators of credit'. They are, of course, creators of credit in the sense in which every lender, even the kind-hearted man who gives a 'little loan' to a needy friend[,] is a creator of credit. But this is not what is meant. By using an ambiguous phrase it is meant to imply that the 'banks' can increase to an unlimited extent the amount of credit current. In this sense the idea is plainly untrue." Leaf, W., Banking, pp. 101–102. Discuss.

6. What is meant by the overvaluation and the undervaluation of currencies? Discuss the relation of these concepts to the doctrine of purchasing power parity and the practical problems of restoration of the gold standard.

7. "Since the fixed reserve ratio system allows the minimum discretion (to central banks) and is designed to produce the maximum disturbance whenever the actual reserve approaches the legal minimum and since the existing minimum of gold reserve percentages could be reduced without in any way weakening the general credit structure, these legal minima should be reduced to a figure well below that which the countries are likely to desire to maintain." New York Times, January 14, 1931. Reprinted from a document published by the League of Nations.
   (a) Why is the League of Nations giving special consideration to this problem at the present time? Answer fully.
   (b) What is the fixed reserve ratio system? Do we have it in the United States?
   (c) In what way or ways may it embarrass central banks?

(d) Do you agree that the credit structure would not be weakened by a reduction in this ratio? Why?

8. "The business cycle is primarily a monetary phenomenon." Do you agree? What writers have advocated this view? Precisely what have been their theories of the business cycle?

9. "In what respects has the Federal Reserve System given the United States a sounder banking system than it had before 1914?"

10. "The depreciation of the monetary standard is a phenomenon of considerable social importance and one whose effects must be regarded, on the whole, as beneficial. To begin with, its ordinary result is a rise in prices. Now a rise in prices is a useful stimulus to production; it keeps the spirit of enterprise on the alert; it encourages a rise of wages; it acts as a tonic; it is a symptom of sound economic health." Do you agree? Answer fully.

(5) OSTRANDER'S CLASS NOTES FROM ECONOMICS 5, MONEY AND BANKING, TAUGHT BY WALTER B. SMITH, WILLIAMS COLLEGE, FALL 1930

ECONOMICS 5

I. Hypothesis
II. Testing
   a. Logical
   b. Inductive
      1. Observation
         (a) General historical
         (b) Statistical
      2. Controlled experiment

Ways and means of payment
   –Source of supply
   –Method of control
Relation between capital and capital accumulation.
Two points of view among U.S. economists
   –Abstract, theoretical
   –Institutional
What are grounds for government interference in monetary matters – why not laissez-faire?

What is the case for Monometalism versus Bimetallism?

What is the merit of metallic currency?

Is Gold really important – Does the value of gold determine the value of the dollar or visa-versa?

What is the future of the gold supply, what are implications for long-time trend of prices – and business cycle?

Do we really believe in Gold Standard – in view of war-time experience?

Do you favor abolition of Greenbacks, and gold and silver certificates – are they wasteful currency, are they inelastic currency?

Do banks create credit, or do they merely lend out deposits? If (1) – have we any problem of scarcity?

[On page 1-A:

Granted we had a standard of value for exchange, is not credit enough medium?

$$MV + M' \, V' = PT$$

How much credit ought the farmer to have? (Too much already?)

Is quantity theory of money and prices tenable?

Do banks provide a 5th wheel to our economic system – or are they vital?

Do we have a pecuniary philosophy of life?]

Is bank credit "inherently" unstable?

Are American commercial banks engaging in too many non-commercial operations?

If money is easily transferred across international frontiers can New York Federal Reserve Bank control the money?

If we have solved problem of credit supply, what does that mean in problem of credit control?

–Are there principles to guide credit control?

–Have we adequate machinery whereby our central bank can control?

Would control of money market, if possible, enable one to control business?

How can one use financial machinery to tax the general public?

Is Branch Banking desirable and inevitable-chain banking?

In view of different British and American conditions – can we borrow their principles?

Are fluctuating foreign exchanges as significant to business as fluctuating internal prices?

Was England wise in returning to the gold standard?

Was France wise to devalue the French franc?

Was Germany wise to repudiate [the] Mark?

Relation between bank rates and foreign exchange rates.
Relation between discount rate and international gold flow.
Ground for close regulation of commercial banking – not of investment banking.
Relation between issuing of securities and business cycle.

Governing circumstances in our monetary history:
  Legislative
  –Establishment of currency – Hamilton
  –National Bank Act – 1863
  –Federal Reserve Act – 1913
  Judiciary
  –Greenback – legal tender
  Decisions of Comptroller of Currency
  General historical background – giving rise to our business practices
  –Frontier characteristics
    –Cheap money demanded
  –Commercially isolated
    –Bankers acceptance was forbidden before 1914
    –Encouraged since then
    –We are producers of an agricultural surplus – exporting them.
    –At mercy of weather.
  Sectionalism

Money – definition – any generally acceptable means of payment.
  (Wealth, generally acceptable in exchange – Irving Fisher)

Means established by law or custom for the payment of debt – Hawtrey.
  Functions
    Medium of exchange
    Standard of value
    Store of value
    Standard for deferred payment
    Stabilizer of the unit of account
  Two ways of thinking
  –Rationalistic – things must be – not are.
  –Institutional – man a product of his environment – of social customs, etc.
    – Veblen

[On page 3-A:

	Legal Tender
U.S.: Gold Coin	full
Gold Certificate	full

Silver Dollar	"unless otherwise specified"
Silver Certificate	"unless otherwise specified"
Minor Coins – silver	limited to $10
Subsidiary coin	limited to 0.25
U.S. Notes	"except [for] import duty and public debt interest"
Treasury Notes of 1890	same as silver dollar
National Bank Notes	none
Federal Reserve Notes	none
Federal Reserve Bank Note	none

Particular Money   Common Money

Money is the product of labor.

Store of value – an instrument for saving one's purchasing power.

    R. G. Hawtrey – Foster and Catchings

    –Money has a peculiar function in our economic life – as this sort of instrument.

    –If we are to store purchasing power we do so by stock, bonds, etc. – not money.

Medium of exchange – very obvious – to facilitate exchange.

    –Facilitate acquiring

    –Facilitate disposal

    –Facilitate period between.

Common denominator of value

    –Orthodox idea – money represents units of utility of various articles.

    –But, if two articles are of same price – money is not the standard by which we make the final decision.

Standard for deferred payment – other means <u>may</u> be used.

Legal Tender

    –If offered – but not accepted – interest stops – no court costs can be assessed.

    –Does not end debt, if refused.

    –Medium which law declares suitable or capable of discharging obligation to pay money.

    –Sometimes given to inconvertible paper – in an attempt to maintain its value.

Monetary Standards

    I. Gold Standard

        1. Automatic

        2. Managed

        3. Gold bullion

II. Silver Standard
III. Bimetallism
IV. Paper Standard
V. Gold Exchange [Standard]

[On page 4-A:

Horace White – very prewar in his ideas of gold.

Demonetization of silver – means discontinuance of the coinage of silver bullion deposited at the mint by private persons.

An ounce of gold or silver will, in long run, exchange for as much of every other commodity, as can be produced or imported at the same cost with itself. – J. S. Mill

I. Gold Standard – automatic. In U.S. 1873.
    –Free and unrestricted coinage.
        (–Not necessarily gratuitous coinage – brassage, seinorage)
        –i.e., buying and selling of gold at a fixed price or ratio.
        –Thus price of gold can never change.
            –Especially when as large a holder as the U.S. Government stands always ready to buy and sell at a standard price.
    –"Automatic" existed before the war.
        –Perfect convertibility of gold into bullion, bullion into gold.
        –International convertibility.
    Managed.
    –Implies control by central bank or Federal Reserve System.
    –Which is in process of formation today.
    –Also a system such as that proposed by I. Fisher – or control of mines.
    Bullion Standard.
    –Convertibility in form of bullion, not coin.
    –To keep coin out of circulation.
    –To insure international stability of exchange par.
    –To withhold gold for reserve.
    Today – on a form of Gold Standard.
    England–U.S.–France–Germany–Italy–Sweden.

II. Silver Standard– China

III. Bimetallic Standard

[On page 5-A:

Quantitative measurements are most important, and are being worked on by everyone in economics today. But they are dangerous tools – must be watched. Rising prices– community not made richer but advantage given to wage earners, over rentiers.
Demand for money – regulated by its necessity to take care of flow of commodities. Unitary demand for money – quantity of goods needing money does not change, supply of money does.]

Index Numbers

$$\frac{\Sigma\, P_1/P_2 + P_1'/P_2'}{N}$$

$$\sqrt[2]{P_1 \times P_2} \qquad \text{geometric mean}$$

–Different systems vary somewhat widely.

$$\frac{\Sigma\, p \cdot q + p'q' + p''q''}{\Sigma\, pq + p'q' + p''q''} = \text{aggregative index numbers – weighted}$$

–Used most widely.

Instead of a "general level of prices" – we can make more progress with levels of prices of two or more homogeneous groups – as exported and imported. –Arbitrarily picked, highly specialized group.

Quantity Theory of Money

$$MV = \Sigma pq \quad \text{or} \quad MV + M'V' = PT \text{ (Fisher)}$$

–Money value of goods equals money paid for them $(pq = M)$ [sic]
–Sum of money values equals money paid times velocity.
–A truism (something too true), nobody denies this.
Value of money directly [sic] proportional to quantity of money in circulation.
–Another way of saying that if you increase the supply the value falls.
–Criticisms–
Pragmatic-empiric

–Only money actually in circulation is significant.
–What of barter – no exchange of money.
–What of trade of goods without money, money without goods.
–"Other things" are never equal in this complex world.

[On page 6-A:

[Assignment]
    First Paper – Origin of the National Banking Act.

    I. General Historians
       Channing, etc.
    II. Banking
        A. F. Davis – Origin of the National Banking System
        C. F. Dunbar – Theory and History of Banking
    III. Digest of Rulings of the Federal Reserve Board, pp. 293–387

    Origin – with view to what preceded it.
    In relation to peculiar events of its time.
    Branch Banking (Free Banking?)
        Notes, Deposits, Charter, Commercial Paper, Reserves.
    Relation to U.S. Government.

[End of assignment]
    [Shall we be clean-and-mechanical, or muddy and true to life?
    Money not in circulation has no influence on prices. – J. S. Mill.
    –Prices do not depend on money, but on purchases. – J. S. Mill]

Hawtrey's Quantity Theory

–A qualification of Fisher's.
–Not total quantity of money (in existence or in circulation) but the unspent
    margin, is important.
–This takes account of individual psychological phenomenon.
Commodity Theory of Money
    Laughlin
    Nassau Senior
    –Money is merely a commodity.
    –Utility of a given object and utility of a given quantity of gold.
    –A very long run theory.
History of Money and Money Standards
    –Considerable amount of gold in ancient time – though much silver in early
        Greece.

–Money substitutes – almost none in antiquity – only clay tablets.

–During Dark Ages, gold disappeared from circulation, silver very scarce.

Gresham's Law.

Bad money drives good money out of circulation.

In Bimetallism the cheaper coins are worth less as bullion than as coin, will drive out the better coin.

–This was first proposed by Aristotle.

–Plato advocated a token currency for domestic purposes.

–Hard money versus soft money men – believe in intrinsic or token currency.

Gold returned to Europe with the new trade with the Orient – first Italy – 1300–1500

–Expanding commerce

–Little change in supply of gold.

1500 – New World mines (silver) occasioned the first big inflow of precious metal to Europe.

19th Century

–England formally adopted Gold Standard in 1819.

  –After long period of fluctuation on a Bimetallic basis – due to Gresham's Law.

  –Accompanied by a change in the ratio of gold and silver – 15:1–16:1 to the disadvantage of silver.

    –England had ceased to have a demand for silver in international trade.

    –Change in relative supplies of the two metals.

–Other countries began to follow England. France 1876, Germany 1871–73, Holland 1876, Scandinavia 1873.

  –Followed by a steady drop in silver as compared to gold.

The U.S.

–Hamilton, 1791, put our currency on a Bimetallic system. 15:1

  –But market ratio was 15+:1

  –Actually a silver standard.

–1834, a change of ratio 16:1, but silver did not come up (15.7:1) to this, thus an actual gold standard.

–1855 – silver coins (except dollar) coined 7% light – making them a freely passing, domestic token coin.

–1861–79 – paper standard.

–1873 – Silver was demonetized.

–Declining prices were hard on debtors – who cried for cheap money – along with silver miners.

–Bland Allison Act – Government had to buy $2 million per month.

–Sherman Silver Purchase Act 1890 – Government had to buy million ounces – price going down.

[On page 8-A:

–Classification
–Mutually exclusive
–Coordinated
–Are unusually arbitrary]
  –Treasury notes of 1890 – to pay for purchase of this silver.
–Cleveland's Treasury was very embarrassed – gold flowing out.
–Spending of Republicans.
–Selling of bonds by foreigners who were afraid of a Silver Standard here.
–About 1900 – formal adoption of Gold Standard.
Paper Money (Prior to War)
  –Government issue, as Greenback.
  –Connection between its gold or commodity value and possibility of redemption.
  –Legal tender power will not sustain its value for long – if over-issued.
  –Inconvertible paper money tends to put international currency out of use.
  –Amount of depreciation measured by its purchasing power over:
    –Foreign exchange
    –Gold
    –Commodities
  –End of paper issue
  –Repudiation
  –Devaluation
  –Return on old basis.

(Banking and) Credit.
  –Implies relationship – between individuals, business concerns, etc.
  –Implies obligation
  –Implies time
  –Getting something now in return for a future promise to pay.
  –Implies confidence
  –Implies legal rights.
Classification of Credit.
  –Basis of borrower
  –Public, Mercantile, Personal, Construction, Bank

[On page 9-A:

All National Banks		
Loans and Discounts	15,000,000,000	short commercial
U.S. Government Bonds	2,704,000,000	
Other Bonds	3,741,000,000	
Overdrafts	15,000,000	

Loans and Discounts
    On Demand
        –One or more individual or firm names   5.76% C[ommercial]
        –Secured by stocks and bonds   17.28%
        –Secured by other personal security   2.54%
    On Time
        –One or more individual or firm names   41.11% C[ommercial]
        –Secured by stocks and bonds   16.49%
        –Secured by other personal security   7.21%
        Secured by improved real estate
        –Farmland   1.24%
        –Other land   4.98%

"Line of credit" constitutes a more or less permanent investment in a business by a banker.]

–Basis of Loaner
–Bank, Mercantile, Personal
–Purpose: Mercantile, Investment, Consumption

Credit is based on <u>confidence</u> in the
    Character – willingness to pay
    Capacity – ability to pay
    –As both are shown in the past and present standing of <u>business</u>.
    –Involves time – which results in expansion and restriction.
    –Line of credit
        –Director decides maximum amount for each customer – loaning up to that amount is mechanical.
    –Credit Analysis
        –2 to 1 ratio between quick assets and quick liabilities – though varies from industry to industry.
        –Cash on hand between 5–15% of quick assets.
        –Notes Receivable, is this a trade custom? – are officers borrowing.
        –How is stock of materials valued – original cost or market value – whichever is lowest.
        –Can real estate be turned into other uses.
        –Trademarks, goodwill, patents – if they have a high earning power, are good.
    Liabilities
        –High amount of accounts payable – they are not taking cash discounts.
        –Are there contingent liabilities.
    National Banks were, and still are, predominantly commercial,
        –But the tendency for investment loaning grows

–This is not as quickly liquid as the old form, nor as safe
–This trend is changing the function of our national bankers.

[On page 10-A: Hour Test – Friday, November 7]

Credit Instruments
–Negotiability
   –Written – signed – payable "to order of"
   –Improves title – giving clear title – regardless of what proceeded.
–Promissory note
   –Written, signed, definite sum, date payable "to order of," unconditional
   [In margin: –Close relationship of bank to borrower.]
–Bill of Exchange
   –Unconditional, order – "to order of", to definite person, signed, definite
      sum and date – payee, drawee, drawer.
   [In margin: Impersonal relation]
–Check – draft on bank.
–Foreign bill of exchange – or domestic.
–Trade Acceptance
   –No bank involved, between individuals or firms.
   –"Accepted" by drawee.
   –Arises out of a commercial exchange of goods.
–Bank Acceptances
Commercial Credit Instruments
–Short time
–Purpose of aiding production – Working Capital
Investment Credit Instruments
–Longer time
–Purpose of creating capital – Fixed Capital
–Bonds

Banking

Commercial Banks
–As National Banks
–But more important State Banks
–Federal Reserve Banks
–Commercial paper houses, banker's acceptance dealers
Investment Banks
–Savings – mutual or stock (Insurance companies)
–Trust company
–Cooperative and building and loan

–Investment bankers proper
–Underwriters
–Bond houses
Commercial Banks
–An institution which accepts deposits – makes loans – Walter Leaf – cloak-room banking
–Defined in terms of functions – Discount, Deposit, Issue – Dunbar
–A dealer in debt – Hawtrey
–Its function is to guarantee the credit of individuals.
  Other lists of functions.
  –Place of safekeeping for funds.
  –Money changers, channels of communication for a currency between government and public.
  –Checking system and clearing system.
  –Shipment of precious metals and money.
  –Collectors of coupons.
  –Channels for collection of notes.
  –Fiscal agents.
  Bank Note
  –A demand obligation – to bearer.
  –Why has bank note banking been so carefully regulated?
    1. Notes in wider circulation than checks – innocent holder must be protected.
    2. Likelihood of over-expansion – bank notes are not very often presented for redemption, cash.
  Systems of banks – note control and issue.
  –Suffolk Bank, Boston – a New England Clearing House.
  –New York Safety Fund System – failed.
  –Fund from all banks – 3% of capital.
  –New York Free Banking Act.
    –Anyone could start a bank.
    –Notes had to be secured by bonds deposited with State.
  –Great variance among multitudinous independent banks.
  –National Banking Act 1863
    –Borrowed from the provisions of the above for its main points.

[On page 12-A:

  Economics studies variables – not constants
  –Real way to study variables is by mathematics – algebra studies the interrelations of a great many variables.

C_1 = overflow cash
K = ratio of derivative deposits to loans
X = loan expansion
  $C_1 = X(1-K)$
C = original primary deposit
R = reserve ratio   [In pencil: (loans or deposits to cash?)]
  $C = C_1 + rC + rKX$

Original cash must provide for overflow (C_1)
–Plus necessary cash reserves against original cash deposit (rC)
–Plus necessary cash reserves against derivative deposits left with bank (rKK)
Solving the two formulas:

$$X = C(1-r)/1-K+rK$$

Amount of expansion is slightly in excess of original deposit.]

Deposit Banking
  Three views on the relation of cash, loan, deposit.
  1. Old fashioned banker – cloakroom banking
    –Banks were middlemen.
    –Loaned the money entrusted to it – for profit
    –Deposits of actual money were only basis of loaning [In margin: loans a
      result of (primary) deposits]
    –Loans could be made only up to the amount of deposits – probably less,
      due to necessity of keeping a cash reserve.
  2. McCleod view
    –Banks could loan about nine times as much as deposits.
    –Adverse clearing house balance would not arise, due to offsetting by other
      banks' checks.
    –But even if every bank were loaning and expanding at the same time –
      overflows all offset.
    –There would be foreign exchange which might start a clearing house
      balance – unable to be offset.
    –Someone might ask for specie – destroying balance.
    –Credit creation.
    –A great confusion of individual banks and banking system. [Single vertical
      line in margin alongside this line.]
    –Thus deposits the result of loans (derivative).
    –What of relation of primary to derivative deposits? – Nothing said in this
      view.

3. Phillips view
   –Analyzes precise definition between banking system, individual bank, primary deposits, derivative deposits.
   –From point of view of individual bank the idea of manifold expansion is not true.
   –But from point of view of Banking System, expansion equals 10-1.

[On page 13-A (Without explanation of source):

599,724,050	Consols of 1930
48, 954,180	Panama Annuals 2^s [Perhaps 2% bonds.]
25,947,000	Panama Annuals 2^s [Perhaps 2% bonds.]
$674,625,230 [sic]	Total of bonds which can be used as security for National Bank notes.
$699,620,652	Total notes outstanding.

Treasury holds as security for these

658,732,988	of bonds
40,887,664	of cash (5% redemption)
699,620,652	

$3,500 →	10,000 →	100,000	28.5 [times
Gold in Federal	Deposits in Federal	Deposits in	expansion]
Reserve Bank	Reserve Bank	National Bank	

But $3,500 gold deposited by National Bank, with $6,000 commercial paper.
Can make only $10,000 of reserve note expansion – this is 2.5 [times] expansion.]

Clearing of Checks
   –Represents a <u>great</u> saving of hard money.
   –Methods of clearing
   –Clearing house
   –Indirect clearing through correspondents
   –Mails
   –Messenger
   –Federal Reserve System
   –Clearance and payment of balances is a most important function of banking.

National Banking Act
   Notes
   –<u>uniformity</u> of design, and <u>value</u>
   –Secured by U.S. Bonds deposited with Treasury (100% of value of notes) – 5% gold redemption fund at Treasury.
   –Taxed state bank notes out of existence.

Defects
–Great inelasticity
–Amount of bonds which could be used was limited – and stable.
–Time necessary to get new bonds and notes issued on them very slow (20 days).
–Just when banks want to expand currency – the premium on bonds goes up
    from increased demand for them.
  –Thus profit is cut, and banks do not want to expand any longer.
(Corrected by Federal Reserve Act)
–Large gold backing – more than in other lines of credit – makes bank notes
    extravagant in its use of gold.
–Provisions were made for the retirement of National Bank notes – but have
    not been taken advantage [of]. [Arrow from "Corrected," several lines up,
    to this line.]
System of Securing Notes
    Percentage specie reserve
    Full specie reserve
    Uncovered issue
    Elastic uncovered issue
    General assets
    Specific property reserve (National Bank Note)
History of Commercial Banking
    1789–1863
–Relatively unregulated state banking
–Two attempts at a U.S. Central Bank
  –Had large control of note-issue
  –Held government deposits
  –But no control of market, no holding of reserves for other bankers.
–Independent Treasury
  –Took government deposits away from private banks
  –Money paid into it embarrassed the credit of the country
  –Having been paid in, it merely sat there – giving no aid to the already tight
    conditions
–Slight organization of investment banking
–Absence of acceptance market
–Usury laws – no possibility of control by discount rate
–Utter decentralization
    1863–1914
–National Bank Act
–Rise of investment banking – Jay Cooke-Morgan
–Decline of merchant banking

–Foreign trade of slight importance
–Growing concern for social control of banking
–Frequent business crises: 1873, 1883, 1893–96, <u>1907</u>
–After 1907, demand for social control
1914 – present day developments
–Commercial banking is undergoing a very rapid change
  –Increased grants of power
  –Can act as trustees or trust companies
    –Competition of State banks drove the National banks to this
  –Can make long-time real estate loans
    –Mortgages on farm land

[On page 15-A:

Large chain stores give <u>prices</u>
Old independent stores give <u>service</u>]
  –For period of 5 years – to 50% of value
–Development of an acceptance market
  –To facilitate foreign trade
  –We were once again great importers and exporters
  –Banks can accept bills of exchange arising out of actual exchange of actual
    goods
  –Banks can, and are encouraged to buy and sell acceptances
–Branch banking – chain banking – mergers
  –1927 – National Banks allowed to create branches within city.
    –If State law allows them
    –Any State banks, becoming National, may keep all their branches
  [In margin: Watch developments]
–Mergers
  –Extend control by combination of branches
  –Causes:
    –Economies of large-scale management
    –Percentage rule for single borrower, is gotten around by doubling capital.
    –More truly <u>efficient</u> service
–Changing relations between New York Money Market and banks of the nation
  –Under old National Bank Act – the reserves of country banks were
    concentrated as deposits in the hands of New York banks.
  –New York bankers could not loan these except on call, for any time of
    tightness would mean that country banks would call for their reserves
  –New system serves to take a great deal of centralization away from New
    York – though short-term loaning is still easiest in New York City.

–An interest in international banking
–Foreign branches
–Increased interest in foreign financing
–Increased cooperation between Federal Reserve Bank in New York City –
and old foreign central banks

[On page 16-A: Functions: If overemphasized tends to justify the things
described – a danger.]

–Commercial banking system is becoming more concerned with long-term
investment – stocks, real estate, etc.
–We are somehow getting a new idea toward banking
–Banking system not our master but a very efficient servant.
Functions of a commercial bank
–Facilitates the process of exchange between production, consumption,
distribution – payment
–Enables us to economize in the use of gold
–Its effect on supply of purchasing power gives it control of value.
–Facilitates capital accumulation and capital formation – in its control of
direction of spending.
–Commercial Paper House
–Buys and sells commercial paper (notes).
–A middleman – buys in one market, sells in another.
–Equalizing interest rates.
–Brings surplus money from one sector to another where that money is
needed.
–Enables small bank to use its surplus – arranging convenient maturities.
–If a business corporation cannot borrow from open market – in times of crisis
and scarce money – to turn back to the bank upsets that banks' predic-
tions, and may result in the corporation not being able to get credit.
Commercial Credit Houses – Installment buying.
–High rate of interest.
–No other place to get loans on automobiles.
–What is effect of increasing amount of installment buying?
a. On production
–Increased production, now.
–But will there be corresponding slump in production, later on?
–i.e., will it not aggravate the business cycle?
b. On consumption
–Increased use of luxuries – more than capability?

Central Bank
1. Holds surplus and reserves of the country.
2. A banker's bank – rediscounting
3. Note issue – currency supply
4. Agent for government – keeps its balances, etc.
5. Redemption of legal tender and lawful money.
6. Control of credit policy
7. Clearance and collection.
–Competitive strivings of banks may put the flow of production in the right directions.
–May increase currency to meet needs.
–But, may inflation beyond needs.

Banking reform
1865–79 – Greenback
1879–1900 – Gold standard-Free Silver
1907 – Tremendous panic
–1908 Aldrich–Vreeland Act – providing for associations of banks to furnish paper money – in crises.
–National Monetary Commission
–Agitation from 1903 to 1913
–During Roosevelt–Taft terms
–1912 Aldrich Bill – not passed.
1913 – Owen–Glass Act – the Federal Reserve System – under Wilson
National Monetary Commission's findings
–Old system undesirable, because
a. Decentralized reserves – no central gold fund – pyramiding.
–Fixed minimum reserve
–No possibility of suspension.
–Drawing on reserve was illegal.
b. Inelasticity of currency.

Federal Reserve System
1. Reserves
Centralization of Reserves
Accomplished through reserve requirements on member banks – 7, 10, 13% on demand deposits – 3% on time
–All of which reserve must be kept as a deposit with Federal Reserve Banks.
–Through sale of capital stock to member banks – 6% of their capital and surplus.

–Gold required behind member bank deposits 35%

–Used as a basis for loan expansion of 93, 90, 87%

–Thus a deposit in a member bank is backed up by 3½% of gold in Federal Reserve Bank.

–Given large aggregates, the averages may be arranged in advance – insurance principle.

–Member banks do not keep excess reserves at Reserve Banks – as they would earn no interest.

–Reserves are built up by:

–Deposit of cash – any lawful money.

–Rediscounting of commercial paper – eligible paper arising out of actual commercial transactions; or agricultural paper.

–Sale of government securities.

–Borrows on its own notes (collateral)

–Sale of bankers' acceptances

Economy of Reserves

At present New York Federal Reserve Bank has reserve ratio of 86.9%.

–Could we stand an inflation to double the present credit – take advantage of the whole reserve – but high prices would bring outflow of gold.

Apprehension point – if with fixed legal reserve limits, when actual reserves get near them the people get scared.

–Other countries have no fixed reserves

–But they have no individualized – "Tom, Dick, and Harry" banking system.

–We may look to a future diminishing of reserve requirements – but branch, or large scale, banking must accompany this.

[On page 19-A:

Can banking policy arrange to take the same amount of goods off the market at all times? – steady flow of monetary purchasing power.]

–Non-member banks can get the benefits of the Federal Reserve System.

–Then what would be the effect of its policy on them?

–One of great weaknesses of system

Economy of Gold

–The more we increase the possibilities of credit expansion – the more we leave behind our old bullion standards – away from hard money.

–Question of banking policy raised – how much credit?

2. Currency

–Federal Reserve notes – issued by Federal Reserve Banks

Security of 40% gold, plus deposit of 60% of

–Commercial paper

–Bankers acceptances
–Bank's notes with government securities as collateral
–Need for currency first felt at windows of member banks – or foretold by graphs of previous experience.
–Elastic currency – to meet "legitimate" needs of business.
–Rediscounting costs member banks something – rate.
–They turn in notes to cancel debts to Federal Reserve Banks.
–Redemption automatic – no bank outside of a district can issue notes of the district Federal Reserve Bank.
–Does value of currency depend on prices, or [are] prices dependent on currency.
   –Federal Reserve Bank Note
   –Issued by Federal Reserve Banks.
   –Designed to take the place of old National Bank Notes.
      –Federal Reserve Banks would buy U.S. bonds from banks.
      –Either change them for good U.S. bonds
      –Or use them as backing for Federal Reserve Bank notes.

[On page 20-A:

"Over-production does not mean production of more than can be sold; but simply production of <u>more</u> than can be sold at the <u>anticipated</u> price or at some lower price that will still cover all the costs of putting goods on the market." – Henry Clay]

Settlements and Collections as a Function of the Federal Reserve System.
–Old system – <u>expense</u>
   –Interest charge – by banks receiving check.
   –Exchange charge – by paying bank.
   –Drafts on the funds by different cities.
      –Draft in New York-St. Louis, etc.
      –Paid by a draft of San Francisco Funds.
   –Indirect routing of checks.
   –Although there were intra-city clearances the nation as a whole was in anarchy.
   –Slow, <u>delay</u>.
   –<u>Risk</u> – possibility of non-payment, possibility of failure of any of the many banks – or the paying bank before payment.

–Since 1913
   –There still exists the clearance through correspondents (10% of total) – and direct clearance by messenger.
   –But the main agency of clearance is the Federal Reserve System. (90% of total).

–Less handling.
–Shorter time.
–Fewer gold shipments.
–Gold settlement fund at Washington.
–Settlements between Reserve Banks are wired to Washington and result in debits or credits to the banks' balances in that fund.
–Par settlement argument
–Federal Reserve Banks are forbidden to accept checks on which an exchange charge has been made.

Federal Reserve System as Banker's for the Government
1. During war
2. In peace time
3. History – since 1846, The Independent Treasury System
–Money withdrawn from circulation – was reserve money – contracted credit.
–Money put out was new reserve money – floated money.
–Great need of a better control of money market.
1. War time – 1917–18
–Federal Reserve Banks extended credit to member banks, individuals bought Liberty Bonds, borrowed from member banks to buy bonds [and pay for] them.
–Thus the government did not borrow directly from the Federal Reserve System, but made the people of the country restrict themselves and their credit to pay for the War.
2. Peace time operations – see [W. Randolph] Burgess.

Federal Reserve Banks and the Money Market.
The Money Market – well organized.
–General features of markets:
–Standardized qualities
–Wide group of demanders and suppliers in close and constant contact – easily
–Nation-wide at least, and a great international organization.
–Divisions of the Money Market.
–Open market – short time
–Rate dependent on play of demand and supply.
–Impersonal, competitive.
Call loan rate   } –greater fluctuation
Bankers acceptance rate   } –is lower – less risk, longer
–Both move together

Commercial paper
Treasury short-time securities
–<u>Open market</u> – long time
–Bonds
–Liberty bonds – in calm times are more profitable than bankers' acceptances.
–Customer's loans – short time – are higher than any other, but [at] call.
–The Bill Market – bankers' acceptances.
–Buyers – Federal Reserve Banks, large banking houses, and large number of miscellaneous organizations.
–Arise out of import and export of actual merchandise – self-liquidating.
–Or out of domestic warehouse transactions.
–A great open market for bills, but the Federal Reserve Banks always stand ready to buy any amount of bills at the <u>Federal Reserve rate on bills</u>.

[On page 22-A:

Structure of the system
Markets
Mechanisms
Policy]

–An <u>alternate</u> market for surplus funds – short time, very liquid, secure.
–Encourages foreign operation in our money market – the bill is a document the foreign bank is accustomed to.
–To date, the bankers' acceptance market is still narrow, – too dependent on Federal Reserve Banks.

Mechanisms for affecting money market:
–Rediscounting commercial paper.
–Rate on bankers' acceptances.
–Open market operations.
–Moral suasion
–Pressure on individual banks
–Publicity
Rediscount rate
–Decided by Federal Reserve Banks subject to review of Federal Reserve Board.
–Objective is not profit – but control.
–Applies to promissory notes of banks, of individuals to their (member) banks.
–Relatively slow change.
–Higher – less mobile than bankers' acceptance rates.

–Lower than rate charged customers – which latter rate charges varies [sic: vary] to some extent with rediscount rate.

–How can Federal Reserve Bank make its rate effective?

–By being sure that member banks are borrowing.

–To sell securities forces them to borrow.

–Unless gold is flowing into country

–Or until Federal Reserve Bank has no securities left to sell.

–Has sold them all

–Government has retired them all.

–There is no perfect correlation between the rediscount rate and the other market rates.

–Tradition against borrowing helps make the rate and open market operations effective.

Credit and Control, Policy

Difficulties with stabilization – what to stabilize?

–Prices

–What prices? some are always going up, while others go down, and others remain stable.

–What of long run tendencies?

–What index method to determine prices?

–Volume of Production

–How to determine the normal rate?

–What we know about volume of production is always too late.

–What to do with steady increase – long run?

–If to allow it – why?

The Business Cycle

–Statistical Facts

–Theories: – Why?

–Hawtrey, [D. H.] Robertson, Fisher–

–Monetary and Banking Theory

–Currency and credit – Hawtrey

–Our Changing Purchasing Power – Fisher

–Schumpeter (German)

–We live in a dynamic world – changes must go on

–Cassel

–Aftalion – over-production

–Socialist

–Maldistribution of wealth

–Lack of purchasing power by workman

–J. A. Hobson

Types of Price Movement
  1. Secular – long time
    –How is banking and currency to be related to secular change?
  2. Seasonal
    –Have we solved the problem of seasonal changes in demand for funds?
    –Concentration of reserve.
    –Elastic currency.
    –Mobility of reserve.
  3. Cyclical
    –Comparative regularity – but irregular in the long run.
    –Does cycle refer only to business prices or to other things as well.
    –Are the things studied internal to the business system, or outside it?
Classic Economic Theory
  –Equilibrium theory – cycle of goods – cycle of payments.
  –Balance between supply and demand in all economic lines – with equality
    of price, wage, etc.
Actual world – all manner of lack of balance.

[Page 25-A:

  Gambling: taking risks that are not socially necessary]
The Business Cycle

  –Rhythmical progress of certain events.
  –No set time of the cycle – from 3 to 10 years.
  –Essence – fluctuations of economic phenomena in time.
  Professor [Warren] Persons – graph
  –Curve A – Speculative curve
  –Curve B – Business curve (heavy industries, outside clearings)
  –Curve C – Money rates
  –Reactions occur in that order.
  –Speculation precedes business changes, but by no precise timing.
  –Business precedes money rate changes, but by no precise timing.
  –Cycle extends over a period from 3 to 4 years.
    –Such measurement depends on the statistics involved – which are arbitrary
      choices.
  –This was pre-war, pre-Federal Reserve System.

At present time.
  Curve A – Speculation (industrials, railroads)
  Curve B – Bank debits, commodity prices.
  Curve C – Short time money rates.
  –New sequence is topsy-turvy.

–Curve A went off on a tangent by itself.

–Level bank rates, level prices.

[Ostrander's class notes show the horizontal and vertical headings for a table but no content. The way the material can be transcribed can introduce error; inasmuch as there is no content, the two heading axes can be shown in such a way that the sub-headings jibe with the headings.]

Prices		Incomes					Production	
Consumer Goods	Production Goods	Finished Costs	Rent	Wages	Interest	Profits	Producer Goods	Consumer Goods
Slow	Rapid	Slow	Rapid	Not much change	Lag			

I. Depression
II. Revival
III. Prosperity
IV. Crisis
V. Liquidation

[On page 26-A:

[Walter] Babson – "statistical P. T. Barnum"]

–Difference of opinion as to what is to be explained.

–What is to be stressed, what is to be included

–What preconceived opinion operates

–Wesley Mitchell and his group in New York City, standard statistics, Harvard Economic Council, and various other semi-official organizations are all investigating the business cycle

–[W. B.] Smith's guess: when all facts are collected – no one thing will ever explain it all.

Theories
    I. Non-monetary
        a. Rain fall (Jevons), H. L. Moore – "Generating Business Cycles"
          –Prosperity of a country depends on farming class and its prosperity.
          –Its prosperity depends to a great extent on rain.
        b. Psychological
          –Marriages and births (Hexter) – some degree of analysis.
          –Pigou's studies.
        c. Uncertainty, ignorance (Hardy)
          –Give rise to oscillations
          –Miscalculations – too much or too little output.
          –Lack of national planning

    d. Innovations and Progress (Schumpeter)
    –New inventions, methods of marketing, marketing materials (automobile boom, 1920–30)
    –Changes in tastes
    –All manner of dynamic changes.
    e. Unequal distribution of wealth – J. A. Hobson – underconsumption of production, which is only increased by any earnings of industry.
    f. Cassel – low rates of interest, high prices of producers goods, rising production (overproduction of producer goods) – surplus of funds and savings brings cycle.
    g. Aftalion
  II. Monetary
    –Fisher – instability of value of dollar
    –Prosperity and depression are results of rising and falling prices – not high and low prices
    –Rising and falling prices a result of money in circulation (and hope of more – Robertson)

[On page 27-A:

Out of our limited supply of factors – we must build an economic system that will enable us to get the maximum good for our social organization.
–Peculiarities of the phenomenon – money, and the peculiarities of the phenomenon – human nature.]
  –Really, a result of lag in rate of interest.
  –When it becomes effective, crisis results.
  –Hawtrey – periodic fluctuation of production and prices.
    –In stable conditions, consumers outlay for goods is just equal to consumers income for services sold.
  –Rise in rate of interest disturbs equilibrium.
    –Cash in circulation.
    –Gold reserves drained abroad in rising prices.
    –Stresses activities of wholesalers and retailers and their reaction to changes in the interest rate – and unspent margin.
Criticism
    –He is singling out a direct line of causation without enough emphasis on other causes.
    –He makes assumption that businessmen are sensitive to discount rate – is this true?
    –Most borrowing is done in long term ways – changes come about in short time rates.
    –America has a line of credit system of banking.

MATERIALS FROM ECONOMICS 6, MONEY AND BANKING AND PUBLIC FINANCE, TAUGHT BY WILLIAM H. WYNNE, WILLIAMS COLLEGE, SPRING 1931

Published below are (1) the continued syllabus for Money and Banking, (2) the syllabus for the Public Finance part of the semester, (3) the final exam for Economics 6 on June 2, 1931 and (4) Ostrander's class notes for both parts of Economics 6.

The lectures on money and banking continue on a sophisticated level. The lectures on public finance are less detailed as to theory and practice than is found in the literature of the field until the time of the course, partly because only a fraction of the semester was devoted to public finance. The covered topics would have been included in a public finance course during the two decades or so prior to the date of this annual. But so would numerous other topics, including many whose practice and theory date from after the second World War.

(1) THE CONTINUED SYLLABUS FOR MONEY AND BANKING

VI. FOREIGN BANKING SYSTEMS
1. English Banking
   a. The Bank of England
   b. The Joint Stock Banks, Overseas Banks, and Foreign Banks
   c. Acceptance and Discount Houses
2. French and German Banking

Read: Dunbar, C. F., The Theory and History of Banking (1929), Chapters 8–10
   Leaf, W., Banking (1927), Chapters 3, 2, 6, 7, and 8
   Andreades, A., History of the Bank of England
   Dowrie, G. W., American Monetary and Banking Policies, Chapter 12

QUESTIONS:

1. Compare the money markets of the United States, England, France and Germany with respect to: (a) freedom of gold movements; (b) flexibility of the currency supply; (c) the mechanism of adjustment of the amount of reserve bank credit outstanding.

2. Why has England been the most important country in the world's money market during the past hundred years?

3. What was the "banking principle"? The "currency principle"? What are the merits and defects of each?

4. What is the relative importance of deposit banking and bank-note banking in the several countries mentioned above? How do you account for the differences?

5. What is the explanation of the long series of bank mergers in England which has resulted in their being a "Big Five" each with many branches? Does the English experience lead you to think that we are likely to have a similar movement in the United States?

6. Do you think that the fact that the London money market makes many loans to finance foreign trade is an important fact in connection with the control of the money market by the Bank of England? Why?

7. Are the central banks of England, France and Germany private institutions or are they owned and managed by the government? What rights do the governments have in each case over the issue of bank notes? Are the governments privileged borrowers?

VII. INTERNATIONAL FINANCIAL RELATIONS (1930–31)
    A. Foreign Exchange under the Gold Standard
        1. Mechanism of foreign exchange
            (a) Pars of exchange, the gold points
            (b) Bills of exchange
                Sources of supply and demand
                Kinds of bills
            (c) Dealers in exchange
            (d) Gold movements
        2. The relation of the foreign exchanges to short time money rates
        3. The relation of the foreign exchanges to the international movements of securities
        4. The relation between the foreign exchanges and price movements
    B. Foreign Exchange under inconvertible paper
        1. Purchasing power parity
        2. Alternative theories
    C. The Bank of International Settlements
        Read: James, F. C., <u>The Economics of Money, Credit and Banking</u>, Chapters 10, 22, and the Appendix.

Escher, F., Foreign Exchange Explained, pp. 1–87, 108–136
[147–174 added].
Keynes, J. M., Monetary Reform, pp. {95–125} [replacing
95–151].
Edie, L. D., Money, Bank Credit and Prices, Chapters 20 and 21.
Hawtrey, R. G., Currency and Credit, Chapters 6 and 7.
Cassel, G., Foreign Investments, Chapter 1.
{Whitaker, A. C., Foreign Exchange
Nogaro, Modern Monetary Systems, pp. 125–156}.

VIII. INVESTMENT BANKING
  1. Long-time lending and investment
     (a) Corporate securities
     (b) Promotion
     (c) Underwriting and the marketing of securities
  2. The stock market
     (a) Relation to investment banking
     (b) Relation to commercial banking
  3. Investment trusts
  4. Savings banks
  5. Trust companies
     Read: [No indication is given as to meaning of #.]
            #Willis, H. P., and Bogen, J. I., Investment Banking, New
              York. Harpers, 1929.
            #Dewing, A. S. The Financial Policy of Corporations. New
              York. The Ronald Press. 1922. Book I, Chapters 1–7, and
              Book II, Chapters 1–4, 7–9.
            #Gerstenberg, C. W. Materials of Corporate Finance. New
              York. Prentice-Hall. 1915. pp. 126–149, 398–414, 421–434.
            #Munn, G. C. The Trend Toward Long Term Investments.
              Bankers Magazine. February, 1929. pp. 181–185.
            #Friday, D. Business Goes to Market. Bankers Magazine.
              September, 1929. pp. 337–339.
            Lagerquist, W. E. Investment Analysis. New York. The
              Macmillan Co. Chapters 10–11.
            [Vertical line in margin alongside last three authors.]

QUESTIONS:

(1) Define: common stock, preferred stock, bond, cumulative preferred stock,
    participating preferred stock, junior lien bond, mortgage bond, collateral trust
    bond, debenture bond, income bond, convertible bond, short term note,

equipment trust certiWcate, rights, promoter, underwriter, and "blue sky laws."

(2) What is the difference between a voting trust, and an investment trust, a trust company, and a trust?

(3) "The older doctrine of bank credit as stated, for example by Adam Smith, would limit the banker to short-term advances of part of the working capital of a merchant. The banker, Adam Smith would hold, may properly lend a merchant funds for the turnover of readily marketable goods, and he might lend a manufacturer also some part of his working capital for the purchase of materials for quick conversion into marketable goods, but he must lend to the manufacturers no part of the funds used to purchase "his forge and his smelting house" . . . The development of the modern stock market has changed the facts and has provided a safe machinery for using commercial banks directly or indirectly for many capital purposes, still keeping them liquid." Anderson, B. M., Chase Economic Bulletin VI, No. 3. pp. 25–26.

    (a) What were and are the grounds for holding the "older doctrine"?

    (b) Do you agree with Anderson's conclusion? Why?

(4) "Because of its effects on foreign exchange rates a long time capital movement will often bring with it a short time movement in the opposite dire ction." Knock, K. A Study of Interest Rates. p. 98.

    Trace the steps whereby a "long-time" movement of capital abroad brings about a short-time movement in the opposite direction.

(5) "One corollary of the easing tendency in interest rates has been the beginning of a recovery in bond prices." The Guaranty Survey. November 25, 1929. p. 10. Why is this true?

(6) "The fact that total (bank) loans have expanded only at the same rate as industrial production raises at least a presumption that the total credit which is being created by loans is going into the support of industry and trade. The difference between the present and a decade ago is that credit is flowing by a different channel."

    Do you agree? Why? What is the "new channel" referred to?

(7) "Under the national banking system, the money forced out of circulation, in periods of low prices and stagnant trade[,] flowed to New York. There it served as the foundation of a rapid expansion of loans and discounts and investments on the one hand and of deposit credit on the other. The New York banks made advances to investors and to speculative buyers of bonds, and, usually a little later, to buyers of stocks. Large advances were commonly

required to finance new issues of bonds . . ." Young, A. A. The Review of
Economic Statistics, vol. 7. p. 33.
   (a) Does the above sequence of events hold today?
   (b) What relation between bank reserves, interest rates, security prices,
       and the volume of long-time credits is implied in the above quotation?
   (c) What circumstances will bring about a reversal of the events described
       above?

(8) "The movement of gold was reversed late in October (1929), an excess of
     imports giving way [to] an excess of exports. . . . Further new outflow of
     gold is rendered probable by the easing in our money market, especially if
     such easing attracts foreign borrowing in considerable volume or leads to
     withdrawals of foreign balances held here, particularly by foreign central
     Banks." Harvard Economic Society. Weekly Letter, November 30, 1929.
     p. 283. Explain.

(9) What is the immediate effect of foreign investment (say, the purchase of
     foreign bonds by the people of the United States) upon the balance of
     trade? What long run effects are likely to arise out of foreign loans?

(10) "After a long period, during which virtually no foreign loans were arranged,
     French banks are about to issue three foreign credits aggregating
     3,000,000,000 francs. . . . While the cash part of the loans will be supplied
     by foreign banking markets the spending which will arise in connection with
     the proceeds of the loans will be allotted to France. British banking circles
     have therefore criticized this method as lending nothing toward the solution at
     the present impasse in the international money market and checking the flow
     of gold from London to Paris." New York Times, February 4, 1931. Discuss.

(2) THE SYLLABUS FOR PUBLIC FINANCE

ECONOMICS 5-6

1930–31.

IX. PUBLIC FINANCE AND TAXATION
     1. Introduction
        a. Definitions
        b. General observations on the relations between government finance
           and the production and distribution of wealth

2. Public Expenditures
   a. Wagner's law
   b. Government and private expenditures contrasted
   c. The facts of government expenditures in the United States
   d. Economic effects of government expenditures
3. Government Revenues
   a. The public domain
   b. Public industry
   c. Administrative revenues
   d. Taxes
      (1) Definitions
      (2) The canons of taxation
      (3) The theory of the shifting and incidence of taxation
      (4) Some important present-day taxes in the United States and Europe
4. Government borrowings and public debts
   Read: Lutz, H. L., Public Finance, Chapters 2, 4, 5, 6, 8, 10, 13, 14, 15,
      16, {17}, 18, 19, 20, 21, 22, 23, 24, pp. 591–610, chapters 27
      and {30}.
   Dalton, H., Principles of Public Finance, Chapters 18, 19, 20, 4,
      14, {15}, 9, 7, 8, 21, 22, 23, 24, 25.
   George, H., Progress and Poverty, Book VIII, Chapters 2 and 3.
   Hoxie, R. F., "The Tariff as a Revenue Measure," reprinted in
      Bullock's Readings in Public Finance {Chapter 20}.
   Comstock, A., Taxation in the Modern State, Chapters 6, 8, 9,
      12, 15.
   Chapman, J. M., Fiscal Functions of the Federal Reserve Banks,
      Chapters 5, 6, and 9.

QUESTIONS:
(1) By what means are public expenditures controlled in the United States?
(2) What is the case for and the case against Federal grants in aid to State
    activities?
(3) What has been the trend of municipal borrowing in the United States in
    recent years? Is it economically desirable that municipalities should borrow
    as much as they do?
(4) What special problems are presented just now by the taxation of automobiles?
(5) In judging the merits of a given system of taxes, which of the following con-
    siderations seem to be the most important, and which the least: Justice,
    econom[ic] adequacy, directness?
(6) If you were anxious to foster the conservation of our timber resources,
    would you favor the taxation of forest lands?

(7) Some "single taxers" claim that Henry George's single tax would cure business depressions. What is the ground for their position? Do you think that it is well taken?

(8) "Borrowing from the currency" is said to be an easy method of taxation; and on the other hand some people claim that it makes the collection of taxes especially difficult. What is the truth in these claims?

(9) Are fiscal monopolies an important source of revenue in modern states?

(10) "Taxation would certainly be a much simpler task if there were not so many curious and roundabout ways of making money." Discuss.

(11) "Taxes are not always, nor necessarily, a discouragement to production. Frequently, they are an incentive, and especially under a good system of taxation, they exert an influence in the direction of increased production in a progressive society." Discuss.

(12) "The purchaser of tax-exempt securities neither evades nor avoids taxation, for the yields on such securities [are] always proportionally lower." Do you agree? Why?

(13) "The population of the world steadily increases. Hence, in case of increased taxation on land, the cultivator of the soil is generally enabled to transfer the burden easily and promptly to the purchasers of the products he raises." Discuss.

(14) "Estate taxes, carried to excess, in no way differ from the methods of the revolutionists in Russia." A. W. Mellon, Taxation, The People's Business. Discuss.

(15) "I have never viewed taxation as a means of rewarding one class of taxpayers or punishing another. If such a point of view ever controls our public policy, the traditions of freedom, justice and equality of opportunity, which are the distinguishing characteristics of our American civilization, will have disappeared and in their place we shall have class legislation with all its attendant evils." A. W. Mellon, Taxation, The People's Business, p. 11. Discuss.

(16) "A current newspaper article states that the people of the United States spend more on automobiles each year than they do on all government services. It is then argued that we ought to spend more on such services as schools, parks etc. Is this a good argument? Is it a valid reply to those who assert that the burden of taxation is too great at the present time?

(17) "To take large amounts by taxation from the rich to increase public expenditures is said to be disguised socialism." Is this true?

(18) "During the World War the United States imposed a tax on the business profits in excess of a certain amount. Opponents of this tax asserted that it (1) raised prices, (2) caused extravagant business expenditures for advertising and the like, and (3) discouraged enterprise." What do you think of each

of these claims? Do you think that they could all have been true at the same time?

(19) Is a protective tariff a good revenue tariff?

(20) There are at least three kinds of value that the economist has to study – value in exchange, value for rate making purposes (e.g., the valuation of the railroads by the Interstate Commerce Commission) and value for purposes of taxation. What, if any, is the difference between these kinds of value?

(21) What are the points of similarity and difference between the single tax and the general property tax?

(22) What is the meaning of the "incidence of taxation" and how is incidence to be distinguished from "general economic effects"? Point out the difference between incidence and effects in the case of important taxes like the general property tax, the income tax, the inheritance tax, and import duties.

(23) What is the capital levy? What do you think would be its effects?

(3) EXAM

ECONOMICS 6

Final Examination   June 2, 1931

PART I. REQUIRED (about an hour)

(1) Write an essay upon equity in taxation; its interpretation, its implications, and its practical applications.

PART II. ANSWER ANY FOUR QUESTIONS

(2) "My own personal view is that business, through the medium of a small turnover tax, could well pay the entire cost of economically running the government, take care of the great national debt, and permit the dropping of all other kinds of federal taxation. Such an exclusive tax would naturally eliminate the personal income tax and relieve business from the burden of providing the additional interest, dividends or profit which it must now furnish to pay the income taxes. In other words I believe that personal income taxes practically amount to indirect business consumption taxes which business must generally find for the individual taxpayer." Meyer D. Rothschild, Chairman of the Business Men's National Tax Committee (1920).

To what extent do you agree or disagree with Mr. Rothschild. Present your reasons fully.

(3) a. During the World War the United States imposed a tax on business profits. State in as much detail as you can the character of these taxes. Opponents

of the taxation of business profits asserted: (a) that it raised prices, (b) that it caused extravagant business expenditures on advertising and the like, and (c) that it discouraged enterprise. What do you think of each of these claims? Why?

b. Hobson in his Taxation in the New State argues that a modern policy of taxation should aim to reach the surplus elements in various types of income. Consider the application of such a policy in relation to (a) excess profits tax, (b) land taxes, and (c) surtaxes.

(4) a. Analyze the incidence of the General Property tax.

b. In the discussion in Congress of the 1928 Revenue Act, it was urged that a reduction of Corporation income taxes would mean lower prices to consumers. Do you agree? Why or why not?

(5) Compare the effects of raising revenue by inflation of the currency with the effects of raising it by a capital levy. Are there any circumstances under which you think the use of the capital levy justifiable?

(6) "The whole theory of public expenditure may be summed up in one sound principle. Private individuals are likely to make better use of their money than governments. The governments should therefore restrict their expenditures to the minimum necessary only for national protection, for the preservation of law and order and for certain indispensable public works."

Discuss this view. In the course of your discussion (a) show what alternative theories or principles of public expenditure have been developed by other writers, and (b) present what you consider satisfactory criteria as to the desirability of various forms of public expenditure.

(7) Discuss the present position and problems of inheritance taxation in the United States. Consider (a) the justification for and (b) the economic effects of such taxes.

(8) Discuss the problem of (a) interpreting and (b) measuring the taxable capacity of a nation.

(4) OSTRANDER'S CLASS NOTES FROM ECONOMICS 6, MONEY AND BANKING AND PUBLIC FINANCE, TAUGHT BY WILLIAM H. WYNNE, WILLIAMS COLLEGE, SPRING 1931

MONEY AND BANKING, CONTINUED

English Banking System
–Joint stock banks
  –No right of note-issue
  –Keep reserve at the Bank of England

–Overdrafts
–Acceptance houses and discount brokers
–For transacting foreign trade
–Discount houses borrow from joint-stock banks; or, if that source is cut off, directly from the Bank of England at the current discount rate.
–That rate is effective if the joint stock banks have not too much surplus.
[Diagram with four circles: northwest one is labeled "J.S.B" (joint stock banks); the northeast one, "B of E" (Bank of England); the southeast one, "D.B." (discount brokers); and the southwest one, "D.H." (discount houses). Arrows run from NW to NE, to SW to SE, and from SE to NE and NW]
French Banking System
–Bank of France founded as private bank
–Soon given monopoly of note-issue.
–Still important in France, because of lack of checking.
–A maximum limit to note-issue, but that limit can be easily changed – has steadily risen since 1914.
–Customary gold reserve is very high.
–Banking operations
–Transfer of funds from one country to another.
–Rediscounting for joint-stock banks.
–Deals in foreign exchange.
–Administration
–Governor and Deputy Governors are appointed by the government.
–In reality a government institution – though privately owned.
–Conditions – Miscellaneous
–Relatively stable discount policy.
–Charge a premium on gold to prohibit export of it
–devaluation, or debasement.
–Payments of the War of 1870 Indemnity were handled by the Bank of France – so as not to disturb the foreign exchange rate.
–During 1914–18 the government turned to the Bank [of France].
–It sold many bonds; loaned directly, in large sums; made this inflation permanent by large issue of notes.
–After war devaluated French franc 1914, 0.25; 1927, 0.04.

[On page 1-A:

The Gold Standard is nothing else than a paper standard whose value is dependent upon the way in which the supply of means of payment is regulated.
–The object of that regulation being to keep the value of the currency at a certain par with Gold.

G. Cassel]

Outside Banks
   –Le Grand Quatre – much like English joint-stock banks.
   –No regulation of their operation – very free.
   –No right of note-issue.
   –They handle issues of foreign securities.
   –Decreased importance since the war.
German Banking System
   Reichbank – established after the Franco–Prussian War
   –Used French indemnities to put Germany on a Gold Standard.
   –Threw silver on the market – price went down.
   –Issued Reichbank notes – though not a monopoly.
   –Before War – a specific limit, might be exceeded on payment of a tax, and
      as long as [there was] one-third gold backing.
   –Since War – (Dawes Plan) limit on amount of loans to the government.
   –40% backing for notes – in gold or foreign exchange.
   –35% backing for deposits.
   –Balances held with Reichbank by other banks are very small.
   –Does a certain amount of rediscounting.
   –Varies it[s] rate often.
Outside Banks
   –Several large banks
   –Are very closely tied up with industry – long-time loaning.
   –A great many scattered and peculiar companies loaning to people for <u>short</u> time.
Foreign Exchange
   –[Foreign exchanage] <u>Rate</u> is the value of money of one country in terms of the
      value of money of another country.
   –Price of one currency in terms of the price of another.
   –Is the connecting link between the price levels of two countries.
Bills of Exchange
   –Cables   clean bill
   –Sight   documentary bill
   –Time – 30, 60, 90 days
Documents
   Bill of Lading – issued by the transporting company carrier.
   Commercial Invoice
   Insurance certificate – to protect holder of documents
   Hypothication certificate – pledges Bill of Lading and other documents as
      collateral
   Consular invoice
   Inspection certificate – B.L.A., etc.

Mint par of exchange – relative gold content of two monetary units.
Gold points – export and import (4.8897) (4.8461)
–The no-profit gold export/import points
–Are not completely stable
–Variations in any of the costs incurred in shipment of gold changes gold points (interest)
–Any shipment of gold[:] time drafts can be drawn against it as soon as shipped.
  –No interest charges lost
  –Thus cable rate is more significant.
–Lower rate of interest will raise gold import rate.
Sterling Exchange – through London
Dollar Exchange – through New York
Franc Exchange – through Paris (?)
<u>Supply of Exchange</u> (payments <u>this</u> way) – rate, down
  Visible (1) Merchandise exports
  Invisible {(2) Remittances of foreigners to the U.S.
  Exports {(3) Expenses of tourists in U.S.
        {(4) Freight
        {(5) War debts payments
        {(6) Interest on private investments abroad
  Long time capital – Foreign investments <u>in the</u> U.S.
  Short time capital – (1) Gold
<u>Demand for Exchange</u> (payments going <u>out</u>) – rate, up
  Visible – Merchandise imports
  Invisible Imports [are]
    Long time and short time capital
[On page 3-A:

  long speculation, short speculation
  –buy, sell   –sell, buy]

–Forward exchange – buying and selling of bills of exchange for the future, dated ahead.
–Hedge – by balancing the sales and purchases.

January 7, 1930		February 19, 1931		
£ Demand	4.86 7/16	4.86 1/16	−0.00 6/16
Cables	4.86 13/16	4.86¼	−0.00 9/16
60 day	4.82 3/8	4.83 13/16	+0.01 7/16
90 day	4.80 ¾	4.82¾	+0.02

–Demand and cables move together
–Increase in demand for sight exchange – raises that rate
  –The various rates tend to remain equal in their amount of discrepancy
  –The spreads depend on rates of interest in two terminals
Arbitrage
  –Simultaneous operations of purchase and sale between two centers with
    different rates.
  –Tending to level out the rates.
  –A "timeless" operation – if in time, speculation.
  –Two-point, three point.
  –As result of the interrelation of all the foreign exchange rates in Occidental
    countries.
Pure speculation – long
  –Contract to purchase in the future at a set price – rates must rise for profit.
  –From standpoint of merchant buying the future, there is no speculation –
    merely good hedging.
  –Has a tendency to iron out the rates (fluctuations) over the period of the
    year.
  –Involving short time investment = purchase of bills.
  –Involving long time investment = buying bonds, awaiting deflation and
    decrease of premium.
  –Most foreign exchange dealers do not speculate heavily – for the most part
    their transactions are simultaneous buying and selling.
    –Foreign exchange market becomes, on the whole, just another means of
      clearance between balances.

[On page 4-A: Ostrander stresses that the following has little if anything to do
          with money and banking, and that it likely was due to (1) an out-
          side professor who spoke on what interested him, or (2) a page
          from another class because he ran out of paper there, perhaps
          American History.
Railroads in the U.S.
  –Role of government in industry.
  –Laissez-faire – not 100%.
  –Public regulation of private business.
  –Government ownership.
  –1830–80 – Laissez-faire in railroading.
  –At first short roads in great number.
  –Then growth of consolidation – competition cutting its own throat.
  –"The public be damned" attitude.
  –Rates – fluctuations, discriminations of place and person, and commodity.

–Financial scandal.

–1880–1920 – First regulations – Grange agitation – regulation in the States.

1887 – First Interstate Commerce Act – put regulation in federal hands.

1890 – Sherman Act.

–Hostility to monopoly, and combination.

–Supreme Court decided against pools – versus competition.

–Northern Securities Case 1904 – holding companies forbidden – versus competition.

–Union Pacific–Southern Pacific – prohibition of ownership – versus competition.

–1917 – The government took over the railroads.

–Executive head (McAdoo-W. Hines).

–Pooling – a single large system.

–1920 – Esch–Cummins Act – Transportation Act of 1920.

–Rates to allow 5¾% in any <u>district</u>.

–Any road making over 6% – one-half of excess would be recaptured by government, for fund for aiding weak roads.

–Pooling agreements may be made with consent of I.C.C.

–Consolidation permitted with consent of I.C.C. – in interest of general welfare.

–General policy – the railroads of U.S. should be consolidated into a <u>few big</u> competing plans – but no power to force this union.

What is advantage of plan for regional consolidation with competition as against regional unification – what is wrong with nation-wide uniWcation? Why no power in I.C.C.?]

Influence of interest rates on foreign exchange.

–Low in London, high in New York.

–Sale of drafts on London in New York – lowers rate, leads to gold import.

–England would raise its discount rates to protect gold.

–Would decrease the possible profit in New York City by increasing the spread between a 90 day and sight drafts in New York City.

–Short time borrowing carried out in market where rates are low.

–Finance bills are sold in high market, money loaned there.

–Low interest rates abroad cause small spread here and vice versa.

–Operations are carried on, not only with an eye to present discrepancy of interest rates, but with an eye on future forecast of interest rates.

–Initiative may be taken from London, from New York, or on joint account.

–Effect of varying interest rates on foreign exchange rate.

–Foreign Exchanges and the interconnections between the national price levels, credit policies, etc.

–Fluctuations occur in response to short-time interest rates.

Long time capital movement

–World market for bonds and stock.

Case I – when stocks are sold abroad for purchasing account, there is no immediate effect on foreign exchange rate – but there will be interest payments, and repayment of loan which will disturb the rate.

Case II – when proceeds of sale are moved to the borrowing country,

    –Due to large supply of bills on London, New York sterling rate goes down, may bring gold import to New York.

–Takes place when there are large differences in the longtime interest rates between two countries.

–Affect gold, bank credit.

Summary of Foreign Exchange under gold

    –Notes kept close to mint par because of convertibility

    –Relative purchasing powers of two currencies over gold

    –Rates are confined within narrow limits by convertibility once freedom of movement of gold – gold import and export points

    –Internationally traded goods tend to equal price – unless tariff.

    –Does not apply to domestic products in short-time

    –Arbitrage in commodities

    –Exchange rates are influenced by all factors entering into demand

    –Not merely commodity demand

    –Exchange rates are influenced by all factors entering into supply

    –Invisible as well as visible.

    –Reparations

    –Interest rates affect both short-time and long-time loaning – thus exchange rates.

    –Short-time interest rates are interrelated the world over.

    –Have pronounced effect on exchange rates.

    –Long time loans affect commodity shipments, exchange rates, gold flow, etc.

Foreign exchanges under Paper.

    –Inconvertibility, paper money is not exchangeable into gold at the banks or Treasury

    –May be convertible into gold in the market at a premium

    –Internal value of paper is its domestic purchasing power

    –External value of paper is the purchasing power of a national currency over foreign currencies.

    –Or the purchasing power a national currency over foreign goods.

    –Depreciation: a. Domestic { over gold
                             { over goods

b. External { over foreign currencies

{ over foreign goods

–Pegging –usually engaged in under paper standard.

–some very large House is given authority to buy and sell all exchange at a <u>given</u> rate.

Devaluation

–Stabilization of currency at a different and <u>lower</u> ratio with gold.

Repudiation

–No redemption (Germany, 1 trillion to one)

–New currency

Restoration

–Stabilization of currency at old pre-paper basis – usually involves deflation.

Deflation

–Increase in purchasing power of currency – <u>planned</u>

Purchasing Power Parity

–Not a <u>new</u> idea with Cassel.

–Price-levels depend on the quantity of money. Rates of exchange depend on relative price levels.

–Using index numbers as gauges.

–This sets a <u>par of exchange</u> around which the rates fluctuate.

–Based on <u>alternative opportunities</u> of getting <u>goods</u>.

–Assumes <u>only</u> the effect of merchandise movements on the exchange rate.

–<u>But</u>:- will quantity of money stabilize price levels by itself?

–Though – why not accept price levels as a resultant of various forces, <u>then</u> apply the purchasing power theory.

–Will the importer have "alternative opportunities" assumed here? – probably not.

–International goods run in channels fixed by natural resources of different countries.

–The price level is only one of a number of forces acting on the foreign exchange rate

–balance of <u>payments</u> also is important.

–Establishes a causal chain – quantity of money→price level→ exchange rate.

–This is not always true.

–Does not consider all the changes possible in <u>reciprocal demand</u>.

In Germany [in its hyper inflation of 1922–23] the sequence is:- unbalanced budget, increased borrowing, buying of exchange, rise of exchange rate.

–There <u>was</u> correlation between prices and exchange.

–But the exchange rates on New York were considerably above the purchasing power parity – going up faster than prices for a while, then reversed.

–Taxes met about 90% of internal expenditures – deficit met by borrowing – but with rising prices, taxes met less and less of expenditures.

–Also very large <u>external</u> expenditures, for reparations, meaning more borrowing from Reichsbank.

–This caused issue of Reichsbank notes, greatly increasing the quantity of currency.

–Germany didn't <u>need</u> more <u>internal</u> currency, but external.

–Foreign speculation in German marks served to <u>sustain</u> the price of the mark.

–But by end of 1922 – confidence left.

–"Flight from the mark" – transference of German savings into foreign currencies.

–This kind of speculation helped the fall of the mark in foreign exchange.

–At first the velocity was <u>under</u> the normal, because of hoarding. The price level rose more slowly than the quantity of money.

–But then, with lessened confidence, the velocity reached a <u>maximum</u>, <u>above</u> the normal. (Hoarded currency had been thrown out.) The price level rose <u>faster</u> than the quantity of money.

–Finally, with a <u>steady</u> velocity – impossible to increase further – the price level in 1922–23 rose <u>with</u> the increase in quantity of money.

–The quantity theory held true only in the <u>last</u> stages of inflation, when the <u>velocity</u> factor had been ruled out.

–The Dawes Plan gave Germany a breathing spell – a chance to forget reparations for a while – a moratorium.

–Coinciding with a repudiation of old currency and issue of a new.

–It fixed a new total [for the currency] – [greatly] scaled down, with very slight payments at first.

–This plan was considered only the first of a series.

–A director of payments.

1919–24 – Summary of Germany

–Unprecedented fall of foreign exchange rates.

–Very great price rise in Germany.

–Lag of rest of prices of purely domestic goods behind price of international goods.

–Increase in prices was not equal with increase in quantity of money – slower at first – prices rose <u>before</u> quantity of money – in last stages

–Velocity of money is an unstable thing.

–The budget was unbalanced – largely because Germany had enormous payments to make on reparations accounts.

–Also because her internal expenses rose in price faster than the taxes could be arranged to the new price levels.

–These two factors brought about increased borrowing by the German government from the Reichsbank.

–And a demand for exchange on New York – abnormal – which drove up the rate, past the parity of the price level.

–Loss of confidence led to "flight from the mark" – accentuating rise in price level in Germany, and rise of exchange rates.

[On page 9-A:

Securities
  {Rights to income
  {Rights to property
  {Rights to control
  Priority]

Investment Banking

–Its role in connection with the accumulation of capital and

–The effect of investment bankers on competition and have they created a monopoly.

–What is the effect of investment banking on the business cycle.

–What is the connection between investment banking and international trade and finance.

Commercial Banking	Investment Banking
–Short-term loans and investments	–<u>Long</u>-term
–Supplies working capital	–Supplies <u>fixed</u> capital
–Expanding credit	–Investment

I. <u>Borrowers</u>

–Issue – (II. Investment Brokers, III. Marketing, IV. Investors)
  –And issuers.

–<u>Government</u>
  –<u>Federal</u>, States, <u>municipalities</u>

–Private corporations

–Public utilities

–Railroads

–Industrials

–Banks and Financial
–Real estate mortgage

II. Kinds of Securities – Investments involved.
  –Stock – Common – Proportionate share to assets.
    –Proportionate share to profits – after other creditors
    –Right to vote.
  –With or without par value.
    Preferred – Right to a specified dividend – cumulative, non-cumulative
    –Prior claim to a share in profits and assets
    –Participating, non-participating
    –Right to vote in occasional cases
    –Convertible, non-convertible

  –Bonds
  –Government, Railroads
  –A certificate of debt by the company to the holder with definite interest
    payment.
  –Gains control in the case that the interest payment is defaulted.
  –"Income bonds" not as definite as the usual bond.
  –Property rights – like a mortgage.
    –Bond holders have rights to seizure of property and sale – if payment is
      defaulted.
  –Collateral trust bond – secured by deposit of other bonds or stocks as
    collateral.
  –Debenture bonds – no specific lien.

  –Securities issued for promotion, operation, reorganization.
  –Financial plan – Amount of capital needed
  –Kinds and amounts of different securities
    –Bonds.
      –Issued only when a company has a steady income in sight.
      –Lower rate of return
    –Preferred stock
      –More agreeable to public
      –Retain control in hands of directors
    –Common stock
      –Large amount – so that control is split
      –Value increases with rising prices
        –Holders' equity increases
  –Investment banks often protect interests of their customers.

III. Ultimate Lender
1. Individual purchaser
   a. Saving
      –<u>Not</u> spent on consumer goods
      –Invested
      –Hoard – by individuals or by banks
   b. Invested money is turned over to corporations involved
   c. Spent by corporation on factors of production
      –Direction of spending in hands of corporation
2. –Savings Banks
   –Mutuals, or stock
3. –Investment Trust
   –Buys the bonds of other corporations – distributes the earnings to the holders of <u>its own shares</u> in the form of dividends.
   –<u>Fixed</u> – announces the fixed panel of stocks which it owns – its each share represents so many shares of each member of the panel.
   –But no possibility of shifting and changing the character of <u>one's</u> investments – aside from total sale of the investment trust shares.
   –Discretionary – a pool of money collected by issuing stock, a board of managers manipulates this as it pleases – for profit.
   –Perfect possibility of change and diversification.
   –But, these managers may speculate wildly.
   –Pay dividends on earnings from other dividends, as well as on earnings from sale and purchase.
4. –Trust Company – an omnibus affair – State charter.
   –Board of trustees for administrating estates and wills.
   –Trustees for bond issues – or registrars
   [Single vertical line along preceding two lines.]
   –Commercial bank functions.
   –Savings department.
   –Selling bonds.
5. Insurance Companies
   –Life – term, ordinary, limited pay, endowment.
   –Property.
   –Casualty.
   –Dual operation of such companies.
   –<u>Insuring proper</u>, collecting small amounts from a large group of people, paying out somewhat larger amounts to a much smaller group, on the basis of the <u>permanent</u> law of averages.
   –<u>Investing</u>, the excess amounts must be saved for future, larger demands and averages.

IV. Middle Man
  A. Marketing of new issues.
    a. –Underwriting (accepting risk and guaranteeing payment).
      –Middle man guarantees to take an issue at a fixed price – the issuer
      has then hedged the risk.
    b. –Selling – middle man markets this issue through the channels which
      make up his organization.
    c. –Investigation – standing of issuing corporation is investigated
  1. –House of First Purchase
    –Underwrites, sells, and investigates.
    –Management, gets rid of part of the risk by distributing the new issue
    among its close business alliances.
  2. Banker's Syndicate
    –A group of business alliances who underwrite parts of the issue, or some
    times bid for an issue at first.
  3. Selling Syndicates and Groups
    –Participate in the risk and selling.

  B. Stock Market
    –Trading in common, by experts (brokers), short or long trading, margin
    trading.
    –Facilitates "availability" – and the possibility of immediate sale.
    –Makes possible collateral loans.
    –Forces a constant evaluation of every stock.

PUBLIC FINANCE

Public Finance

Development of Taxation
  –Probably in a rough parallel to development of parliamentary government –
  freedom of contract.
  –Is partly [a] problem of government.
    –Expression of demands of sections of the populace, expressed through their
    organ, the State.
  –Economics is, most generally, the study of Costs – as against Economic
    Welfare.
  –Cost: Money cost; Real cost: labor, natural resources, capital saving,
    Managerial enterprise; Opportunity costs.

–Economic Functions of State

Mercantilists – building up the national State, government supervision and control of industry and money.

Physiocrats – believers in Natural Rights and the Natural Order – first laissez-faire advocates.

Adam Smith – Opponent of government in business, attacked legislation in favor of special groups, in opposition to business.

> – "The Invisible Hand" – individual man's own selfish desires lead – by the aid of God – to the good of the whole society.

> –State's activities limited to – defense, administration of justice, public works.

J. S. Mill – Modification of Smith, wobbling, especially in middle life.

> –Government out of business – essay "On Liberty".

> –Violation of division of labor.

> –Self-interest necessary for incentive (but, leads to predatory actions).

> –But government should take care of coinage – things striking everyone.

> –Money demand is not sufficient to get produced all that should be produced.

> –State ought to lay down rules and regulations in all cases where one person takes over the rights of another (corpora tion – stockholder).

> –State should give to citizens those things which he cannot get by merely desiring them (as peaceful Sabbath).

> –State should undertake all those things which are so large that individuals are timid to undertake them.

[On page 14-A:

Wagner – law of increasing State expenditures.

–An intensive increase of State activities and functions.

 –Old duties constantly being performed more efficiently.

–An extensive increase of state activities and functions.

 –New duties are being constantly undertaken.]

Modernist version

> –Dalton – principle of maximum social advantage in view of the character of the natural resources, and industrial and technical development.

> –Effect of government's action on

(1) Production,
  –in quality and quantity (savings, organization)
  –in direction of expenditure
(2) Distribution
  –Equality
  –Marginal utility
  –Regularity
  –Certainty
Government Expenditure
  –Wagner's Law of Increasing Expenditure
  –Increase of welfare expenditure.
  –Widening of the trade area.
  –Fostering of cultural growth (education).
  –State carrying on of activities too large or not favorable for private operation.
  –Government expenditure versus private expenditure.
    –Government – for immaterial; private – for material.
    –In matter of profits, especially.
    –Government – authoritarian expenditures; private – no authority – flexible.
    –Government – long run expenditure; private – short run.
    –Government – adjust income to expenditure; private – adjust expenditure to income.
  –Facts of Expenditures

U.S. Federal Government	1927
–Military functions	31.8
–Public debt	51.0%
–Internal security	2.0%
–General government	2.7%
–Rules and Regulation	3.3%
–Public works	7.3%
–Miscellaneous	2.0%

  –Wars – past, present, and future account for most of expense
  –Tendency for government expenses to vary with economic condition.
    –To go up, but not to come down.
  –Increase in expenditures – for regulation and supervision – welfare.

  State Expenditures
    –Highways – Education – Welfare – Collective effort.
    –General government – protection.
  Municipal Expenditures
    –Protection – police, fire, sanitation, etc.
    –Education, Charity.

Classifications of expenditures.

–Real expenditure versus nominal expenditure (bookkeeping transfers).

–Ordinary and extraordinary – Budgetary versus borrowing.

–Productive versus unproductive.

–Reproductive – not bringing national utility

–Non-reproductive.

Classification of Revenues (Receipts)

1. Commercial – revenue in return for a distinct service given to public at its voluntary instigation.
2. Administrative – fines, etc.
3. Transfers.
4. Taxes – compulsory revenue in return for general functions of the State.
5. Loans

1. Commercial

a. History of acquisition of Public Domain [In U.S.]

–Disposal of Public Domain

–1796–1820 – Sale on credit.

1820–60 – Sale for cash.

1861–90 – Homestead Period.

–Land grants – to railroads, schools.

–Conservation

–Revenue from this source – not much (Have we encouraged our farmers in land speculation?)

–Has it been advisable to transfer subsoil rights?

b. Industry

–Reasons for government in business – not necessarily to make money – but to promote general welfare.

–Fear of monopoly in certain lines.

–For military reasons.

–To bring in revenue (in certain cases).

–If only the government could furnish capital – but, more truthfully – when there are not enough profits in sight to attract private industry – yet the undertaking is needed.

Adam Smith's qualifications

–Small capital – small risk – not much loss if it failed

–Simple administration – low view of public intelligence

–Immediate and regular return – is any return needed?

–Industry is not an important source of public revenue.

2. Administrative

–Fine – no relation to ability to pay

–Of a semi-compulsory character.

–Fee – "special assessments" – license.

Problems – division of assessments for private and public benefit.

–Excess condemnation – for revenue

   –Right of eminent domain – used to take more property than is really needed – then selling surplus.

3. Transfers – Grants-in-aid

   –A transfer of funds from the treasury of the central authority to the treasury of the local authority.

   –Central authority lays down rules of expenditure.

   –Decentralized spending.

   –A compromise – there should be, in one sense, centralized spending, at the same time a form of local autonomy is desirable.

   –Really, a transfer of funds from rich sections of the country to poor sections.

   –Establishes a certain amount of national equality of standard of living, etc.

   –Has advantage of economy of collection.

   –Disadvantage – log rolling – granting "plums."

4. Taxation

   –Compulsory contribution, levied on the individual by the State – for the benefit of the collective expenditure (levied irrespective of the benefits received).

[On page 17-A:

Diagram, with rate on vertical axis and amount of income on horizontal axis; nature of four types of tax schedule indicated: Progressive: rising straight line, originating slightly to the right of the origin on the horizontal axis. Regressive: falling straight line, originating up on vertical axis. Proportional: horizontal line parallel to and just above horizontal axis. Degressive: curved line, originating at point of origin, rising and then flattening.

Several lines below diagram: Plato, Rousseau, Militaristic, St. Thomas Aquinas.]

–Direct tax – borne by the person on whom it is legislated.

–Indirect tax – passed on to someone else, not mentioned in original legislation.

–Base – thing on which the tax is levied.

–Rate – ad valorem – according to value.

   –specific – according to quantity.

On income:

   –proportional – everyone pays the same proportion of his income.

   –progressive – rate increases as income rises.

   –degressive – as income increases, the rate increases, but by progressively decreasing increments.

   –regressive – rate decreases as income increases – (as tariff).

Adam Smith's canons of taxation
–Taxes should be levied equally.
–Each person should contribute in reference to his ability – that ability would be based on the proportion of benefits received under the protection of the State.
–Taxes should be certain – as to time, manner and quantity of payment.
–Taxes should suit the convenience of the taxpayer.
–Should be economically collected.
Lutz's canons of taxation
–<u>Fiscal adequacy</u>
–<u>Economical</u> – Low cost of collection
              –Minimum disturbance of money market.
–<u>Equitable</u> – Principles stated – no personal prejudices
–<u>Elastic</u> – Able to be adjusted.
–<u>Simple</u>
–Diversity
–Flexibility – Not embedded in a constitution.
              –<u>Should</u> be statute law.
Physiocrats – agriculture alone makes a surplus – that surplus should be appropriated by taxation.
–Principle of expediency.
–Reaction to the chaos and injustice of feudal taxation.

[On page 18-A:

    Taxes on commodities
    –Under competition
    –Under monopoly
    Taxes on income: to labor, to land, to capital
    Taxes on sales
    Tariff]
Distribution of Taxation
–Cost of service – taxpayer should bear cost of the service he receives.
–How determine cost – is it just?
–Leave them as you find them.
–Don't disturb distribution – reactionary.
–Is it economic? (Emotional)
–Benefit rendered – taxes should be levied where the benefit accrued.
–How determine benefits?
–Why give benefits – to be taxed away?
–Ability to pay – each person to pay taxes according to his ability.

–How measure that ability?

–Property – bondholder, etc. escapes.

   –Indebtedness on land makes property tax extremely heavy – matter of equity.

–Gross income – on net, after deductions and exemptions.

–Real income, or money income.

–Income from effort, or income from "unearned" sources.

–Exemptions

Incidence of Taxation

–Evasion = criminal dodging.

–Shifting = economic dodging.

Taxes on Commodities

a. Under competition

Case 1 – conditions of constant cost (real) [Diagram with two horizontal lines each intersecting downward sloping curve. Vertical difference on vertical axis labeled "tax" and indication that imposition of higher of the two lines also lowers quantity on horizontal axis.]

   –The price will be raised by the amount of the tax – the supply would be cut down, as it is very easily under constant costs.

   –In the short run, until the supply is lowered, the tax would rest on the producer.

   –The amount of capital and labor shifted to alternative fields [inserted in pencil: if elastic demand] would cause other prices in those other fields to fall – increased supply of factors.

   –Under conditions of inelastic demand, there would be increased money outlay in this field, which would restrict the amount con sumers could spend in other fields – lowering price in those fields. But, this increased price would affect general price level – as it is an element. And, it would raise costs in other fields, in so far as they buy this commodity.

Case 2 – conditions of increasing cost (tax on commodities) (opportunity costs, diminishing returns) [Diagram erroneously drawn by Ostrander; has AB and CD on different lines. Correct diagram would have two upward sloping lines, the top line resulting from imposition of tax. Intersection of single downward-sloping demand curve with top upward sloping line is marked A; B is point on bottom upward sloping line where perpendicular to horizontal axes from A crosses it; D is point where demand curve intersects initial (lower) upward sloping curve. C is point where line perpendicular to vertical axis from D

crosses vertical perpendicular line from A. AB is amount of tax; AC is tax-caused rise in price. B<D is due to lower costs at lower output.]
–The tax causes a raise in price (CD), but not by the amount of the tax (AB), i.e., CD<AB [sic].
–The lower supply put out, is produced at a lower cost, so that tax added to 1000 units produced at $1.00 per unit, will really be applied to a lower output, say 800, at a cost of production of 90¢.
–The extent to which the tax can be shifted depends on the extent to which the supply can be reduced – or demand increased.

Case 3 – conditions of decreasing cost (tax on commodities) (internal-technological-economies, external-growth of industry as a whole – economies). [Diagram with two downward sloping cost curves and downward sloping demand curve intersecting them from above. Original intersection (of demand curve and lower of pair of curves) is labeled A and point above A on perpendicular drawn to horizontal axis is labeled B, i.e., amount of added tax. Point of intersection of upper downward sloping curve and demand curve is labeled C. E is point of intersection under C where perpendicular drawn from A to vertical axis intersects perpendicular drawn from C to horizontal axis.]
–According to the diagram, the added tax (AB) causes a rise in price of CE, or more than the amount of the tax – CE > AB.
–But, since there are decreasing costs as supply increases, the most efficient firm will drive out the others, leading inevitably to monopoly.
–The total supply would be reduced, not by cutting down each producer's output somewhat, but by making it easier for the most efficient to buy out the least efficient.
The results of this sort of study from diagrams
–The benefits of mathematics – to realize the given:
–The study of variables – dynamic society (though over-simplified).

[On page 20-A:

$$P = ay^{1-n} - acy^{-n}$$

Market value – equilibrium between buyers and sellers
Tax value
Rate value
Property tax – a tax on ignorance and honesty]

b. Under monopoly

Case 1 – Constant cost [Diagram with two horizontal curves, upper one raised by amount of tax; no labeling, no labels on intersections.]

–Tax would be borne partly by consumer, partly by monopolist, depending on the elasticity of the demand [curve].

–The more inelastic the demand, the more that can be shifted.

–Tax per unit of commodity output.

–Tax in a lump sum on profits – usually paid by monopolist because he is making a maximum profit – it is easier to pay lump tax if supply is not altered.

Effects of a tax – on flow of income, on distribution among factors)

Taxes on Income – from wages, rent, interest, proFIts.

Wages – taxes on special ability are equivalent to taxes on monopoly profit

Interest – quasi-rent (return to owners of fixed equipment), interest proper.

    –Tax on a given factor in a given field – will decrease the income earned by that factor in other fields.

    –What is the effect of tax on interest on volume of saving?

General Property Tax – used by States.

–Difficulty of assessment – corruption, what sort of valuation to use.

–Evasion very possible.

–Inequality between individuals and sections.

–In New England the administration is decentralized; in South and in West is centralized – State and local Boards of Equalization.

–This tax is in the state in which the property (tangible) is located.

–But, it is not equal; incentive to evasion; hard to administer; Boards are not efficient; is regressive in practice.

–Its application to railroad property.

    –How determine value? – How apportion interstate taxes?

Personal Income Tax in U.S. – Federal and State.

Normal rate – surtax rate.

–Has been since 1798 in England – used during Civil War time, then again after 1913 (Amendment).

–Normal rate – graduated rate on all income above exemptions. 1½–5%.

–Surtaxes – 1–20% – begin with $10,000 income.

–Difficulties – What is income? Can it hit the direct income of the farmer, who "raises his own"? No.

–Is appreciation in the value of property, income?

–Should gross or net income be taxed?

–Assessment and collection.

    –Individual (easy) and "at source" (is it truly just – if graduated?)

–Individual returns needed too.

–Earned and unearned.

–What is the effect of this tax on prices.

–In short-run, negligible.

–Long-run, affect prices through affecting quantity of savings.

–What is the effect on the standard of living.

–Lowers the standard of living of the rich.

–Raises the standard of living of the poor – through government services for his benefits.

–What effect on saving and enterprise?

<u>Poll Tax</u> – regressive, unjust, easily evaded, discourages voting.

–A universal tax on every citizen of the State over 21.

–Its only value lies in forcing <u>everyone</u> to help support the State.

–Is certain, fixed, relatively convenient, economical to collect.

<u>Taxes on Corporations</u> – there is a Federal 12% tax in excess of certain credits.

–Not always just to the individual stockholder.

–Comparatively easy to administer.

<u>Excess Profits Tax</u> – tax on business profits above some sort of normal; exemptions for normal revenue, and 10% of new investment, then very highly progressive taxes – 80% maximum. (War profits Tax)

–Very good revenue yielder.

–<u>Just</u> – since War profits were windfall profits, since individuals should not profit from a national war.

–Easy, cheap – difficult to determine new investment.

–Injustice between concerns with fluctuating and steady prices.

<u>Excise Tax</u> – What is definition?

–Have been decreasing in fiscal revenue.

–Lutz says it should be levied on consumer's goods, not necessities. Should be spread over a wide area.

(Export) or <u>Import Tax</u>

–Will be borne by domestic consumer – to full amount of tax, if the demand does not fall with higher price – inelastic demand, and all of the goods <u>must</u> be imported.

–Domestic price will rise, but by less than the amount of tariff if the domestic producer of the good can sell it at less than the foreign cost plus tariff – while expanding production.

–Price will not rise at all

–If substitute is used, no more importation.

<u>Inheritance tax</u> – or estate tax

Federal

–Minimum exemption, graduated rate above that.

–Acts as equalizer with State taxes.

–Fiscal adequacy – below 5% (3.5%) in U.S. – 9% in England

–Not regular – not responsive.

–Social justice – equalization of wealth.

   –Possibilities of injustice between payers of the tax.

   –Frequent transfers.

   –If tax is levied on estate – that is injustice between the recipients, and between the degrees of inheritors, and in the case of residuary legatees.

–Effect on saving.

   –If insurance is taken out on the amount of the tax – saving is increased.

   –Decreases ability of the legatees to save.

   –Rignano – heavy tax on <u>inherited</u> wealth increasing with number of times it changes hands.

   –Light tax on earned income.

   –Administrative difficulties

   –Evasion easy.

Single Tax

   –<u>Rent</u>, a payment for use of natural resources (Taussig), is differential, arises because of differences in the fertility of land – marginal land yields no rent.

–Henry George says rent is a gift of God.

–Shown in varying fertility.

–Society gives land a value which is a Godsend to the owner – he having done nothing to raise value.

–Rent from these two sources is unearned – should be taken by the State.

–Labor theory of property – right to income only when labor has been expended on land.

–Single tax on land rent cannot be shifted.

But, – are there "natural rights" in the case of land?

   –Or are there not expedient social rights?

   –On the <u>benefit</u> theory, the landowners pay for the social value of the land, taxing away the value accruing to land because of the State.

   –But lots of recipients of the government's benefits, yet not owning land, would not be taxed.

   –On the <u>ability</u> theory – those who have no land would not be taxed – yet they have ability.

   –As the owner of money and investments.

   –As the possessor of an extraordinary brain or physique.

–Are not certain men aided by the social state – why not tax this socially produced rent value?

–The tax is not elastic – would it be fiscally adequate after one or two generations?

–Would tax mostly the small rural farmer. [In margin: Etc.]

5. Public Debts – Loans

–A modern development (although government borrowing is old).

–Difference between private and public debts one of degree.

–Perpetual life of the State.

–Easier for State to repudiate than individual to bankrupt.

–State can give its debt special privilege.

  –Tax exemptions – Circulation privilege

–Does government borrowing increase or decrease the national wealth.

–What would private individuals do with their funds if the State did not tax them?

–Adam Smith said it decreased it.

[On page 23-A:

By the process of paying interest on loans can the cost of a war be postponed, or must the cost be paid at once?

–Is it internal or external borrowing?]

Why does the State borrow?

–To acquire funds to meet temporary deficits until taxes come in.

–Stabilizes tax rate.

–There should always be a treasury deficit.

–Emergency financing – as war.

  –Taxes force the rich to economize.

–Sometimes the tax yield is a more reliable revenue.

–Patriotic fervor makes heavy taxes bearable.

–Heavy taxes keep the public credit good.

–Only during the war can war profits and excess profits taxes be collected.

–Taxation stops inflation.

–If compulsory military service – why not compulsory capital service – [capital] levy.

–Industrial purposes.

–There is much to be said for occasional and casual borrowing – as an alternative to keeping a surplus.

–For slight deficit keeps Congress on its toes.

–If a government borrows, does it postpone actual payment until a future generation?

–In case of inflation, by printing presses – the civilian purchasing power is cut, and actual payment is made by certain classes, at that same time – rentiers, wage earners.

–In case of borrowing,
  –Of borrowing merely detracts from national savings, it is only a transfer of purchasing power – no inflation.
  –But if borrowing creates inflation – as was the case with the latter issues of Liberty Bonds, then certain classes pay for the war at that time.
  –But [incomplete sentence]
  –Taxation, in latter days, will probably come from the lower classes, to pay interest, etc. on bonds which will gravitate to the rich.

–People are more willing to be taxed during a war – if too much borrowing, public credit loses caste, – borrowing is uncertain, even profits taxes can only be gotten at during war, etc.

–(Perpetual) or terminable debt
  –long term, floating debt.
–Short-term – emergency, tax anticipation
  –Get lower rate in the future.
      But will the public continue to accept a floating debt? (Cf. France, 1919–26)

–Treasury bills are sold at a discount.

Short term
  Demand Notes – Greenbacks
  Treasury Warrants – pre-dated check
  {Treasury Notes – fixed percentage interest
  {Treasury Bills – sold at a discount
  –For tax or loan anticipation.

Long term – Civil War Bonds (reissues), Panama Canal Bonds, Liberty Bonds
  –Tax-exemption – Does the government gain or lose?
    –Government gains on tax exempt bonds by being able to market them at a lower rate.
  –But this enables people to pay lower income taxes.
    –Surtaxes on some ordinarily tax-exempt bonds bring in very little.
    –[C. O.] Hardy says the taxes lost just about equal taxes gained.
  –Is it not inadmissible to adopt a system which you do not know how much it costs?

–Repayment of debts.
–In U.S. – by applying proceeds of debts from abroad.

–By applying surplus.

–Capital levy – non-recurrent progressive tax on an individual at a given date.

–Not always non-recurrent, not always progressive.

–Advocated to cut down heavy national debts.

–If – one class holds the national debt – they are paying enough tax to pay their own interest.

–Why not cancel both. This would take away possibility of capitalization of interest and of the amount of the bond – it would no longer be worth anything (except amount of future payment capitalized at length of time).

–Would this improve the public credit?

–Would it equalize distribution of wealth?

–What is the relation of this to the price level? – If capital levy during time of price level under which debt was incurred – good.

–Get rid of possibility of lowering price level and increasing burden.

–Disadvantages

–Would it hinder saving?

–Psychological effects?

–Effect on securities market?

–Problem of assessment (same as General Property Tax).

–How has it worked?

–Not badly.

Budget – Administrative plan – review of past appropriations.

   –Providing for auditing, etc.

   –Providing for future expenditures and reviews.

–Very weak in this country – weak executive, Congress can do anything it wants.

Social Reform and Taxation

–What do you want to accomplish?

–Aims of social policy are imponderables.

–Taking wealth as a means.

–Are we getting maximum production?

–Of a right quality.

–Of proper regularity.

–Do we have good distribution?

–Do taxes affect factors of production? – rent?

–Does a given tax tend to increase of decrease the supply of factors?

–Taxes to get rid of wrong kinds of goods.

MATERIALS FROM SENIOR SEMINAR, ECONOMICS 7, TAUGHT BY WILLIAM JEROME BALLINGER, FALL 1931, AND ECONOMICS 8, TAUGHT BY W. EDWARDS BEACH, SPRING 1932, WILLIAMS COLLEGE

Warren J. Samuels (Editor)

Some information concerning the seniors seminar and its professors was provided in Volume 22B of this Annual as part of the brief biography of F. Taylor Ostrander, and is not repeated here.

For the fall semester's course, Economics 7, taught by William Jerome Ballinger, the final examination, all that is available, is published here.

The other documents published below are Ostrander's class notes and the mid-term and final examinations for the spring 1932 second semester of the senior seminar, Economic 8, taught by assistant professor W. Edwards Beach.

Not published here are Ostrander's notes on his readings – interspersed among the class notes – of the following:

> J. S. Mill, *A System of Logic*, 1851, Book VI, chapters I, II, III, VI, VII, VIII, IX, X.
>
> W. Ashley, "On the Study of Economic History, 1893," [*Quarterly Journal of Economics*, vol. 7 (January 1893), pp. 115–136].

Further Documents From F. Taylor Ostrander
Research in the History of Economic Thought and Methodology, Volume 24-B, 183–207
Copyright © 2006 by Elsevier Ltd.
ISSN: 0743-4154/doi:10.1016/S0743-4154(06)24024-0

F. C. Mills, "On Measurement in Economics" [possibly *Statistical Methods Applied to Economics and Business*, New York: Holt, 1924; see Index to Economic Journals, Homewood, IL: Irwin, 1961, vol. II (1925–1939), p. 388].
A. A. Young, "On F. C. Mills," and "Economics as a Field of Research," *Economic Problems, New and Old*, Boston, MA: Houghton Mifflin, 1927.
W. M. Persons, "Statistics and Economic Theory," *Review of Economics and Statistics*, vol. 7 (July 1925), pp. 179–197.
T. Veblen, "Why is Economics Not an Evolutionary Science?," *Quarterly Journal of Economics*, vol. 12 (July 1898, pp. 373–397.
F. D. Graham, "International Trade under Depreciated Paper: The United States, 1862–1879," *Quarterly Journal of Economics*, vol. 36 (February 1932), pp. 220–273.
F. D. Graham, *Exchange, Prices, and Production in Hyper-Inflation: Germany, 1920–1923*, Princeton, NJ: Princeton University Press, 1930.

Of Ostrander's notes summarizing other student's reports on the following topics only those of Burnett and of Ostrander himself are transcribed here. The list of reports is as follows:

Mark W. Cresap, Jr., South America and Latin America (Oil, Exports, Control of Panama Canal).
F. Taylor Ostrander, Intergovernmental Debts Owed to the U.S.
Robert B. Reeves, Jr., Trade Rivalries on the West Coast of South America.
Robert H. Burnett, International Cartels.
William M. Payne and Robert A. Buddington, Jr., Population and World Peace.
George H. Pierce, International Economic Policy of Soviet Russia.
John H. Kerr, Free Trade and the Depression.
Charles A. Baez, Jr., Economic Position of the United States in Latin America.
Adie A. Stevens, Reparations.
2:D. Douglas Swinehart, Some Causes of World Industrial Depression.

Ostrander's notes from Beach's lectures will be of interest depending on the concerns, or interests, of readers. Perhaps the most significant relevance of Beach's lectures, especially in conjunction with various lectures by Palyi, is their illustration of a particular theme: that while monetary and banking factors have distinctive interest as such, their roles, and therefore our interest in them, is specific to the monetary standard and monetary and banking system in place. The reader need only reflect on how different various considerations would appear if the context were, instead of the gold standard, a floating exchange rate standard with inconvertible paper currency. Institutions may not be everything, but they matter.

FINAL EXAM FROM SENIOR SEMINAR, ECONOMICS 7, TAUGHT BY WILLIAM JEROME BALLINGER, FALL 1931, WILLIAMS COLLEGE

ECONOMICS 7

Final Examination   February 2, 1932

PART ONE

(to be answered by all – write one hour)

1. Discuss the causes of the world's business depression. Must recovery be along lines that will endeavor to create an international order with
   a) International planning?
                or
   b) National planning and international competition?
   Discuss the difficulties of each course.

PART TWO

(answer three questions)

2. Is international investment more or less hazardous than domestic? Why, or why not?
   a) How can we make international investment safer?

3. Which should be paid first:
   a) Reparations
   b) European private debts to the United States
   How, if at all, can either be paid?

4. Do you believe that a tariff should
   a) Be for revenue only?
   b) Equalize the costs of production when differences are due to
      1) Different working and social conditions
                or
      2) Cheaper production due to a better technique of production abroad
   c) Shut out foreign goods entirely?

5. If it was economically advantageous for England to devaluate the pound, why wouldn't it be a good thing economically for the United States to have a devaluated dollar?

If a little devaluation of the dollar and the pound would be a good thing both for Britain and the United States, why shouldn't both the pound and the dollar be devaluated to extreme limits?

6. Answer specifically:
   a) What is the amount of governmental indebtedness to us from Europe?
   b) What is the amount of private indebtedness?
   c) How much money have we lent abroad since the armistice?
   d) How much money has the United States in Germany?
   e) What percentage of our loanable funds have been exported since the armistice per annum?
   f) How has Germany paid reparations up to the Hoover moratorium?
   g) What has been the trend of German foreign trade since the war? Has she had a favorable or unfavorable balance of trade or payments?
   h) How much money has the United States invested in Latin America? How much is in default?
   i) A devaluated currency acts as an invisible embargo on exports in the country whose currency is devaluated. Why, or why not?

NOTES FROM SENIOR SEMINAR, ECONOMICS 8, TAUGHT BY W. EDWARDS BEACH, SPRING 1932, WILLIAMS COLLEGE

The materials covered in Economics 8 are principally methodology, cost and supply curves; and especially international trade, the English £ and the Gold Standard, and post-1926 overvaluation of the £. Beach was well prepared to teach the latter subjects: His *British International Gold Movements and Banking Policy, 1881–1913*, Cambridge, MA: Harvard University Press, 1935, had been awarded the David A. Wells Prize for 1930–1931.

The following includes Ostrander's class notes, selected student oral reports, and the midterm and final examinations.

1. NOTES

Economic Methodology
   –The methods of approaching an economic problem.
   –The Classical School – mostly deductive.
   –The Historical School – looking at facts.
   –The Statistical School – more facts.
   –Without deduction you cannot use facts – analysis requires deduction.
   –The Veblen or Institutionalist School – social background.

–We are now interested in the <u>manner</u> by which these men <u>arrived at</u> their conclusions.

–Their admitted or unadmitted assumptions.

–Ferret out and recognize the assumptions involved in any <u>method</u> or <u>statement</u>.

–Economics, being complex, involves many opportunities for assumptions.

–We must look for assumptions, not only in economics, but also in the writings on methodology themselves.

Economics as a subject

–Earliest economists were philosophers.

–Up to 19th century, economists were mainly interested in something else – even Adam Smith.

–With Ricardo, there begins to be men whose <u>primary</u> interests are economic.

–But bourgeois, too – J. S. Mill.

–At first, economics had been a <u>branch</u> of <u>moral philosophy</u> – the science of wealth, of income, etc.

–Even today, economics has a border field with <u>ethics</u>.

–It is impossible to study economics <u>deeply</u> without getting into <u>ethics</u>.

–Any statement of <u>judgment</u> brings it in.

–But it is possible to make a purely <u>mechanistic</u> study of certain functions or institutions.

–Such an economist does not have to be a philosopher at all.

–Although some of the assumptions of the mechanists may <u>include</u> ethics.

–As economics becomes mechanistic, it becomes a science very like <u>physics</u>.

–Mechanical causal relation.

–But is more nearly akin to <u>geology</u> (paleontology).

–A study of growth, of particular organisms.

–i.e., economics should be treated from the point of view of the institutionalist.

–Economic institutions as organic.

–Theory changes with changes in the institutions.

–Also, the method must be nearly akin to that used in geology.

–Economics has been broken down into small fields – many of them overlapping with other subjects. [Arrow pointing to third line below.]

–<u>Sociology</u> – study of general human relations.

–Economics is a general branch of it.

–Different fields have adopted different <u>methods</u> (<u>statistics</u> are sometimes regarded as a separate subject). [Arrow pointing to here.]

–Beach can see it only as a <u>method</u>.

–Example – the same correlations can show a lag from one point of view, or an advance from another point of view.

–Neither prove <u>cause</u>.

–Harvard Statistical Society points out relations but does not use correlation as a method.

–Correlation shows tendencies – but it does not establish the causal relation.

–Economist regards statistics as a methodology which can be used in any subject.

–Used in economics to a certain extent.

–Economic statistics and history are often much the same.

–Science is (a) experimental or (b) deductive according as the effects of causes, when cojoined [incomplete in original]

Class

–Science – approaches a certainty – like and dislike very absent.

Art – like and dislike predominate.

–Differences are only of degree.

–For pragmatic purposes, it is helpful to distinguish a temporary difference of "kind."

–Beach holds that economics is nearer the sciences than the arts.

  –Pragmatic study of institutions are very much akin to a science.

  –Even though these institutions are based on psychological motives or on ethical considerations.

  –The economic study of psychological motives or ethics – as these enter into it – is nearer an art.

–Mill does have a basis for building up a study of economics on scientific grounds – then what method.

–Method of Concomitant Variations.

–Has a large influence on the statistician's view of economics, today.

–Statistics does not give certainty.

  –Often, our trust in statistics is a result of observation and experience in other than the statistical fields.

  –Thus we cannot substitute the statistical method for all others as a universal method.

    –For example, we could not trust a pure mathematician to do statistical work in economic data – for his random choices would have to be conditioned by some knowledge of economics.

–Veblen must have an Associationalist psychology to explain his institutionalism.

–Equilibrium must itself represent change.

–Were the Classical schoolmen teleological?

  –Beach thinks no – they were determinists, positivists but not teleological.

–It is the Socialists and J. B. Clark, and Carver, who are teleological.

–Ricardo was very nearly a determinist and positivist.

–Veblen attacks this too.

–To erect a taxonomous structure is of no use, for the institutions will soon change, and the former laws can no longer apply.

–Beach says no one can be entirely deterministic or entirely teleological – nor can anyone entirely escape either.

–The positivist approach is not evolutionary.

–The normal is ever changing – calls for a different type of economic theory – a larger use must be made of induction.

–Would Veblen ever get a science of economics?

–Could an economic determinist be a Behaviorist?

–Tyndall: It does require imagination, even in compiling pure facts.

–What we call imaginative-dreaming is only another dogma or form of thinking.

–Deduction is a form of imagination.

[At this point the notes from lectures are interrupted by notes from John Stuart Mill's *System of Logic*; Ashley's "On the Study of Economic History;" Mills's "On Measurement in Economics;" Allyn A. Young on Mills and on "Economics as a Field of Research;" Warren M. Persons's "Statistics and Economic Theory;" and Thorstein Veblen's "Why is Economics not an Evolutionary Science." (References given *supra*.)]

Class

–Law of Necessity

–Given stimulus, character and disposition, and motive, – we could predict the actions of men.

–Very akin to a natural law.

–Art – no possibility of quantitative measurement – feeling involved – aesthetic principles involved.

–Science – purely exact, logical, no sensation.

–While laws in economics may not be true, it can be of help to formulate general principles.

–Viner – on thinking:

–Aesthetic

–Deductive

–"Thobbing," so-called thinking, but based on prejudice.

Cost – and Cost or Supply Curves.

–Beach does not accept comparative cost in international trade.

–He uses a different concept of domestic costs from which he arrives at a different concept of international trade.

–Long run cost.

–Secular changes – complete revolution in methods of production.

–We have no cost curves which represent this sort of change.

–Long-run normal – no specific length of time.

  –Sufficient time for all the dynamic forces which would result from a given change to work themselves out – absence of friction from new changes.

  –What happens to cost as a result of a change in demand (in the schedule sense).

  –Brings in the problems of constant, decreasing and increasing cost.

  –Repercussions on other industries in same class.

  –And repercussions of such a change on the side of cost of production of the instruments of production – and repercussions on interest rates, etc.

  –These forces are supposed to work themselves out in the absence of new inventions.

  –Only forces he [Beach] considers are those in existence at the time of the first impulse we consider, and the forces set up by that first impulse we consider.

[In margin: – To trace one impulse we must assume a state of equilibrium, or a static state to begin with.]

–Short-run normal.

  –Actual length of time is not an important factor.

  –Applies to those problems where labor and liquid capital can fluctuate, but where fixed capital remains stationary.

  –Involves changes brought about by, say, a change of schedule-demand, but without its having time to affect fixed capital.

  –Raises problem of the distribution of overhead cost.

–Market cost.

  –Cost is really not involved in market price.

–We are speaking only of money cost – without going behind it.

  –Classicists said there was an actual similarity or relation between money cost and real cost.

  –Particular expenses – cost curves.

    –Expenses of producing particular units. Or of goods at different times.

    –Expenses of producing an average of goods for particular plants.

    –Problem: Do we speak of marginal costs, or average costs.

  –Long-run normal supply curve. [Diagram with two downward sloping curves, one dotted, intersecting one upward sloping curve and two vertical lines, one dotted, from intersection points.]

  –Particular expenses, average cost (bulk line).

    –At a given time – this is Beach's interpretation.

    –Average cost of production of a commodity by a firm, at a given time.

–Variability of price at margin as output varies.
–Gives rise to variability of expenses within a plant as output varies.
–But this neglects the time element.
–And it cannot be compared to the other particular expenses curve which
   is at a given moment of time, with given internal and external economies.
–The curve can show the marginal costs.
–Or the average costs of different companies.
–These, at a given moment, cannot be different.
[In margin: "or representative firm" with one further word indecipherable.]
–The other kind of curve – of expenses within one industry at varying times,
   with changing output – is a <u>normal supply curve</u>.

Interpolation – filling-in between known facts.
Extrapolation – extending beyond the end of known facts.

<u>International Trade</u>
  –Absolute advantage

U.S.	5 days labor = 10 kegs beer	
	5 days labor = 30 bicycles	
Germany	5 days labor = 20 kegs beer	
	5 days labor = 15 bicycles	

$$2/3 \text{ beer} = 1 \text{ cycle}$$

–But:– there is absolute advantage in case:

$$1/3 + \text{beer} = 1 \text{ cycles } (1/3 \text{ beer} = 1\text{-cycle})$$
$$\text{or } 1/3\text{-beer} = 1 \text{ cycles } (1/3 \text{ beer} = 1 + \text{cycles})$$

–Trade could proceed with advantage to both countries with any proportion
   between these two.
–What of the method? Is it possible to study these simplified conditions, then
   add qualifications? – or does the addition of qualifications cause changes
   in the original simplified case?
–Assumptions:
–Perfect mobility of labor <u>within</u> a country (a) geographical, (b) between
   industries.
–No mobility of labor in international field.
–No change in the demand in the <u>schedule sense</u>.
–Constant cost.
–Barter trade.

–Equal differences of cost:

U.S.	5 labor = 20 wheat
	5 labor = 10 beer
Germany	5 labor = 10 wheat
	5 labor = 5 beer

–It <u>might</u> be advantageous for Germans to move to the U.S.
–If difference were physical.
–But not if difference <u>were</u> racial.
–Where there are equal differences of <u>cost</u> –
–There will be, in stable long-run, <u>no trade</u>.
–If introduction of money causes different prices – there will be trade, offset
    by gold, which will influence prices and bring about, again, a position of
    equilibrium with prices the same, and <u>no trade</u>.
–Sectional price levels – important in theory of international trade adjustments.
–With shifting of goods.
–Domestic commodities – are there any?
–Influence of goods on world price level makes them international; also
    possibility of substitution makes goods international.
–If there were no domestic goods, price levels would have to be the same all
    over the world.
–What of services – these are domestic because we have <u>assumed</u> them to be
    immobile.
–Mechanism= <u>a chain of events</u> which will lead to a certain result.
–Non-competing Groups: – not offset.
–Conditions of <u>cost</u> (labor cost) no longer rule the terms of trade – but
    reciprocal demand plays almost the whole part in international trade.
–Capital
–Varying <u>costs</u>
–<u>Simultaneous cost curve</u> – of all or several of the firms.
    –Particular expenses curve.
    –<u>Given movement of time</u>, with <u>given output</u>.
–<u>Normal cost curve</u>.
    –Showing marginal costs for <u>different amounts</u> – or as technological
    conditions change – but no new inventions.
–<u>Historical cost curve</u>.
    –In industry <u>and</u> agriculture – taking a given output – <u>every</u> unit in a single
    firm costs the same. It is necessary to change the output, within a firm, to
    change the cost per unit. To say that to produce <u>five</u> bushels costs $1.00,
    but 10 bushels $0.75, is not to say that the first 5 of these ten cost $1.00.

–But there are differences <u>between</u> firms at a single amount of output
–Taussig assumes <u>uniform</u> costs.
–With no change in demand or output – this implies a simultaneous cost curve.
–But with change in demand – there is implied a normal cost curve – with changes of costs.

[Diagram, with two rising curves, both starting from point D on vertical axis. From arbitrary point B on easternmost of the two curves (DB), line perpendicular to vertical axis intersects it at point C and intersects westernmost curve (DA) at point A. Line drawn perpendicular to horizontal axis from point A intersects axis at point N and crosses easternmost curve (DB) at point E. Line drawn perpendicular to horizontal axis from point B intersects it at point M.]

–<u>When output is</u> OM, MB is cost which settles price. Then curve DB is a simultaneous cost curve (or particular expenses). NE is the cost of the output of the firm at that position (N) of total output.
–When output is ON, NA is cost which settles price. Then DA is the particular expenses curve, CB is the <u>normal cost curve</u>.
–Uniform cost may exist with <u>increasing</u> returns.

[Diagram, downward sloping curve, marked CD, with interior points F and B, to which correspond, on vertical axis, points E and A, respectively.]

–At <u>any</u> point of output, the simultaneous cost curve is a straight line, or AB or EF. CD is a normal cost curve – showing increasing returns.
–Uniform cost must exist with constant cost.
–Simultaneous cost curve is a straight line, at any point. Normal cost curve is also a straight line.
–We have been assuming a uniformity of the effectiveness of labor.
–But now we see that as total quantities are changed, the cost changes, and the total (or national) effectiveness changes. [Double vertical lines in margin beside this point.]
–Gross and Net Terms of Trade – Tribute.
Case I. – Demands of <u>each</u> country for the other's product is very elastic.
  –Country receiving tribute pays more for its total amount taken.
  –Country paying tribute pays less for its total amount taken.
  –Tribute easy to pay.
Case II. – Both demands inelastic.
  –Country receiving tribute pays smaller total sum.
  –Country paying pays larger total.
  –Tribute virtually impossible to pay, in goods.
Case III. – Receiving country has <u>in</u>elastic demand for paying country's product.
  –Paying country has <u>elastic</u> demand for receiving country's product.

194   WARREN J. SAMUELS

–Each country pays the other a smaller total sum.
–But tribute is not provided for, still not too hard to pay – easiness
  depends on relative states of elasticity and inelasticity.
Case IV. – Receiving country has elastic demand. Paying country has inelastic
          demand.
–Each country pays the other a larger total sum.
–Tribute not provided for.
–Easiness of payment depends on relative states of elasticity and
  inelasticity.

–Cost of production of an exported commodity must be considered in relation
  to the costs of production of all other countries exporting that commodity.
–With possibility of trade adjustment, in different proportions, due to different
  costs of production and the elasticity or inelasticity of the world demand.
–Taussig admits sensitivity or lack of it in banking systems – as a qualification
  of the classic theory.
–But he is essentially a classicist.
–Dependent on a quantity theory of money theory [sic].
–John Williams – most monetary phenomena are short run.
  –Things like the quantity theory of money are long run – cannot be applied
    very fruitfully to short run phenomena.
–Taussig claims to be a Ricardian.
  –Beach says the Classical theory is found in Hume, Thornton, and Mill – but
    he doubts whether Ricardo ever held the "Classical theory." [Single ver-
    tical line in margin beside this point.]
    –Not in the Principles is this found, but in the other writings and in his
      testimony.
  –Williams and Angell have worked out a different analysis of international
    trade adjustment – based on short-run analysis, and on purchasing
    power.
  –When a loan is made, the borrower has an immediate credit made to his
    name in the banks of the lending country – i.e., added purchasing
    power (even though expressed in foreign money units).
  –Specie flow not necessary. If lender withdraws his purchasing power to
    his own country – the price of bills is bid up – instead of specie flow,
    there will be adjustment made by other means.
    –By arbitrage of one sort or another.
    –By speculation – in securities, bills, balances, etc.
  –Changes in interest rates are much more important as means of bringing
    about adjustment than price level changes.

–Taussig is applying what <u>may</u> be true as a long run theory to short run conditions.

–Movements of price levels are slow acting.

–<u>Beach</u> thinks international capital movements are quicker than domestic income movements.

–Imperialism is a perfect accompaniment of such international mobility of capital.

–International trade is a concomitant, or following development of international mobility of labor and capital.

–Labor is <u>as</u> mobile internationally as it is nationally – sometimes more so.

–The important movements of labor are in relation to important new discoveries.

–Effect of all this – is to question the doctrine of <u>comparative</u> cost.

Canada – Viner

–Faults with orthodox theory.

–A priori method.

–Dependence on quantity theory.

–Dependence on strict interpretation of effects of gold movements.

–Mechanism by which change in terms of trade is brought about

Hollander: discrepancy between imports and exports is made up by exchange rate fluctuations.

–Viner disagrees.

Editor's Note

The provenance of the notes on dumping that follow is unclear. They continue in Ostrander's handwriting (with a new pen) but they are organized differently as a series of six paragraphs numbered in Roman numerals. They relate to the first nine of Viner's fifteen-chapter book on Dumping, where the chapters are in Roman numerals. (Viner, originally a Canadian, published his book, *Dumping: A Problem in International Trade*, in 1923 (Chicago, IL: University of Chicago Press) when he was a young assistant professor of Political Economy at University of Chicago. Viner's *Memorandum on Dumping* was published in 1926.) Most of the paragraphs are almost exact copies of certain sentences in Viner's original text. They seem to summarize quite correctly some of the main points that Viner makes. They are not in the same order as in the original as three historical chapters are omitted.

At the point where these paragraphs start, Ostrander has written in the left margin "Cresap" (the name of one of his classmates); and Cresap's name appears twice again in two of these paragraphs, in the form of Ostrander's notes or comments Cresap must have made, e.g. "Cresap doubts ... "; the second comment is interesting: "Cresap criticizes ... " Viner for studying elasticity in dealing with the domestic market, but omitting any mention of elasticity when dealing with foreign markets.

These comments recorded by Ostrander are the only words other than Cresap's careful summaries of Viner's views on dumping. Otherwise, there is nothing new or personal.

Whether these summary paragraphs were ever presented orally to the class, or whether Ostrander copied them from a paper written by Cresap, and why Cresap wrote a paper on dumping are now unanswerable.

It does not appear that Cresap's paragraphs are the oral report that Beach assigned for the course, because Cresap's paragraphs on dumping are on a page *prior* to Beach's assignment of written reports with oral summaries. Moreover, Cresap presented an oral report on a Latin America subject in the oral report section, later, but it does not have the format or style of the dumping paragraphs.

These paragraphs are part of Ostrander's notes and therefore are reproduced here.

Mark Cresap was the son of a high executive at Hart, Shaffner and Marx. After military service during World War II he co-founded the early consulting firm, Cresap, McCormick and Paget; at the age of 45 he was President of Westinghouse Corporation. Ostrander fondly recalls that Cresap came to Washington in 1941 as a First Lieutenant in the Quartermaster Corps, and left in 1945 as a full Colonel, with two battle stars, the Legion of Merit and Letter of Commendation; his early death at 53 was a great loss.

The Cresap summary follows.

Dumping – Viner
["Cresap" written in left margin alongside following text.]
   I. –"Sale at prices abroad which are lower than the current prices at home."
       –i.e., national discrimination.
       –"Spurious" dumping, freight dumping, do not come under above.
       –Concealed dumping does not.
  II. –Classification of Dumping by Time.
       –Sporadic –
          a. –to dispose of casual overstock
          b. –unintentional
       –Short-run or intermittent
          c. –to maintain connections in a foreign market
          d. –to develop trade connections in a new market
          e. –to eliminate competition
          f. –to forestall competition
          g. –to retaliate against reverse dumping
       –Long-run or continual.
          h. –to maintain full production from plant facilities without cutting
              domestic prices
          i. –to obtain the economies of large scale production without cutting
              domestic prices
          j. –purely mercantile dumping – (Socialistic – Russia)
 III. –Influence on prices of dumping country
       –Comparative monopolies dump – not pure monopolies.
       –If one firm is producing a large share of the total world supply, they will
          not dump – because of its effect on the world price.

–Sporadic dumping not of much importance.

–Short-run dumping – in classes c, d, e, f, h – no influence on domestic prices.

–Cresap doubts Viner's assumption as to h.

–g – may have an influence on prices.

IV. –Profitability of dumping to the dumper

–Sporadic – is profitable

–Short-run – difficult to say it is profitable

–The long run effect might be profitable

–But under increasing costs – short run dumping cannot be profitable in short-run

   –Gain possible – drop in unit cost x total output before dumping (is greater than) > excess of the average cost of production after dumping x units sold at dumping price.

   –Cresap criticizes: domestic market is set out and studied with its elasticity, the foreign market is set out and studied without any mention of its elasticity.

[In margin: Systems]

V.   –Consequences of dumping in the home country

–Gain from dumping may be offset by loss from monopoly prices.

–Long run dumping may be beneficial.

–Gains to consumers balanced against loss to producers.

–Dumping is abnormal – as are dumping prices.

–Long-run dumping is equivalent to an advantage of trade to the country dumped on.

VI. –Viner does not consider dumping of enough importance to warrant a protective tariff against it.

–Free traders split.

–Tariff is no real protection against dumping.

–Bounties are the chief causes of dumping.

[RESUMPTION OF CLASS NOTES ON BEACH'S LECTURES]

Form of Reports

   –Readable style – typewritten.

   –Bibliography – of books <u>used</u>.

   –Sections and Chapters.

–Footnotes, for important statements.

–Table of Contents – "Author's" name.

Reports are to be presented orally – but not read.

A principle has nothing eternal – is only an adaptation of thought to life. When life changes, the adaptation of thought to it, or principles, must change.

The situation in which England finds itself.

–Forced off Gold Standard at time it has 20 billion dollars worth of foreign investment.

–Having come to the aid of Germany and Austria has great short term investments in them. – (How much?)

–Its situation resembles that of many banks in this country [US] – frozen assets.

–Domestic drains on Treasury – revenues diminished.

–National government – to reduce unemployment insurance, to increase many taxes.

–Balance of international payments?

–French have helped loan on short term to Germany and Austria, but mainly to England.

–They have loaned very little on long term in the last two years.

–French method of using its financial power is to further its political policies.

–Little Entente (Russia before the War).

–American loaning is three quarters on this hemisphere.

The English Pound – theoretical problems

At beginning of War – Gold Standard abandoned.

–Governments want to hoard gold, trade is disrupted and becomes a means of supply only. Industry runs as a service, not a profit basis.

–But going off the Gold Standard in times of war is entirely different from going off the Gold Standard in times of peace.

–Devices in hands of England for controlling gold:

–Discount rate

–Ratio of tolerance – give out light sovereign.

–To bring in gold.

–Discount rate – low.

–Free interest on gold shipment.

–Premium on gold imports.

–Discount rate does not affect the market until the supplies of cash in the market are low or have to be renewed.

–This does not affect the exchanges unless they are near the [gold] points.

–Reasons pro and con for returning to old £ level.

Pro
–Pride in integrity of British £.
–Financially virtuous
  –To pay creditors in full £'s.
–Security holders and holders of money generally.
  –Repayments of British debts to them.
  –Repayments of all their income.
  –Wanted those kept up.
–Lower prices for consumer.
Con
–Producers would benefit from inflation.
–Savagery of the Gold Standard.
–Was the new trade up to the old £.
Banker's Pool – as National Credit Corporation.
  –To liquify the frozen assets of banks.
  –As mortgages, on land and real estate.
  –In Federal Reserve System member banks this would not be over 10%.
  –Bonds and stocks.
    –U.S. bonds are still good.
    –But from the banker's point of view the bond and stock price level is the most important price level in the country.
  –Assets in failed banks.
  –Many possible degrees of unfreezing these.
  –Federal Reserve System cannot undertake this for it is founded on a definition of short term commercial transactions, with a few exceptions (U.S. bond and agricultural paper).
  –Bank with frozen assets can give its note to this corporation and get cash.
Gold
  –How much monetary gold? What percentage increase expected?
  –Why does gold distribution change?
    France
    –Balance of payments – trade and invisible.
    –Interest rates, insecurity abroad.
    –Debt payments, conspiracy (political pride) – conquest of Europe by franc.
    U.S.
    –Debt payments – favorable balance of trade – great exporting.
    –High interest rates.
      –Harrison [New York Fed president?] tried to get rid of gold – put down rate relative to England by cheap money was gobbled up by stock speculators – leveraging gold.

England

–Losing gold.

–Deflation at home – trouble with labor at home, trouble with colonies, loss of their markets, and new competitors Germany and U.S. – who fit supply to the climatic demand.

–Inflation and revaluation of currencies of England's competitors.

–Giving them an advantage in foreign and domestic markets.

–Costs of production.

–England has no waterpower for electricity – has oil and coal.

–Lack of nationalization in basic industries.

–Too many in upper wealth brackets?

–Capital sent abroad – needed at home.

–Individual proprietor still exists.

–Results of England's going off the Gold Standard.

–Depreciated Sterling acts as an invisible tariff on imports.

–Will benefit the debtors of England who are in debt to England.

–Wages are thus put down – automatically.

–Balance budget – temporary?

–Cause of going off Gold standard.

–Forces beyond her immediate control.

–Deliberate intents.

–Advantages of going off.

–Lower real wages, costs of production, thus increase its ability to compete in foreign market.

–A form of tariff on imports.

–What now?

a. Would redistribution of gold help?

–Not necessary; if she succeeds in new competition in foreign markets, it will flow in of itself.

b. Nationalization – still necessary.

c. Vitalization of Eastern markets.

–3/5s of world's population is on silver.

–Oil (Deterding [Sir Henri Deterding, chairman of Royal Dutch Shell]), tobacco (Cunliffe), shipping, silver interests, imperialists (to hold India).

–In India and China, there were 7 billion ounces silver (1929) – worth 4½ billion dollars; 1930, it is worth 1,800 million.

–Mines are not producing too much silver.

–During War, England paid her balance to India in Silver, who hoarded it.

–Then she (India) went off the Bimetallic Standard dumping her silver on the market.

–China complicated – production impossible with War – no good roads.

–Pittmann Plan – Silver Conference – a huge silver loan to China – to enable roads to be built.

–<u>But</u>, this would only further reduce the value of silver.

–Brownell Plan – [He was] head of copper smelters – copper is a by-product of silver – by <u>joint cost</u> it must bear the total cost while silver is worthless.

–No country to sell any more silver under 0.51 [51¢/ounce].

–Unless price gets above 0.58 [cents], when India can sell. [This sentence is thought to state the Brownell plan.]

[At top of next page: Interconnection of planned economy and the tariff.]

–Bimetallism is <u>impossible</u> unless on a completely international scope.

–And there it result[s] in terrific inflation, if mint ratio anywhere <u>above</u> market value.

–If <u>at</u> market ratio, there would be no use of doing anything.

–What of using silver for new <u>uses</u>?

–Electric conduit, etc.

–But one industry, in picking up, ruins another.

–In order to attack supply of silver, it would take 10 years.

–Irving Columbia Trust Co. plan.

–No paper [money] under $5, force silver into circulation.

–This is giving specious <u>value</u> to silver, at the involuntary expense of some parties.

d. Lower tariffs, get rid of [German] Reparations.

–First, a tariff for revenue, then for infant industry; then, in U.S., a tariff to "equalize the costs of production," but it is impossible to discover these costs.

–Now there are those who say – let's have economic isolation, put on such a high tariff – unscientific – to keep out everything.

–[Beach on] Ballinger – the cause of the crisis is the unmanageability of capitalism. It has gone on unabated and without a mind.

–Destructive competition.

–We have been overpaying capital.

–Maldistribution between <u>mass production</u> and archaic distribution.

–World market is most chaotic of all.

–Capitalism has either got to be made to work in a competitive way, or through a planned economy.

Reparations and War Debt

–Is there capacity for paying both war debts <u>and</u> private debts? Even then should there be payment[?]

–If only one can be paid, which should it be? – It should be decided on the
locus of the burden.
–If neither can be paid – that's all there is.
–Would 20 year period of waiting do anything?

Cancellation of Reparations
–There may or may not be connection with war debts.
–No connection if it is possible for Allied governments to pay their debts out
of trade surpluses, and accepting a lower standard of living.
–Tests – convenience, good business, moral.

Economics of Peace
–Land-hungry nations – Japan, Italy, India.
–Acquisitive nations – hunting natural resources.
–What is limit to standard of living[?]
–U.S.–Great Britain, Germany.
–Providing for excess of population.
–Birth control
–Infanticide, contraceptives, education
–Higher standard of living, diversity
–Invention and large-scale business
–Foreign trade
–Seizure of new territory

Gold Hoards and Depressions
–No absolute scarcity of gold today – only unequal distribution.
–Loss of America's gold to France or Swiss does not affect that unequal
distribution (U.S. 80%, Swiss 16% [?])
–Defaulting of German short-term borrowing from England – was the principal
reason for England's going off the Gold Standard.
–Deflation – punishment of debtors.
–Position of France is largely due to the devaluation of the Franc to a position
lower than justified by the world price conditions.
–If the U.S. gives a turn to the cycle, at home, this will react on the world
condition.
–U.S. must help herself to help the world. (Hoover)
–Cut down purchasing power of dollar (Commons, Fisher, Douglas, etc.)
–Fight the deflation by monetary means.
–Lower discount rates do not achieve results.
–Nor buying of securities.
–Credit creation by pumping currency into circulation.

–But this cannot go to <u>savers</u>, but must go to <u>spenders</u>.
–No necessity for giving up Gold Standard.

Problem of Risks
Primary risk
–Expectation of profits – will it be realized.
–Combated by knowledge of the market.
–Combated by change of risk-interest.
–Risk on the <u>problem of payment or transfer.</u>
–Nationalistic discrimination
–Offset when fear of retaliation arises from other foreign investments.

<u>Read</u> – <u>European Union</u>
–Security from intra-European war.
–Neutralization of Europe in world conflicts.
–Protection against invasion of [by] Russia.
–Compete with U.S. and Great Britain.
–Why not work <u>through</u> the League?

2 STUDENT REPORTS

[Ostrander's paper was on equity aspects of payment or non-payment of inter-governmental debts owed to the U.S., or private post-war borrowing by foreigners. The following are his notes for his oral summary of his report.]

INTERGOVERNMENTAL DEBTS OWED TO THE U.S.
by F. Taylor Ostrander

–Is there capacity to pay both these war debts <u>and</u> the post-war private debts?
–If there were such capacity, would it be to the advantage of the U.S. to receive both payments?
–If only <u>one or</u> the <u>other</u> of these debts could be paid, which should be chosen?
–Ought it not to be decided with respect to the <u>locus</u> of the burden?
–which classes in this country would be most affected by a cutting off of one or the other?
–which classes abroad would be most affected by cutting off of one or the other?
–relation of direct burden on taxpayers to indirect burden on taxpayers through the condition of industry and banks.
–would taxpayers ultimately suffer from either?

–If neither could be paid
    –would a 20-year period of waiting do any good?

[Robert H. Burnett's oral report on international cartels is reproduced below
because the topic relates to the treatment of cartels in Henry Simons's Economics
201.]

INTERNATIONAL CARTELS
by Robert H. Burnett

–Definition   Liefmann, Domeratzky
    [Robert Liefmann, 1874–1941, and Louis Domeratsky, 1881-, each wrote
    several books on cartels, among other works. Domeratsky's were chiefly
    US Department of Commerce publications.]
    "A cartel is a voluntary association of independent enterprises with common
    interests and aims for the joint regulation of production and distribution."
    –A pool, perhaps?
    –Not a trust, combination, etc.
    –Is monopolistic.
Classes
    a. Territorial
        –domestic
        –international
    b. Price
        –simple, but many disadvantages
    c. Production
        –fine and compensation
    –Characteristics
    –Mass production and great capital
    –Standardized product
    –Where overproduction has existed
    –Resultant of price-cutting
    –Based on natural resources or other limiting factors
    –Practical Difficulties
    –Individual and national jealousies over quotas
    –National bodies are weak
    –National and racial factors complicate
    –Some countries are industrially underdeveloped
    [Alongside preceding four items, in margin:
    –Limited number eligible
    –Monopolistic difficulty
    –Changes and compromises, impermanence]

–International Cartel Growth and Development
–Not especially recent; 114 before War, doubled since.
–Influence of Tariff
   –Might hinder – make them needless.
   –Might help.
   –Were both attempts to meet about the same situation.
   –Dumping brings cartels, which bring dumping in neutral markets, which results in tariffs there.
–Examples – Continental Steel – Copper, Potash
   –A production cartel
   –Fines and compensation
–Test of 1930–31
   –Did not stand up well
–Judgment
   –International combination will probably be more efficient.

3 EXAMINATIONS FROM SENIOR SEMINAR, ECONOMICS 8, TAUGHT BY W. EDWARDS BEACH, SPRING 1932, WILLIAMS COLLEGE

MIDTERM EXAMINATION

ECONOMICS 8

Hour Examination   March 29, 1932

Answer two questions

I. "It has already been mentioned that Wagner recognizes three theoretical problems in political economy, namely, the description of economic phenomena, their arrangement under types, and the explanation of the causes upon which they depend. He adds, however, that the three problems really constitute three stages of a single problem, and that they must not only be all of them as far as possible solved, but also in the order in which they are given. Political economy, he goes on to say, would be, if still a science, at least no independent science, but only a part of historical science and descriptive statistics, if – in accordance with certain tendencies of the historical school – it were to limit itself to the first of the three problems. The second and third really constitute the special and chief problems of political economy, for the solution of which the first was merely preparatory; and it is only when the second and third problems are reached that political economy becomes a really independent and theoretical science."

What would Mill have said with respect to this position? Would Ashley agree with it?

II. Can we say that economists in accepting Marshall's definition of economic laws as statements of tendencies are accepting the statistical view of nature?

III. "The instinct which leads working men in discussions on economic questions to return constantly to the ethical aspects of them is a sound one, and Economics will gain rather than lose authority by discarding the Mid-Victorian pose of the one and only science of society."

"It is important for us all to understand that economic laws are neither moral nor immoral; they are inexorable. To accept them as such is the first business of any one who would serve his fellow men."

Are these statements necessarily inconsistent? Discuss.

IV. "The greatest error of individual psychology is the suggestion that man thinks. What thinks in man is not he but the social community of which he is a part."

Compare the views of Mill and Veblen on this statement.

FINAL EXAMINATION

ECONOMICS 8

Final Examination   June 9, 1932

PART A

Write an essay of about one hour on the basis of one of the following quotations.

I. "It can fairly be said that the classical writers never worked out the elements of their system into a complete theory of international prices as such. The constant effort was to go behind the phenomena of money prices, and to explain the facts in other terms."

II. "Trade history shows that in international exchanges it is always the industrial nation which gets rich."

III. "The Ricardian theory teaches that gold tends automatically to distribute itself among gold standard countries in such proportions as to equalize its purchasing power over commodities."

IV. "Large sections of the British people have unconsciously worked for the benefit of the foreigner and the British colonist, never realizing that their own country sorely needed all the capital that their labor could create."

PART B (About one hour)

Answer two questions.

I. Discuss the place of "sectional" price levels as a factor affecting the mechanism of international trade adjustment.

II. In what respect does international trade resemble exchange between noncompeting groups within a country? Wherein does it differ?

III. What modifications of international trade theory are introduced by variations in cost as between firms, and by changing costs for an industry in both the short and the long-run?

PART C (About one hour)

Answer two questions.

I. "The fluctuations of purchasing power par are due to currency conditions; the deviations of actual rates from this par are due to commercial and political conditions." Discuss.

II. Describe briefly "pegging" and the gold exchange standard. What connection is there between them?

III. What principles of the mechanism of trade adjustment are illustrated by the Franco-German Indemnity?

F. TAYLOR OSTRANDER'S NOTES FROM GEORGE YOUNG'S REVIEW OF POLITICAL THEORY, POLITICAL SCIENCE 4, WILLIAMS COLLEGE, SPRING 1930

Warren J. Samuels (Editor)

INTRODUCTION

These notes are from a course in Political Science. The question sensibly arises – Taylor Ostrander raised it – as to how such a course relates to the history of economic thought. A short answer runs, in part, as follows. (1) In the real world, in juxtaposition to specialized academic disciplines, the polity and the economy both emanate from the legal–economic nexus. What is political and what is economic are matters of selective perception and sentiment. Generally speaking, economic activity takes place within and impacts on politics, and vice versa, the topics of politics are largely, though not entirely, matters of economics. (I have published extensively on the topic; see, especially, "The Legal–Economic Nexus," *George Washington Law Review*, vol. 57 (August 1989), pp. 1556–1578.) At the deepest level, the economy is comprised of property rights, duties, immunities, powers, exposures, and the other elements of Wesley Hohfeld's model; and the structure and distribution of these is established, and continually reestablished, at the constitutional level, in part through judicial decisions. Judicial review in matters

Further Documents From F. Taylor Ostrander
Research in the History of Economic Thought and Methodology, Volume 24-B, 209–311
Copyright © 2006 by Elsevier Ltd.
All rights of reproduction in any form reserved
ISSN: 0743-4154/doi:10.1016/S0743-4154(06)24025-2

of economics, and perhaps all other areas of life, is the principal means through which constitutional change is effected, as courts approve or disapprove of the actions of other branches of government. Much of the foregoing has become the domain of Political Science.

Decisions and/or decision making about economic policy (narrowly, resource allocation) tend in practice to get combined with issues of decision-making structure (power). That is an aspect of the twin processes of working out (a) optimal allocations of resources and the structure of rights and (b) the structure of rights (power) governing the actual allocation. (2) Not only is the legal–economic nexus influenced by and influences these twin processes but it is also similarly connected to the continuing working out of the nature of the state. In any event, political–economic analysis cannot assume a given state without (a) ignoring the evolution of government, legal change and the processes involved therein and (b) by improperly equating the state as a pure concept with existing states (as it tends to do with markets) render many if not all political and legal change non-optimal. One key point is that changes in governmental organization correlate with changes in the interests included in decision making. Indeed, if no such changes in inclusion ensue, the organizational change is potentially evasive in nature and intent. Another part of the answer is the example provided by the work of such scholars as James Buchanan, Friedrich Hayek, Vilfredo Pareto, Max Weber, Amitai Etzioni, Charles Lindblom, John R. Commons and others, including Adam Smith, who have worked out systems of thought in which economics and politics, both broadly understood, are part of a general or more general system.

In the first Archival Supplement (1989) in this series, I published lectures by John Dewey on moral and legal philosophy. Dewey's and George Young's lectures illustrate a further part of the answer: the quality of the presentation of their work and thoughts.

Only obvious corrections and minor stylistic changes have been made in Ostrander's class notes. My editorial remarks are contained in square brackets. Ostrander wrote his notes on one side of a sheet, marked 1, 2, 3, . . . n. On the back of a page, facing the next page, numbered 1-A, 2-A, etc., he occasionally continued his note taking; but also occasionally entered other notes. The former are treated as regular notes; the latter are marked within brackets. I have occasionally broken the text a few lines into the next page in order to fit the bracketed material into the text and maintain continuity.

The following section discusses Peter H. Odegard and Telford Taylor, two of Ostrander's three other Political Science professors. Then, apropos of Political Science 4, a short biography of George Young is provided, followed by two examinations from the course, comments on Ostrander's notes, Ostrander's notes from the course, and two outlines he developed to better fix its coverage in his mind.

DIGRESSION: OSTRANDER'S OTHER COURSES IN POLITICAL SCIENCE

Taylor Ostrander had other courses in Political Science at Williams College and he had them from remarkable professors. He had Political Science 1-2, Comparative Government, during the Fall and Spring semesters of 1928–1929, as a freshman. The course was taught by Peter H. Odegard, an Assistant Professor in his first year at Williams. He was assisted by Telford Taylor, a Williams graduate earlier in 1928. Ostrander thinks that Taylor lectured about one-quarter of the time in each semester. Ostrander also had Political Science 5, American Government and Politics, in the Fall of 1929, from Odegard, who was to leave in 1930 for Ohio State as full professor. The following biographies of these two teachers partly reproduce and partly expand upon those incorporated in the biography of Ostrander published in Volume 22-B (2004), pp. 168–170.

Peter H. Odegard (1901–1966) was born in Montana of Norwegian immigrant parents. His undergraduate education was at the University of Washington, where he studied under Vernon B. Parrington and others. He received the doctorate and taught in the Department of Public Law and Government at Columbia University, where he studied with John Dewey and Arthur Reed Powell, among others. After teaching at Williams College, he taught at Ohio State (1930–1938), Stanford (1934), Amherst College (1939–1945) and, after serving as President of Reed College (1945–1948), went to the University of California–Berkeley where he initially served as chair for seven years. His presidential address to the American Political Science Association centered on Political Science as the overriding discipline embracing the findings of the social sciences as government produces form and order within the society. Odegard was a member of several Presidential and other national commissions, e.g., on migratory labor, UNESCO. He was bipartisan in his work with both major political parties, while a critic of the House UnAmerican Activities Committee. He achieved a national reputation for his year-long lecture series, "Structure and Functions of American Government," on Continental Classroom.

In private memoranda and memoirs Ostrander has written that "Odegard's teaching style was highly provocative and iconoclastic. He was a 'radical' but only in his tough-minded realism, his way of seeing and saying things that were not usual in those days. He awakened, fascinated and often shocked his students." Although Ostrander has written that he experienced "political and even religious apostasy" as a result of Odegard's teaching, there is no sign of why he did so in his course notes. He comments, "Just as Odegard was disciplined in keeping to the basic topic of the course, so I must have been disciplined in keeping my class notes, for I seem to have written down only things that strictly related to 'Comparative Government.'" Because he finds, disappointedly, that his notes from Political Science 1-2, "Comparative Government," do not provide a record of Odegard's mode of teaching, he feels this two-semester set of class notes does not justify publication. The notes will be deposited in the Williams College Archives along with all his other William's class notes. Ostrander finds that his notes from Political Science 5 do reveal much of "Odegard's personality, his sarcasm and wit," recording "many of his sharp, even outrageous, sayings" (for example, he is recorded as saying of Second Ballots that they were "Devised by English to keep them from thinking too much." Nonetheless, he feels that Odegard "at his core, . . . was sensible and sound. This course was largely based on material to be published in Odegard's *The American Public Mind* (New York: Columbia University Press, 1930). The working title of the book at the time Ostrander took the course, based on the book, was "Public Opinion." Ostrander feels that publication of the book makes unnecessary the publication of his notes, since the course so closely followed the book. The book was published six months after the end of the course. Of Political Science 5, Ostrander has written in a memorandum,

> The course was pure vintage Odegard! He saw the essence of the new America that was being formed by all the techniques and technologies of American modernity. He was brilliantly perceptive in describing (acidly) the forces and problems, the strengths and contradictions, the follies and strengths of American public culture.

Ostrander feels that "An essence of Odegard's view of things, as covered in the course and the book, can be glimpsed in three paragraphs of the Preface to his published book." The book's table of contents reads as follows:

I. THE FOUNDATIONS OF PERSONALITY
II. SOCIAL BEHAVIOR
III. THE PILLARS OF SOCIETY: THE FAMILY AND THE CHURCH
IV. THE PILLARS OF SOCIETY: THE SCHOOL
V. THE FOURTH ESTATE
VI. POLITICAL PARTIES AND THE POPULAR WILL
VII. PRESSURE AND PROPAGANDA
VIII. THE ARTS AND THE AUDIENCE
IX. CENSORSHIP AND DEMOCRACY

The three principal paragraphs from the Preface to the *American Public Mind* are the following:

> Why do we behave like Americans? Whence come our ideas and ideals? What are the forces which mold our minds? Is the family bankrupt, the Church decrepit? Who controls our schools, and what do they teach? What newspapers and books do we read and how do they

influence our behavior? Are the movies and the radio enervating or elevating? Do our political parties adequately represent our opinions on public questions? If not, why do they endure? What function, if any, do lobbyists perform? Are we helpless victims of high-pressure advertising and propaganda? Is there an American Public Mind, and where is it to be found? These are questions which the following pages attempt in part to answer.

"The private citizen today has come to feel rather like a deaf spectator in the back row," says Walter Lippmann. "[Public affairs] are managed, if they are managed at all, at distant centers, from behinFd the scenes, by unnamed powers." What are these powers, and whose are the invisible hands pulling the strings which make the puppet public dance?

There has been an excess of laudation and lampooning of the public. It is a far cry from Aristotle's belief in the divine wisdom of collective humanity to the cruel cynicism of George Moore, who assures us that "Humanity is a pigsty, where liars, hypocrites, and the obscene in spirit congregate." Public opinion has been called the "voice of God" by romantic democrats and "the muttering of a great beast" by self-styled aristocrats. Obviously it is neither. Nor is it a disembodied spirit which mysteriously governs in a democracy. It can be heard, its influence can be seen, and it can be understood. Public opinion is not a phantom and it should not be made a fetish.

Several questions of interest to the political economist are raised by Odegard's Preface. How would economics look if social preferences were assumed to be manufactured rather than given? What about Political Science? Whatever Adam Smith meant by the Invisible Hand it was not some power behind the scenes pulling the strings of public opinion. How would Smith's total system look if an Invisible Hand were operative in his three domains – moral rules, law, and markets? How does one distinguish a definition of reality from cynicism? May not the cynic's definition of reality be accurate? Is Odegard a cynic or a visionary or a wishful thinker when it comes to public opinion?

Ostrander also writes of Odegard, "He didn't call himself an atheist, but his opposition to organized religion was part of his concept of political science." He reports that he, from a family of Christian Scientists, was so initially aghast at what Odegard was saying that about two weeks into the course he sought to transfer to another section. After a lengthy conversation with his Dean, in which the latter said, "Taylor, these are some of the ideas you've perhaps come to college to hear; I don't think you ought to change," he remained and within a month or so became an Odegard "disciple."

Among Odegard's other books are *Pressure Politics* (1928), *American Politics* (1938, 1947, 1974), *The Power to Govern* (1957), *Religion and Politics* (1960), *American Government* (1961, 1964, 1966), and *Political Power and Social Change* (1966).

Odegard's career was, in a sense, in part a sequel to or continuation of this course that Ostrander took at Williams College in `1929–1930. For example, he gave a Stafford Little lecture at Princeton University in 1941–1942 on "Propaganda and Public Opinion." He was then at Amherst College.

The sequel to Ostrander's experience with Odegard is to be found in the courses he took from Frank Knight at Chicago a few years later, notes from which have been published in this annual in volumes 22B (2004) and 23B (2005).

The final examination in Political Science 5, given on February 1, 1930, is as follows (no examinations are included in Young's text):

1. A. Compare (using outline form) the Articles of Confederation with the Constitution having in mind especially:
   a. Amending Process
   b. Executive organization and leadership
   c. Organization and powers of the legislative branch
   d. Judicial system
   e. Separation of powers
   f. Bill of Rights
   B. Illustrate briefly how custom and usage have affected the form and functioning of the Constitution of the United States.

                                                                                          40 Minutes

2. Assume that you are a candidate for public office (you may choose any office from city-councilman to president): How would you organize your campaign (both for nomination and election)?
   Upon what principles would you proceed in appealing to the voter?
   Give illustrations of the type of appear you would make.
   What difference would it make in your tactics if you were running for an office with a wider (or narrower) constituency, or in a different part of the country from the one you have chosen?
   B. "The twin rights of association and advocacy are fundamental in a democracy." How far are these rights realized in America?
   C. Describe the methods employed by pressure groups to achieve their ends. How are they related to political parties? Do they constitute a healthy or unhealthy growth in a representative democracy? Why?
   (Choice of B or C.)   55 minutes

3. A. Suppose the State of Massachusetts were to adopt a statute making it unlawful for any manufacturer, mine or quarry operator who regularly employs children under the age of sixteen in his plant, to export his products outside the State of Massachusetts. The law does not apply to goods shipped to foreign countries.
   Is such a statute constitutional? Why? Reconcile your opinion with the decision in Hammer versus Dagenhart (the child labor case discussed in class).

Would it make any difference if, instead of prohibiting such exportation, the State had merely laid a heavy tax on the products of child labor intended for export?

B. From what, if any, provisions of the Constitution does the Supreme Court derive its power to pass upon the constitutionality of acts of Congress and the State Legislatures? What, if any, check is there on this power?

Mention and evaluate some of the proposals which have been made to limit the court's power in this respect.

45 minutes

4. A. What power has Congress over the conduct of campaigns and elections for national office?

What limitations are there in the Federal Constitution on the states' control of the suffrage? How effectively have they been enforced?

What, if any, limitations are there in the Federal Constitution on the police powers of the states? Illustrate. Is there such a thing as Federal police power in this sense? (Police power must be taken to mean here legislation in behalf of the safety, health and morals of the community.)

B. Under what provisions of the Constitution have the powers of Congress been most widely extended? Give illustrations.

What are some underlying causes of this federal centralization?

40 minutes

Question 3.B is noteworthy in at least two respects. First, this exam, given on February 1, 1930, is concerned with judicial review and proposals to limit the power of the court in this respect. This was during the Hoover administration. (Ostrander's father's Valedictory Address at Union College in 1902 was on the subject "Judicial Usurpation of Legislative Power.") Second, a recent book, Larry D. Kramer's *The People Themselves: Popular Constitutionalism and Judicial Review* (Oxford University Press, 2004), would remove the power of the court to determine constitutional issues and locate it in either the legislature or referenda. (Kramer is dean of Stanford Law School.)

Telford Taylor (1908–1998) was born in Schenectady, N.Y., on his father's side a relative of Edward Bellamy, author of *Looking Backward*. He graduated from Williams in 1928 and from Harvard Law School in 1932. He then served with the Department of the Interior, the Agricultural Adjustment Administration, the Senate Interstate Commerce Committee, and the Department of Justice. During the Second World War he served in Europe as an Army intelligence officer. As a chief deputy to Justice Robert Jackson he wrote the prosecution rules for the Nuremberg trials and later, when Jackson returned to the Supreme Court, succeeded him, with the rank of Brigadier General, as Chief Counsel for War Crimes;

as such, he prosecuted German government officials, military officers, doctors and scientists who experimented on prisoners of war, and industrialists. He fought for the trials and the concept of "crimes against peace" to have permanent judicial and prosecutorial status; and for the principles that crimes against humanity could be punishable even if not related to war, that aggressive war (war-making itself) was an international crime and not a right of sovereignty, and of gradations of guilt.

Telford Taylor then went into the private practice of law. He became a professor of law at Columbia in 1962, also joining the faculty of the Cardozo School of Law in 1976.

He was an outspoken critic of Senator Joseph McCarthy, whose ostensible investigations into Communism had become, as Taylor put it, "a vicious weapon of the extreme right against their political opponents" and made McCarthy "a dangerous adventurer." Taylor served as legal counsel for some of those prosecuted. He later was a critic of the Vietnam War and of the conduct of John Poindexter and Oliver L. North in the Iran-Contra affair and its aftermath, as well as of the genocide in the war in Bosnia and of Soviet criminal courts as courts of terror. He considered that the bombings of Dresden and of Nagasaki, but not of Hiroshima or Hanoi, probably constituted war crimes.

Telford Taylor was known not only for his prosecutorial role at Nuremberg and as an expert on the law of war, but as an advocate of an international criminal court. He sought the creation by the United Nations Security Council of the International Criminal Tribunal for Crimes in the former Yugoslavia. The first permanent International Criminal Court was passed by a Diplomatic Conference in Rome on July 17, 1998, two months after Taylor's death (it still awaits ratification).

Taylor authored *Grand Inquest: The Story of Congressional Investigations* (1955), *Two Studies in Constitutional Interpretation* (1969). *Nuremberg and Vietnam: An American Tragedy* (1971), *Courts of Terror: Soviet Criminal Justice and Jewish Emigration* (1976), *Munich: The Price of Peace* (1979), and *The Anatomy of the Nuremberg Trials* (1992).

GEORGE YOUNG, A BRIEF BIOGRAPHY

In his sophomore year, during the Spring 1930 semester, Taylor Ostrander took Political Science 4, A Review of Political Theory, from Sir George Young (1872–1952). He inherited his baronetcy in the year 1930. Young was not as outstanding as Peter Odegard and Telford Taylor in their respective fields but nonetheless worldly and impressive. Young was then in the process of finishing his book, *The Pendulum of Progress: An Essay in Political Science and Scientific Politics* (1931). Educated at Eton and universities in France, Germany and Russia, Young had a series of diplomatic appointments, including Attaché, Chargé d'Affaires, expert delegate and First Secretary, between 1896 and 1924, in locations such as Washington, D.C., Athens, Constantinople, Madrid, Brussels, and elsewhere. He taught political science and international law in several U.S. colleges and universities. He also served as Professor of Portuguese and Examiner in Ottoman Law at London University. A prolific author on diverse topics, often taking advantage of opportunities provided by his diplomatic postings, his prior publications included *Nationalism and War in the Near East* (1915), *Portugal Old and Young* (1917), *New Germany* (1920), *Diplomacy Old and New* (1921), *Constantinople* (1926), *Egypt* (1927), and *Freedom of the Seas* (with J. M. Kenworthy, 1928). He contributed "Europe and the United States" to Quincy Wright (Professor of International Law at Harvard Law School), ed., *Interpretations of American Foreign Policy* (Harris Foundation Lectures, 1930). He subsequently published *Tales of Trespass* (1932), *New Spain* (1933), *Poor Fred; the People's Prince* (1937), and *Federalism and Freedom; or, Plan the Peace to Win the War* (1941).

CHARLES FAIRMAN, A BRIEF BIOGRAPHY

In the last semester of his senior year, Ostrander took a one-semester course in international law with Charles Fairman of the Political Science Department. Ostrander still remembers it to be an intriguing course but also tough, of law-school caliber, as was the text. Fairman had a splendid education and a remarkable career. He was at Williams College only during the period 1930–1936 and must have been the intellectual equal of the same level of his fellow faculty members. Born in Alton, Illinois in 1897, he received the BA in 1918 and the MA in 1920 from the University of Illinois. From Harvard he received the PhD in 1926, and SJD in 1938, having received his LLB from the University of London in 1934. He taught at Pomona College and Harvard prior to his six years at Williams College. At Stanford University he achieved professorships in political science and law during the period 1938–1953. Thereafter he served as Nagel professor of constitutional law at Washington University during 1953–1955, and professor of law at Harvard until 1962, thereafter Emeritus professor of law. At various times he served as a Carnegie Fellow of international law; a consultant to the Hoover commission on the organization of the federal branch of government; member of the Social Science Research Council; a Gugenheim fellow and SSRC faculty research fellow; and the recipient of various honors, e.g., an honorary fellow of the American Society of Legal History. Among his publications were Fourteenth Amendment and the Bill of Rights: The Incorporation Theory (1970); American Constitutional Decisions (1948, 1950); Law of Martial Rule (1930, 1943); Mr. Justice Miller and the Supreme Court, 1862–1890 (1939, 1966, 2003); and books on Civil War reconstruction, and the electoral commission of 1877. Fairman died in 1988.

COMMENTS

Apropos of Young's statement that the older philosophers "tell us what they thought in their time – not about our own time," insofar as the world has changed, from monarchical to democratic government and from rural, agricultural, landed-property societies and economies to urban, commercial and industrial, non-landed property societies and economies, one cannot expect ancient, medieval and pre-modern philosophers to enable us to construct theories pertinent to our day from their theories. One can sense that the fundamental problem of princi-ples of authority, freedom, and order are universally and timelessly relevant. But the language in which they are expressed, especially the definitions built into the words themselves, will reflect the preconceptions of their day and not ours. The same is true of economics. Mainstream, neoclassical economists prefer to think that economic agents have given, unchanging preferences and that the economic theory of today can be applied to any period, the logical equivalent of assuming that the economic system is unchanging. Different ages have different, as well as common, interpretive problems. The definitions of words – like property and liberty – change over time, in part as economic experience and ideology change. These changes of definition introduce further problems of interpretation for the jurist and the econ-omist. The nature and significance of property changes – even though the word remains the same – when property no longer conveys participation in govern-ment, although it now raises questions of participation in governance.

One further point has two facets. The point concerns continuity. When Plato and Aristotle tell us about their time, it is clear that they react differently to the same experience: Plato the Idealist, and Aristotle the Realist. The first facet is that a given reality or status quo can, and likely will, be interpreted differently on the basis of different perspectives; e.g., a given reality can elicit different pictures of utopia. The second facet is that Idealism and Realism are two perspectives which are common throughout history.

Young presents a methodological introduction. Here Physics is treated as the model of science. Of interest also is the possible mutual relationship between methodology and circumstances external to Political Science, with greater emphasis on the power of external circumstances. When Young writes that man, a political or social animal, must "live in an organic, dynamic community," he only implicitly raises the problem of continuity versus change; when he says that man "must either contribute to its life or to its premature death," he need not be taken literally.

Young has an ambitious procedural role for Political Science. He juxtaposes nationalism (loyalty to state; patriotism) to socialism (loyalty to class) as two conflicting driving forces. The role of Political Science is to enable individuals to analyze the two and to apportion loyalty between them. Several points: (1) More recent writers would say that these are two conflicting ideologies. (2) Also these writers would not necessarily equate nationalism with statism. (3) Loyalty to state in relation to class will depend on such variables as (i) degree of societization or acculturation by individuals, (ii) whether or not one's state was controlled by one's class, and (iii) cognitive dissonance, e.g., conflict between one's induced belief system and one's perception of reality. (4) Some economists and political scientists, policy analysts all, contemplate such a role for either or both disciplines, especially an economistic political science. (5) The social preferences involved are altogether more complex and subtle than are preferences for goods and services.

In Ostrander's class notes on Young, the lectures only hint at and largely omit the psychology and the processes of manipulation of psychology that drive the history of states. On the other hand, Young treated controversial topics, topics of enormous importance, in a clinical, dispassionate way. These phenomena, however, do not just happen. Their genesis and course of development is complex and laden with political and economic conflict. Saying so amounts to raising the issue of the conflict between generalizations transcending individuals and descriptions of individual behavior.

One controversial topic that Young treated in a clinically dispassionate way is imperialism. He seems to have treated imperialism as a fact of life, independent of the rationalizations given out for public consumption in order to manipulate political psychology. Three lines are very suggestive. One is that "Imperialism is the peculiar religion of conservatives." The second, in relation to international financial agreements that set up international institutions, maintains that international finance tends toward imperialism: "Objective in character=imperialism." One wonders what Young thought, after the Second World War, of the Bretton Woods institutions. Young died in 1952. Whether it was too early for him to perceive their role in governing the economies of the world one can only guess. The third is in regard to the statement recorded in the notes that "As soon as a nation becomes an empire, it loses its democracy." Here one wonders what Young might have thought, after the dissolution of the Soviet Union, when reference to the U.S.

as the world's lone super power goes from the *is* of its super power status to the *ought* of affirming its international military ventures, including the idea of "preventive war," and somehow must abort critics' claims that the U.S. is acting less like the live-and-let-live of a democracy and more like the aggressive dynastic state of olden times.

After discussing the allies' "complete international industrial organization for shipping, supplies, encirclement, blockade," Young is recorded speculating,

> –No reason why civilization should not have free trade, international organization, etc.
> –It has already been proven most effective.

Young himself provides three reasons: "no emergency urge," private opposition and U.S. isolationism. His discussion can readily be seen as statist; it can be said, however, that the U.S. wanted to return to its pre-War modes of international statism, in cooperation with private economic interests, rather than venture into the unknown. U.S. businessmen, in particular, did not see international affairs in terms of high political theory; they sought a "return to private trading." Young's mentality, because of his diplomatic background, in which international relations are worked out within the state sphere (albeit with the private sector involved), was very different.

At one point the notes read:
> Idea that Germany had – that Russia has – was to organize the state along economic lines – this will do away with the need for a political organization.

It may be speculated that if one means by "political" having to do with power, or decision making, organizing the state along putatively economic lines will require decision making both in the organizational stage and thereafter during operation. Doing away with the state – as per Karl Marx, Murray Rothbard or, seemingly, Young – is an illusion, a matter of misleading definition.

Altogether one receives here a very different conception of the nature, history, and theory of the state than one finds in economics generally or in the subdisciplines that study the state. How representative Young's ideas were for his time is another matter, on which this editor will be silent.

As wide-ranging as is Young's course, missing are analyses of various meanings of key terms and the consequences of using one or the other and of the various objects to which a term can be applied. Perhaps the best example – because the term and concept are repeatedly used by Young – is "democracy" and included among the objects can be right to vote, free press, etc. On the other hand, Young makes a fundamental point when he is recorded as saying,

In Political Science we have the difficulty of terms which remain the same – while changing meaning.

–We are inclined to use the word "Democracy" to represent all that is good.

We are inclined to classify everything as good or bad according to its similarity or dissimilarity to our own customs and ideas.

We are having some difficulty in getting away from these old-fashioned – clumsy – ideas of government.

Also, one does miss much recognition of the struggles that have transpired over the distribution of power in society and over changes therein. Only rarely do the notes record that something, for example, "was a result of the struggle between the people and the prince."

In his discussion of the separation of powers, Young is recorded as saying,
There are no clear cut divisions in existence
–Tendency to break down the existing divisions
–In interest of efficiency

Both of the first two points are true and important; all branches of government make law/establish rights, i.e, legislate. The third point is true in one respect and possibly another. Efficiency is a function of rights; different structures of rights yield different allocations of resources, etc. Agents do not act with a view to producing social efficiency; they act with regard to enhancing their position in the structure.

The notes include a five-word statement that may help in comprehending a very complicated thinker:
Rousseau – romantic sentiment – cynical realism
The very next line states perceptively,
French Revolution – not a revolt against property – but against privilege
The proposition is largely correct but requires two caveats: that privilege is not seen as property, and that property is not seen as privilege.

Young presents a broad array of political theories most of which is prescriptive – say, discussion at the constitutional stage – and only some of which is descriptive or explanatory. In earlier times, when theology entered more prominently, two key issues were, first, what is attributed to divine intent, and, second, the relative scope of divine and human decision making, respectively, i.e., what is God's domain and what is left for man, or vice versa. Here, the key issue is what is to be established by way of theory and constitution – of theory embedded in constitution – and what has to be worked out by actual participants and not set down in advance. The latter – the working out – also applies to the interpretation of theory and constitution. Actual results will ensue from both theory/constitution and pragmatic working out. Young provides an important historical example of this:

- –Central authority maintained by the class dictatorship through Communist Party – outside constitutional structure
- –A pragmatic result of the War, not in original theory

Shortly thereafter, Young's discussion of Hobbes and Austin includes the following:

- –All legal organs and associations live only within the limits of the license conferred by the state.

Here we have combined the two issues, first, freedom versus exposure to others' freedom – freedom to versus freedom from – and, second, who controls the state in determining the continuing resolution of the first issue.

The most pervasive strand of thought in Young's lectures seems to have been the class nature of government and indeed of all of governance, private and public. The foundations of modern society, his lectures further stress, lie in the institutions representing property and proletariat (working class). Vilfredo Pareto's political sociology is not mentioned by name (nor is that of many other early 20th century writers) but his themes reverberate throughout the lectures, albeit without the cynicism and sarcasm.

The Soviet Union in the years following World War II was seen by Western experts as having a cyclical pattern in its planning system. A period of centralization was followed by a period of decentralization, the form and structure of each phase varying from cycle to cycle. Young's lectures seem to provide a predicate for this when he is reported to have identified the Soviet system as representing regional interests. One also senses a recognition that the Soviet Union's political and economic leadership substituted for "property" – i.e., if property is power meaning decision-making participation, the leadership is the new form of property.

One of Young's conclusions with regard to "Progress" is striking. Instead of assuming one theory and/or practice of government – one political theory – as the normative basis of his description or evaluation, his position is given as,

- –Nothing definite or absolute
- –Is something entirely relative

Pervading Young's interpretation of the history of political theory is his equivalent of John Stuart Mill's (and others') idea of the "spirit of an age." For Young, the term is "idea," as in the idea of progress. Practice and ideas mutually influence each other; so too do they and the major institutional structures, the "legs" of a system, such as property and the organization and control of the human labor force.

Young pursues two interpretations of "theory." One is theory in the sense implications derived from first principles or premises. The second is theory in the sense of taxonomic and other systems intended to make sense of practical experience. One historical connection between the two types of theory is that practitioners of the first tended to be influenced by their work under the second. Which is to say, that the two are intermingled, in both the history that Young discusses and in his own discussions. Thus, the questions in Test III relate to considerable empirical material but have a significant substratum of theory. The latter is more conspicuous in the Final Examination but the former is amply present as well.

TWO EXAMINATIONS FROM THE COURSE

POLITICAL SCIENCE 4
Test III   March 28, 1930

1. Give a classification of Empires and show how this may allow an estimate of (a) success, (b) survival of British in (1) Canada, (2) India.
2. Give chief characteristics of (1) Roman Empire, (2) British Empire, and chief differences between them in (1) origin, (2) objective.
3. Define differences between Federation and Confederation and describe the different developments of Federations, giving examples.
4. Give (1) classification and (2) brief characterization of the various International organizations and also estimate the present function and future possibilities (1) of the International Bank, and (2) of the International Labor Office.
5. What effect did the war have on International institutions and how may peaceable economic and financial relations cause war. Give examples.
6. Give a general outline of the triple character of the League of Nations and describe the course of its development.

POLITICAL SCIENCE 4
Final examination   June 5, 1930

No more than eight questions to be attempted, including at least one of the first three. A full mark will be given for six questions well answered. Starred questions are suitable for answer, in part, by a diagram.

1. Distinguish between the political philosophies of (a) Plato and Aristotle, (b) Stoics and Epicureans, (c) Constantine and St. Augustine.
2. What were the most characteristic contributions of (a) Machiavelli, (b) Montesquieu, (c) Rousseau?

3. Mention the leading political philosophers of (a) the individualist, (b) the collectivist, (c) the socialist schools in the 19th century, with a few words of comment on each.

*4. What is Political Science? What is its past and present position in respect of ethics and economics, and what is its utility?

5. What are the various factors of nationality? What is the relation between nationalism and imperialism, and what are the tendencies of federalism?

6. Define sovereignty and describe shortly any recent (a) ideas, (b) institutions affecting its principle.

*7. What is (a) the historic and (b) the philosophic theory of the origin of the State? What is your own idea of a State in respect of its controlling, cooperating, and conflicting classes?

8. What are the various powers of popular government, and what are its main faults in the United States and United Kingdom?

*9. Review briefly the various schools of socialism and syndicalism in the present day (post-war) and outline the attempts to establish new forms of social democracy (a) by evolution (b) by revolution.

10. What is the present position of the churches in Europe?

*11. What is the history of the idea of progress, and what is your own idea of it? What are the principal forces working for progress and how do they work?

F. TAYLOR OSTRANDER'S NOTES FROM GEORGE YOUNG'S REVIEW OF POLITICAL THEORY, POLITICAL SCIENCE 4, WILLIAMS COLLEGE, SPRING 1930

February 10.
Political Science
–Not a science such as mathematics.
–No technical terminology.
–Only everyday terms used.
    –Often have several different connotations – Democracy, etc.
        a – Moral Sense (Dewey, Public and Its Problems)
            –An idea (not an alternative) of community life.
            –Clear consciousness of community problems.
        b – Principle of Government–Political Sense
            –Popular government, with idea of sovereignty of the people.

c – A <u>National Sense</u>
  –Republican or Constitutional government.
  –<u>Representative</u> government
  –No democracy without it (an English or U.S. viewpoint)
–The oldest of all mental activities.
–Attempt to construct an organization of social control. [Vertical line at left of this sentence.]
–A long and elaborate history.
–One would expect to be able to trade a constructive course of Political Science theory – but we can<u>not</u>.
–So intimately connected with our society, life, prejudices, a true philosophy is very difficult to get.
–You can<u>not</u> construct a practical, modern, applicable theory of Political Science from study of <u>older</u> philosophers.
–They tell us what <u>they</u> thought in <u>their</u> time – not about our own time.
–Most books are concentrated on the ancient authorities.
–We shall get as much out of them as possible – but not give our entire attention to them.

[On page 1-A:

Russians are materialistic Utopians.
  Reaction in America – going East – Revolution in Russia.
  Great names are ones that were acceptable to the people of their time – usually conservative.
  Dryden called Aristotle's reign of thought a "grand tyranny."
  Burke – reaction to French Revolution – pessimistic.
  J. Bentham – optimistic.
Democracy – basic principle is the equal right of all to hold office and determine public policy. Will Durant, on Plato
(Political Sense)
–Means perfect equality of opportunity – especially in education.
Aristocracy – means rule by the best.]
–Has great influence on all other studies, etc. Aristotle's classification so powerful, we did not get the theory of the world going around the sun (astronomical) for 1500 years after it was first put forth.
  –We must clear out minds of lags, handovers, prejudices, etc. – to fully get this true theory.
–Has been taken up in two ways.
–Practical Politics.
–A priori Propaganda.

–From general principles – one builds up a practical system.
–Having built up a practical system one preaches it, urges it, etc.
Utopias – Plato's Republic
   Thomas More's Utopia
   Samuel Butler's Erehwon
Present day ones [Utopias]:
   Russia
   Prohibition
   League of Nations
   Henry Ford's economic experiments
–From Aristotle and Plato we can get a great deal of the foundations of
   modern political theory.
–Plato – a thinker – radical
–Aristotle – a planner – conservative – realist
–Importance of Aristotle is subjective
–Each one reflects the age in which he was living – or reacts to it.
–Give us an idea of how men's minds have reacted to various events.
–Political Science as a Science.

[On page 2-A:

   Sociology
      Ethics (Ideal of conduct)
      Political Science (Ideal social organization)
      Ideas (Principles)
         Present-(Past) (philosophy)
      Institutions (Politics)
         Present-(Past) (History)
      Economics (Ideal form of house keeping)
   "We shall keep the past where it belongs – in the background."
   Exogamy – a rule of marriage – not to marry within blood.
   Ethics – ideal of conduct for man – as a whole
   Political Science – ideal of conduct for man – as parts of a whole?
                           –Acting individually.
                           –Acting within a group.]

Political Science as a Science
   Hobbes and Machiavelli laid all human institutions to war.
   –But Sociology – to take the totem group, shows exogamy not only for breeding
      purposes – but to keep peace – the totem group was organized for peace.

Hobbes and Maine have said that the old men were given authority for purposes of war – but Sociology teaches us that they were given their authority for purposes of peace.
Association not brought about for war – but for <u>production</u>.
History formerly considered the growth of the science of war – from a time when everyone fought individually.
–But present-day discoveries show [incomplete]

Political Science originates very largely in Ethics
–Morals
–Influence of Ethics has been very dominant
–Attempt to apply Morals to political theories – American Constitution – French Constitution
Last great revolutionary age was at end of 18th century – produced the American and French constitutions – also English reform constitution.
We are now in another great revolutionary age – not based on Ethics so much – but on Economics.
Switch over from Ethics to Economics is having a great effect on Political Science – giving greater materialism – less morals.
–But Economics is also switching over from former materialism (Laissez-Faire) – and being subjected to all sorts of Ethical considerations.
Present day constitutions have rights of man still – but also rights of classes.
Since the War, Political Science has been very much linked to Economics.

[On page 3-A;

Will Rogers – a reproduction of the King's Jester
–Jester appointed by the community to tell the truth to the King – as no one else dared to do so.
–Being entirely disqualified from active political life
–In course of time he became a very great political factor – of great benefit
What is an aristocratic state – opposite Democratic?

"Patriotism is the last refuge of the scoundrel" – Dr. Johnson]

Until the War – Political Science was very closely related to History. Political Science was treated in various ways.
Philosophic Method – <u>a priori</u>
–Very easily degenerates into ideology – Plato, Bentham, Rousseau, Butler.

Comparative Method
–Most scientific
–Logical induction and examination
–Combination of practical and ideal – Aristotle, Burke.
Historical Method
–"History without Political Science has no Fruit.
–Political Science without History has no Root."
History has also gone through a change
–Not concerned with facts as facts
–But with facts as forces, or functions of forces.
We have to deal with Political Science as a Science – although it will be a
    long time before it comes to be treated in same way as Physics.
–Has great use in practical life. Man is a political–social animal
–Has got to live in an organic, dynamic community – must either contribute
    to its life or to its premature death.

Patriotism
–One of the uses of Political Science is to teach how to use our Patriotism.
–Varies in definition
    –A sentiment of loyalty to the state.
    –Loyalty made up of a lot of different loyalties – sub-loyalties – city, county,
        race, country, school, religion
    –Generally one is leading
    –Patriotism can be divided
–Very difficult and dangerous to restrict loyalty.

[On page 4-A:

            Same Question[?]
    Class – Two nations – no intercourse – not governed by same law – don't see
        things the same – are muchly disliked
            –The Rich and the Poor (Disraeli)
            Plato wrote – every city is divided in two, the Rich and the Poor –
            who are always warring.
    Books – Hernshaw – Gilbert Murray – Harold J. Laski
    [Last two pairs have downward sloping line through them.
        -Past   -Past   -Present]

Political authorities have all along prepared the state as a body politic – the
    body – an entity.
–How then apportion and apply one's loyalty – bad view.

Loyalty to the spirit of one's country
–Instead of to the body politics
–Over run by patriotic hymns
  –That one's country is the only free one
  –And selected by God for that purpose.
Test of patriotism – is service – always tendency towards sacrifice
Political Science will tell us what is real service and when sacrifice is
  necessary.
Poorest real servitors are usually those who are the loudest patriots.
A longer view
  Conflict between loyalty to one's country versus loyalty to one's class.
  Two driving forces – conflicting
    Nationalism   Socialism
    –Patriotism   –Loyalty to <u>class</u>
    –Loyalty to state
  Political Science – will enable us to analyze and apportion between these.
  [Single vertical line alongside preceding four lines, commencing with "A
  longer view"]

1. History of Nationality
   –So long as Roman Empire and Papal Authority existed – nationalism could
     not take shape
   –Began with the Reformation and downfall of the Roman Empire.
   –First evidences were in <u>Empire</u> not narrow patriotism
   –Joan of Ark – first French patriot
   –Machiavelli
     –A realist, stating facts.
     –An appreciation, in advance of his day, of the great moral forces – at work
       – saw nationality

[On page 5-A:

[Diagram: Two overlapping ovals, one north-south, encompassing, north, règime,
and alongside, revolution, and south, religion, and alongside, religious view; one
east-west, encompassing, west, race, alongside, minorities, and east, region, alongside, rebelling colony. Nothing labeled in center; comprises circle tangent to four
lines of overlapping ovals plus an X touching points at which ovals cross.]

   –The ideal state would be a circle, as that in the center.
   –Very few, however, are that perfect – but have some tendency towards ellipses
     [ovals, above].
   –If these ellipses break off entirely, it results in dissolution, or war.]

–Grotius, Puffendorf, <u>Hobbes</u> – Leviathan
–Nationality – different meanings in different languages
–Nation – a State
–Nationalism – A political force
[Bracket along both sides of preceding two lines]
–Nationality – A legal term
  –A law of nationality – greatly varied with different countries
  –A political term
    When carried to its logical end – Socialism

2. Nation – no really established definition
                            Historically

Character or clan   1 People of the same <u>race</u>
Country   2 People of the same <u>region</u>
Central government   3 A regime – covering all types
                             of government
Culture   4 A religion of nationality
                            –Moral feeling, apart from the others
                            –Has its own priests

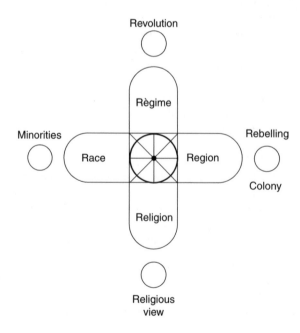

–Propaganda
–Moral force
–Bismarck took these into consideration, all
these points, building the nation around
them.
–Cavour in Italy
–The above numbers show the relative weight
– today.
–Applied to U.S., 4, 3, (2), ((1))
–Applied to British Empire (except India), 1,
3, 4, 2
India, 2, 3, 4, (1)

U.S. 4 3 | 2 1 | Nation

B.E. 1 3 | 4 2 | Not a nation, a nationality [British Empire]

India 2 3 | 4 1 | Nationalist movement
A nation – where first two are greater than the next two
National movement, an attempt to shift balance from right to left.

France is a nation

Ireland (past)	4, 1, 3, 2	–Nationalist movement
(present)	4, 3, 1, 2	–A nation
Russia (R.S.F.S.R.)[*]	3, 4, 1, 2	–A nation
Jews	1, 4 – no 2 or 3	–A nationality
Jews, in Palestine	4, 3 |1, 2	

[* Ostrander originally wrote U.S.S.R. Corrected to R.S.F.S.R., Russian
Soviet Federation of Socialist Republics]

[On page 6-A: "When I was writing a History of Modern Egypt" [quoting George
Young]

3. Two most important elements in present-day nationality are artificial: regime,
religion
–Can be altered or added to – as in Ireland today
–Language
–Courts
–Institutions
–Race and religion only 'needed to start with, can soon be overstepped';
and a real nation developed.
–No need or use of war.
–What if the Negroes followed Ireland

4. Nationalism is elementally political
   –Not so much economic.
   –A political ideal – or force.
   –Nation, a political idea
   [Single vertical line in margin alongside preceding two lines, at which an arrow, further to the left, is pointed.]
   –Economic control does not mean very much.
   –England had it over Ireland.
   –The Austrian Empire was an economic group.
5. Usual course of development is from nationalism – to – a nation – to – an empire
   –As shown in England–Germany.
   –As in Russia today – taking months where the others took years.
   –Some exceptions.
      –Egypt became a nation without any awareness of nationalism
      –Nationalist movement has started up, [at] last – forcing England to let it go.

[On page 7-A:

"Imperialism is the peculiar religion of conservatives." – George Young
In 17th century the French were four times as large and strong as England
      20 million – 5 million
   18th   25 million – 7 million
   19th   30 million – 9 million
      After Industrial Revolution [incomplete?]

	Irish	England	
19th	7 [million]	9 [million]	
After Industrial Revolution 4.3		43	38]

6. Close connection between ideal of nationalism and idea of democracy
   –Both popular movements.
   –Both come into collision with conservative traditions.
   –Had to fight on together against a common enemy.
   –The original moves for nationalism were made by Political Liberals (Democrats).
   –No longer true.
   –Nationalism has become saturated in most Western countries.
   –No longer connected with democracy.
      –We need less nationalism (and more democracy (?))

–Extreme nationalism–imperialism and extreme democracy–socialism came into a very definite collision – are pulling together only in Russia – but even there it is eccentric.
1. Analysis of Nationality–Race
→ It <u>must</u> begin with a <u>dominant race</u>. Question of <u>Fertility</u> – growth of the race.
–Necessary for starting and continuing the nation.
–A very fertile race will largely alter the problem – English was a very fertile race.
–Fluctuation of fertility is very important.
–A Nation going down in fertility is <u>nervous</u> – occupying itself with national defense – France at the [indecipherable words].

[On page 8-A:

Nordic legend invented by
a Frenchman – [Arthur Gobineau, The Inequality of Human Races, 1915]
–Taken up by Germans
–Poetic expression by Wagner
–Philosophical expression by Nietzsche
–Legend has some basis in fact

As soon as a nation becomes an empire, it loses its democracy – becomes aristocratic]
–If the fertility is increasing the nation is willing to drop armaments, etc. – (as Italy at the Conference?)

<u>Forcefulness</u>
–Very strong bond in holding together a nation.
–Invent legends, etc., to create this feeling of force.
–Nordic Myths (England and U.S.) – by nature a ruling class.
–Greek myths in Greece.
–Can be given legal expression.
  a. In immigration laws, etc.
  b. In recruiting the ruling class.
    –Drawing from source of the race.
    –As Mamelukes in Egypt – belong in Georgia.
    –As British in India.
    –Civil Service.
    –No miscegenation.

Fluidity – adaptability (successful)
  –Ability to improvise under stress
  –Change in national church
a) Ethnic changes – actual changes in race type

Nordic	(rulers)
Mediterranean	(artistic)
Alpine	(agrarians)

  –England: have Nordic and Mediterranean
  –France: have all three
  Nordics contribute character
  Mediterraneans contribute culture – artistic, melancholy, mystic
  Nordic – optimistic, strong
  –A race developed under the same conditions – through long ages.
b) Economic changes
  –Rural to urban
  –Effect on physical size – smaller bones in cities
  –Effect on mentality – became more quick-witted
  –However, the city-type became more hardy, able to stand more gaff
  –Political ideas in industrialized sections, are far in advance of those in
    rural sections
  –Women have altered their status – have already acquired equal political
    rights
  –"If all women got together to vote as women, they could put men out
    of power."
  –Have not had prophesied result – have even increased the virility and
    masculinity of the customs.

[On page 10-A:

Intellectual literature of Russia – for past 100 years – shows the evidence of a
servile race.
Dr. Louis Berman – The Glands Regulating Personality, 2nd ed. rev., 1928.
James Bryce – Race Sentiment as a Factor in History, 1915.
Arthur Keith – Nationality and Race from an Anthropologist's Point of View,
1919.
Arthur Dendy – The Biological Foundations of Society, 1924.
Madison Grant – The Passing of the Great Race; or, The Racial Basis of
European History, 4th rev. ed, 1922]

–Are on their way to economic equality.

–Change from young to old.

–Tendency is to favor the aged over the young

–As civilization proceeds, the death rate drops, as does the birth rate
[In margin to left, with single vertical line alongside: "Proceeds" – in
    what sense? – True if meaning standard of living, education, etc.]

–Population increases faster among the old, than among the young.

–If young feel too cramped by old – who have gotten a preponderance,

   –There will be a revolution.

   –Plato proposed to <u>double</u> every old Senator with a young one.

   –We have done this to some extent – by young secretaries.

  c) Enfranchisement – or Emancipation

   –When race goes from a position of subjection to supremacy

   –Great change in national character [Single vertical line in margin
    alongside this line]

   –Servile race – cruel, sly, crafty

   –As Greece, Russia, Ireland

 2. <u>Regionalism</u>

   –Change of national type produced by change of region

   –Irishman to America, Americans to Italy, Englishman to Australia

   –Connection between physical types and glands

   –Places one lives a most important element in determining allegiance.
    [Single vertical line in margin alongside this line.]

[On page 11-A:

"For thousands of years the Old World has accepted government by a privileged class. Even under democratic forms it is held that experience in government is an advantage." (P. W. Wilson, New York Times, February 23,
1930)

Bodin.
"The first thing an Englishman does when you give him a job is to invent a
machine to abolish the job. Then he builds political institutions to prohibit
his working the machine too long."]

People have always been interested with effect of <u>sea</u> on human character.

–Plato agrees with modern viewpoint – sea breeds <u>duplicity</u>, cunning

–Hypocritus wrote a thesis on "Air, Water, Land" 500 B.C.

<u>Climate</u> has important effect on race <u>characteristic</u> – mountains big and virile.

Soil has important effect on character of race – Scotch – thrifty, frugal – poor soil

Theories that northerners are more hardy, southerners more intelligent. In between have both qualities

–Bodin. [Arrow from "Climate has. . ." to this line]

Montesquieu – carried those theories rather too far – in application to England

English climate supposed to be cause of their energy.

–But Young says that Englishmen are naturally lazy, and climate makes them lazier.

  –Energy a result of reaction to climate

  –Sport necessary – playing game – rules

  –Eats too much.

Climate may also have an effect on political institutions

–Bad climate leads to collective development – clubs, homes, sitting around fire, talk, etc.

–Good climate leads to little development.

[On page 12-A:

"Quite as much geography as Joan of Ark that created the French nation."]

–Climate not very reputable any more – as an element.

Shape of a country – and internal composition does have affect on the political institutions and national characteristics.

[Alongside in margin: (Effect of good harbor, and favorable sea-coast)]

[Arrow from "Shape of a country" to the following in margin:

           Climate

Shape: {Content

        {Coast Line

        {Contour

        Contagion

        –Primarily geographic

        –Secondarily economic and political]

–Greece – Submerged coast – many mountains – led to city-state

–France – very level, no harbors, i.e., indentations of coast line – homogeneous nation – not sea-faring

–Russia – isolated – different social and political institutions from the rest of the world.

–Rhineland – not a state or nation – but has its own culture – Germany has changed character as the center of rule moved out of Rhineland toward the north (Berlin)

Contagion – has great effect on growth of state

–Black Death in England – most important

–Often linked to sea-faring nature of an indented coast-line.

An Island is important

–Islanders grow quicker in mental and moral lines.

 –Not held down by sluggish countries

–The navy shows this – as sailors take on islanders' characteristics

 –Revolutions have often started in sailors' mutinies

  –England – in Napoleonic Wars

  –Russia – first sign of revolution in seizing of a battleship in Black Sea

  –Germany – Bismarck was terrified by navy – nucleus of revolution in 1919 was in the navy.

Sea-faring people become imperialists

–By economic laws

–Because to some extent internationalists

–More the imperialism grows, the less the nationalism [Single vertical line alongside in margin]

 –Country indulges in easy and lucrative job of governing others

  –Neglecting home government

  –Shaw's apple-cart on wrong tracks – it would be good for England, to have the seat of empire moved to Washington – would be first chance in 200 years for real home government.

Regionalism has connection with plur[alism] and unitarism [?] of state.

[On page 14-A:

Two things are keeping things going in the world today – national and social forces.

[Double vertical lines alongside in margin]]

Basis of nation was the joining of like regions.

New state grew up

–With disappearance of Papal authority towards the South, and city-state towards the North.

–In between these two (i.e., France and England) originated the geographical, regional state – <u>unitary</u>.

–We shall hope to proceed further – and attain again to a <u>new</u> form of pluralism.

3. <u>Religion</u>
    –An association against unknown and feared elements.
    –Nationalism also an association
    –The two are inseparably connected in the development of civilization
    –That [if] one thing wrong, affects the whole, is a result (as finger hurting affects the whole body) – likely to result in many helpful aids to society
    –Nationalism–Religion, together
    –City-States of Greece all had Gods of their own
    –Emperors then tried to make themselves the Gods – as Nero – but failed
    –Then chose Christianity as the national religion – much the worse for Christianity

    –National movement sprang up at the Reformation
    –International religion – of Rome – put up a good fight against their separation of Christianity – tried to use persecution – but failed – Inquisition
    –The new nationalities grew very quickly
        –Again concentrated the national religion on the King
        –Deify the King
        –Also in Republics – deify the public heroes.
        –Crown came into conflict with the national idea – through its dynastic aims which were usually contrary to national aims
        –Democracy much better suited to such a national religion
            –There were democratic Demi-Gods, long before the Democratic State – Robin Hood – Drake

    Nationalism as a force is quite recent
        –Montesquieu had no idea of it
        –Only since about Rousseau's time
        –The growth of the French nation put it into effect (Executive) – Danton – Napoleon
        –Written about by Rousseau
        –In Germany – Stein, Bismarck, Hegel
        –In America
        Jefferson and Hamilton – exponents
        Washington and Lincoln – executives

[On page16-A:

Sanction – a coercive clause, some means of enforcement – such as "putting teeth in the Kellogg Pact"
[The following is on page 16-A, but may be a continuation of lectures, though possibly a digression.]]

F. W. Maitland (Laski) Otto Gierke (Political Theories of the Middle Ages)

Idea of Organization
  Society thought of as an animate body – organism – anthropomorphism
  –Members thought of as parts of a living organism
    –The Whole independent of parts, welfare of individual sacrificed to that of body
  vs
  –Whole lives and exists in the members, every amputation of a member gives pain to the whole
  –State a mechanism constructed of atoms
    –"Like a human body, (from which) if the little finger should be cut [arrow to preceding parenthetic interjection], it would not be a perfect body, but a monstrosity (from Latin)
Idea of Monarchy
  –God was considered as monarch – office of every particular wielder of lordship was considered a lone [?] God
  –Tendency to exalt the person of the ruler
  vs
  –A public office – service rendered to the whole body
  Sovereignty – Popular
  –Limitation of monarchy to "rights of the community"
  –Was connected to idea of a Ruler's sovereignty – foundation for most diverse constitutional systems.
Religion of nationalism is strongest when connected with democracy.
  –The first man to recognize the religion [of nationalism] was a reactionary Frenchman
    –"The wise legislator will make his political theory a religion"
    –Brought in idea that an unwritten constitution is very much stronger than a written.
    –Democracy has no strength – is a mere association – no sanction
      –Can never succeed without some strong executive, as President – contrary to its theory

[Single vertical line in margin alongside preceding line; beyond it is: Religion of nationality concentrated in one person.]

–Can have no permanence in democracy.
–Most modern expression is that the religion of nationalism must be active and working in every form of national life.
–Must be spread over every person in the nation – through national, state, county, town governments – through industry, culture
Religion of nationality as a force concentrated on a state
–With a National Frontier
–Preached in Press, through schools
  –Necessary in a young country
  –Out of place and dangerous in an old state
    –Leads to armaments, etc.
    –Leads to a "religious test"
    –In certain national dogma
    –Disqualifying if your religion is different from the state religion – conscientious objection
[On page 17-A:

Germans are, taking them by and large, the most civilized and cultured people in the world.
[Preceding likely a digression. The following – through "communes below it" – possibly a continuation of lecture.]]

Idea of Popular Sovereignty
  –Based in the people – ruler elected
  1. Ruler's subsequent sovereignty
  2. Divided sovereignty
  3. Popular Sovereignty
    –Monarch like a Republican Magistrate
  –Continued recourse to (3) had effect on the minds of the people – preparing them for later developments – Reformation – Democracy
Idea of Representation
  –From Rights of Rulers and Rights of Communities
  –Core idea of a State with representative institutions – Body Politic to "represent" the whole
  –Monarchy took on a representative character
    –The Emperor represented the Empire
    –Assemblies, Election

State – a community which recognizes no external superior [single vertical line in margin alongside]
–Is "communitas perfecta" [perfect community or fellowship] (Aquinas)
–No community above the State, only communes below it.
National religion must be kept in bounds, or the most appalling results will ensue
–As happened during the War [World War I] in all countries
–As the Hindenburg statue in Berlin
–Liberty Loan drives [in U.S.A.], etc., etc., etc.

4. Règime
   –One of two most important elements today
   –Government begins as a system of customary conventions, traditions, etc.
   –But once a people have given themselves a framework of government, it has great effects
   –In respect to public law
   –On language – court language becomes the official language
   –On literature – religion of the regime is mirrored in the writing – Shakespeare made democrats demigods
   –On national life
     –Coloring it greatly
     –As the American Constitution's effect on the point of view of the U.S.
     – legal attitude shown in legal mind of the Americans
     –Make-up of American mind as a result of regime
       –Draws from British the representative idea
       –From French the ideal of equality and liberty
       –From Colonial governments a strong distrust of an executive
   [Continued below]

[On page18-A:

Outline

Patriotism
Nationality
   History
   Nation
       Race   –clan
       Region   –country
       Règime   –central government
       Religion –culture

Analysis of Nationality
  Race
  –Fertility
  –Forcefulness
  –Fluidity (Ethnic change, economic change, enfranchisement)
  Region
  –Climate
  –Content – coastline – contour – contiguity
  Religion –(nationalism)
  –History
  –As a force is quite modern
  –Strongest in connection with democracy
  –National frontier
  Regime

<u>Nationalism (general sense)</u>:

Nation	Nationalism	Nationality
–State	–Force	–Status
		–Moral
		–Legal
	Race	
	Region	
	Règime	
	Religion	

<u>Empire</u>

1. Nationalism	2. Imperialism	3. Internationalism
Conquest	Colonization	Conscience
–Corruption	Commerce	
–Cruelty		British Empire
–Collapse		(Nothing exclusive in any Empire
		–may include any or all)
Confederation]		

–Social force here is largely individual.
  –In England, the discontented man is mainly concerned with his class – not
    himself.

–Effect on respect to private law
  –What entitles one to be a national of a country (subject in law).
    –Great diversity of laws in different countries.

–It would be greatly desirable if nations could get together and decide on a standard basis.

–How to decide on a woman's nationality.

–Only 5 states put women on a par with men (Russia and 4 South American countries) [Plus United States: not included since it was understood to treat women as equal to men]

–She may lose it [established nineteenth century rule that on marriage to a foreign man a woman lost her original nationality and acquired that of the foreign husband] on marriage.

[Set of numbers referring to earlier chart and accompanying discussion.]

Imperialism – Empire
1. Empire the development of a nation.
   –Comes from the desire to assert one's dignity and parity or supremacy.
   [Single vertical line in margin alongside this line]
   –Edward the Peaceable first used title of Emperor to assert this national dignity.
   –Richard II
   –Henry VIII – asserting his temporal power against the Pope – asserted England an Empire.
   –Maximilian – in Mexico, thought he would make his weak position stronger by calling himself Emperor.
   –Kings of Portugal – driven out of Portugal and set up in Brazil – called themselves Emperors.
   –This is relatively unimportant

[On page 19-A:

"We are on the road from Nationalism to Internationalism by way of Imperialism."]

2. Imperialism
   a. By Conquest
      –Roman Empire
         –Began by conquest purely – no confederation
         –Took Roman law and legions with it
         –Roman peace – giving the world a chance at progress
         –Started while there was still a Republic at Rome
         –Started with a high degree of conscience
            –Foreign envoys got no salary – only "representation" – as our envoys today
            –Expected to do things from a sense of civic duty

–Corruption began with the farming of taxes by the envoys to get money

–This was landed-on [opposed] by the Republic very heavily, with severe laws

–A parallel case to Russia today – much work expected for little pay

–Had to make their fortunes

–Under Augustus the whole system was transformed

–Large salaries – colonies under the Senate

–But as the government at Rome grew more corrupt, the colonial empire once more became corrupt

–When the Empire was split, the whole thing broke down

–"Rome sacrificed her domestic freedom to her domination over other peoples" – Bryce.

–Steady transfer of power from polis [?] to the plebes.

–Comparison between ruling class of Britain and [Roman] Senate – is false

–It should be the landed gentry of the 18th century with Senate

–Ruling class today compared with a later date

[On page 20-A:

Junquero – Portuguese poet

"I went through the Spanish–American campaign as an observer for the British."]

(1) Corruption (Roman Empire) – an almost inevitable result of conquest

(2) Cruelty – Spanish Empire a very good example of empire by conquest

   –Were going to cross the Atlantic and save the souls of the poor Indians

   –In principle – perfect

   –But the practice was bad – they made slaves of Indians, exploited them, or killed them

   –Present day "White Man's Burden"

      –Very good ideal (?)

      –But it has resulted in some very bad effects

      –It always brings its own retribution

      –Keeping an eye out for the "divine justice" of history, we see many examples

      –British in slave trade

      –Started on an economic basis

      –Without thought of moral harm

      –Eventually the public conscience revolted – determined to put a stop to it

–Retribution for that has not in any way been paid – lies [as a] potential in the <u>colored</u> problem in U.S.

–Suppression of Spanish cruelties in Cuba, was cause of our intervention there

–Was a very important factor of our going to war

–Led to collapse (final) of the Spanish Empire

(3) <u>Collapse</u> – an almost inevitable result of empire-by-conquest

–Quickened by cruelty and corruption

–More violent the conquest, the more sure the collapse

–May be staved off by introducing culture, as the Romans did

–Or by intermarrying, as the Portuguese did

–Culture, if brought in, will last long after the collapse of the empire-by-conquest

–As Portuguese culture in India

–Spanish culture in Philippines, etc.

b. By Confederation

–Based on sea power (instead of military power or conquest) – sanction in the existence of a navy

–Primus inter pares – Athens, Delos [Single vertical line in margin alongside this line]

–Slowly evolves into an <u>empire</u> upheld by the <u>sword</u>

–And in time it perishes by the sword

–As shown in fact that loss of navel and military power by Athens resulted in breaking up of the Empire – which would not have been the case, if it had remained as a confederation

–British Empire is not following the path of Athens

–Is getting more and more loose – a true confederation

–Less reliance on the sword

c. By Commerce and Colonization

–Extreme wealth that this brings

–Causes extreme danger of corruption and cruelty – ending in collapse

–Carthaginian empire followed this course – its culture leading to cruelty

–Commerce only temporary – Colonization lasting

–<u>British Empire</u> – was in its origin very largely a crusade for freedom of the seas

–Against claims of Spanish and Portuguese

–Who had a material advantage in previous start

–Who had a moral advantage in a Papal Bull, dividing the New World between them

–Spanish conquered the Portuguese and took over their claims

–The Spanish Armada combat was brought on by this rivalry for the seas – and was accompanied by a declaration by the Pope as to Elizabeth's legitimacy – but this failed to arouse the English people

–Then became a race for colonization of the New World

–Between English, Dutch, Spanish, French

–French were wiser than the others

–Giving a [sic] plenty of government support to the colonies

–Gave their culture to the Indians

–Went in with a much greater insight into the true problem and outcome – but it was the English ability to colonize that won

–Dutch went into the race for commerce – thus gaining temporary conrol – but were soon overcome by the superior colonizing ability of the British

–Spanish were mainly concerned with making conquests – and turning the Indians into Spaniards

–Lost out to colonization of English

[On page 23-A:

Cromwell was the founder of the British Empire

–Had a strong international imperialism

–Had a very strong element of national imperialism

Capable of conquest – cruelty

–As shown in his treatment of the Irish – tried to exterminate them – failed

Present French Empire is one of conquest

–Are cruel – bombardment of Damascus

–Are using their servile, foreign troops for military service in Europe – will bring its own inevitable retribution

Empire by Commerce – which never became an Empire, because there was nothing but Commerce – Hanseatic League]

British emigrated because they wanted to – were men of independent means – got along very well without government aid

–Civil War between Puritans and Nobility, Revolution of 1668, gave to the emigration a great release of vitality, which accompanied their colonization

British Empire began with the Revolution of 1648 [?]

–Also American Revolution of 1776

–Pact signed by the Mayflower pilgrims [was] one of the first Imperial documents

–Canadian revolt was another landmark – Durham's Report (1846) was
  another Imperial document
–Making him the grandson of the Empire
Conquest comes into this Empire in a secondary way
–British Empire was gained in a fit of absentmindedness
–Muddling into possessions
–Drifting into Imperialism
–Commerce
–Mercantilist theory – keeping colonies as markets
–An attempt to assert control over colonies
First breakdown of Empire was resistance to that theory – no revolt against
  the King
American War of Independence saved not only their own liberties but those
  of the English

[On page 24-A:

Diagram of British Empire: inner circle with London at center, area labeled
United Kingdom; area between inner and outer circle labeled Commonwealth.
Surrounded by inner set of circles labeled India, Newfoundland, New Zealand,
Australia, Union of South Africa, and Canada; and by two outer circles, labeled

British Empire

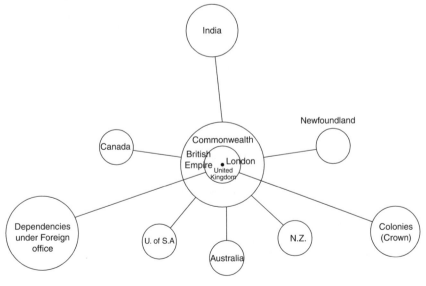

Russian Empire

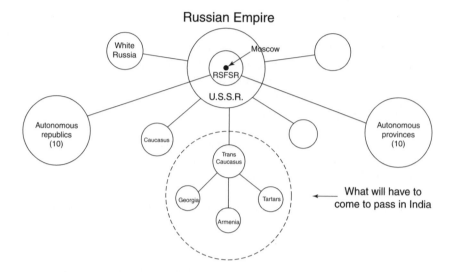

Dependencies under Foreign Office, and Colonies (Crown) each connected by straight line to outset circle.

Similar diagram of Russian Empire: inner circle with Moscow at center, with area labeled "RSFSR", inner circle labeled, first, Autonomous Republics and, second, Autonomous Provinces, "(10) of each." Area between inner and outer circle labeled USSR. Outer circles surrounded by set of circles, connected by straight line to outer circle, and labeled White Russia, Caucasus, and Ivan's Caucasus the latter with lines to three circles, labeled Georgia, Armenia, Tartars. Alongside latter is statement, "What will have to come to pass in India."]

–Otherwise King George III might have founded an autocracy.

–A curious throwback from commerce to politics

Present movement to have free trade within the Empire

  –Would break up this Empire

    –Destroying sentiment – put it on a commercial basis

    –Other dominions would resist English manufactures

Present make-up of the British Empire – a loose confederation

1. Dominions
2. Colonies   (more autonomous than [arrow to next line])
3. Crown Colonies
4. Dependencies – Colonial Office – (little democracy)
5. Dependencies – Foreign Office (protectorates, mandates)
6. Waste Paper Basket Collection – some military, some navel – Home Office
7. India – an Empire (possibly already a Dominion)

  –Has just grown – no artificial construction

–Something on this scale is a very living organism – the only kind that can endure

–On this plan (or lack of plan) only, can a world superstate be formed [single vertical line in margin alongside preceding statement] – Russian Empire – almost international

[On page25-A:

Equation for Imperialism (ethically and historically in [the following] order)
1. Conquest
2. Commerce
3. Colonization
4. Confederation

British Empire

Canada 3,4,1,2	–likely to carry on
India –now [1930] 2,1,4,3	–in bad shape
–after a [?]	
–Simon report 1,4,3,2	–at a balance
	–anything likely
Portuguese Empire 1,3, (incomplete)	
Philippines 2,1,4,3	–not in such good shape

Empire

Nationalism → Imperialism → Internationalism
1. Executive
   –Federations, confederation, real and personal union, international association
2. Economic
   –Internationals of Wealth and Work (Finance and Labor)
   –Public
   –Private
3. Ethical
4. League of Nations
   –Policy, Peace, Progress
   –Executive (Council), Ethical (Assembly), Economic (Commissions)]

Three phases through which an empire usually passes
–1st-Dependencies looked upon as states, to be exploited
–2nd-Discovery that exploitation is unprofitable

–Colonies looked on as encumbrances
–"Millstones hung about our necks" – Disraeli
–3rd-Last stage – colonies extension of the mother country – ought to be
 reincorporated
[In margin alongside first two, words and arrows indicating that the U.S. is now
in the first stage and soon to be in the second stage]

Internationalism
–Lies mostly in the future, at present
–No maps and charts
 –Those that these are, are like maps of unexplored countries
 –blank space
 –with imagined utopias
 1. {Politically
    {Executive
    –Real union
     –Austria–Hungary before War
      –A legislative ruling both, manned by delegates sent up from national
       legislatures
     –Norway–Sweden
      –Central legislature
      –Broke up when Norway wanted a hand in foreign affairs
    –Personal union
     –Hanover – to the United Kingdom
     –British Empire is on its way from a real to a personal union

[On page 26-A:

Confederation	Bundestat
Federation	Statenbund
Federation vs Pluralism]	

–Federation (foedus – Latin word "treaty")
 –Most centralized
 –Based on a treaty
 –Very close, practically unbreakable contract
–Test for determining whether federation or confederation
 –Whether it is possible to break up federation, by secession of one or more
  units – if so, it is a confederation
 –Principle of federation
  –Modern society has divided itself up into very definite national states
  –With fighting frontier
  –Has drawn down from above all the former imperial powers

–Has drawn up from below all powers of local government

–Is a strongly centralized, <u>unitary</u> state

–<u>Federalism</u> is attempt to draw up again to internationalism

–<u>Pluralism</u> the attempt to drop down again to local units

–Montesquieu – "a convention by which separate states agree to form a larger one"

–[Alexander] Hamilton – "an association of states forming a larger one"

–U.S. began as a confederation, grew into a federation, has become a unity state

–States are not states but provincial governments

–Swiss call their provinces cantons to avoid this confusion

–Is generally a sovereign, unity, State

–Approximating closely a nation – but does not require race and region

–Makes possible the forming of a strong national government with different races

=Canada–English–French

South Africa–English–Dutch

Switzerland–French–German–Italian

[On page 27-A:

India is in both evolution and devolution

–British provinces an evolution

–Provincial governments

–Indian Nationalist Movement

–Native provinces are straining to get back their former power]

–Federation – (1) a unifying process – getting rid of distinctions – the U.S. – or (2) a process of decentralization, due to national differences and conflict – United Kingdom

–Gradual recognition of real differences

–two processes in federation

(1) Evolution

(2) Devolution

Evolution – a <u>definite</u> journeying back from internationalism to nationalism

Devolution – from national to internationalism

–Can go on at the same time – as they are in Great Britain today

–Australia – evolution

–Imperial Conference – devolution

–Federations within the Empire are following the evolution of the U.S. – while the Empire as a whole is devolving to a League of Nations

–Test for Federation or Confederation

–Whether it is diplomatic or democratic
–Democratic – Federation – U.S.
  Diplomatic – Confederation – British Empire
–Original concept of the League of Nations was that it should be democratic
–But as it is today, it is diplomatic – thus a very loose confederation
Advantages of Federalism
–Makes for efficiency
–Economizes overhead
–Energy
–Often tends toward an economic unit, rather than political
Importance of Federalism
–Leads to a reorganization of the country along the lines of an economic entity
Disadvantages
–Weakness of central government in war
–Possibility of civil war
–Federal principle encourages formation of nations within the Federation,
  which have no raison d'etre.
Most political scientists conclude in favor of Federation –especially when there
  is any variety within its borders
Differences between Devolution and Decentralization
–Devolution, interpreted in terms of nationalism (home rule) [In margin:
  Ireland]
–Decentralization, interpreted in terms of social legislation [In margin: powers
  to counties]
–Confederation
–Usually in movement – either toward devolution or evolution
–In Great Britain
  –Actual movement is toward a looser union – devolution
  –Although the entire efforts of the ruling class have been in the opposite
    direction
–International Associations
–On a diplomatic basis – League of Nations – Postal Union
 a. Public, governmental, supported out of public funds
    –About 24
    –Postal union, telegraph union, railroad organization, navigation, general and
      special
 b. Private – supported by voluntary funds – about 500
    –Scientific, literary, artistic, scholarship
 c. Official agreements dealing with private rights – patents, trademarks, copyrights
    –Until the War, were all transactions through the Diplomatic Missions

–League of Nations is peculiarly fitted to do this work
–Article XXIV – very sweeping inclusion
–Has not been given any use

2. Economic
   –Most important in tariffs – economic frontiers
   –Economic internationalism can only come about through lowering or removal of tariffs
   –A movement in Europe to make it a tariff-less country – like the U.S. – has failed so far
   –Tariffs are now about one-third higher than before the War – are imposed for shorter terms
   –Control of finances – internationally
   –Control of foreign political governments through control of the economic life
   –U.S. since the War:– shifted from being a debtor nation, to amount of 4 billion, to a creditor nation, 3 billion
   –Attitude of American government – pay off your debts, or scrap your dreadnaughts

[On page 30-A;

Principal advocates of international economy were South Americans.]

–Where money has been loaned from one nation to another
   –In case of threatened bankruptcy, bailiffs, or receivers, are put into the debtor nation
   –Or international action without receivership
   –Can one go to war?
      –[Henry] Palmerston said, No – about 100 years ago – but has been done by many countries, since
   –Does it lead to imperialism?
   –Haiti
   –Financial control
   –Threat of war – third party
   –Venezuela, third party (U.S.) – opposing Great Britain and Germany
   –We wouldn't let them collect, but do collect ourselves by threat of war
–Internationals of Finance [sic]
   –Tend toward imperialism
   –Combines of big international banks to share out loans
   –Loan may be interrupted politically

–Loans depend on relative rates of interest in different countries
–Economic aspect
   –International agreements (financial) set up international institutions
   –Objective in characterr = imperialism
   –Prussia, before War, had treaties with England and Russia – was under
     international control
   –Spheres of economic influence are bound up with spheres of political
     influence [Single vertical line in margin alongside this line.]
   –Partition of Asia Minor during the War
     –Special secret treaties among allied powers, made during the War
     –Divided Asia Minor, into economic spheres – a slice for each power
   –War showed what a pooling of sources of supply can do
     –Allied powers had to internationalize their war organization – for efficient
       working
     –Same thing could be done in peace.
   –During War the Allies developed a complete international industrial
     organization for shipping, supplies, encirclement, blockade
   –Cornered the world, in scope – especially after U.S. entry, 1917
   –Controlled first munitions, then materials of every kind
   –Delegates from each nation appointed a central executive which conducted
     and controlled international supplies and trade – each department pro-
     duced a balance sheet
   –From this it may be seen that no real economic reasons inhibit that again
     today
   –No reason why civilization should not have free trade, international
     organization, etc.
   –It has already been proven most effective.
–After the War, fearing a collapse, these same international organizations
  refrained from disbanding
   –Against terrific private pressure
   –Allies pooled their interests against private interests
   –But dissension of the U.S. from world politics had very serious results.
     U.S. withdrawal, after the War, into its old shell of isolation, broke up
     the War pools.
   –Return to private trading – no international assistance
   –Any new return to that most efficient system must be worked out under
     the old competitive methods – no emergency urge.
–Thus, the force of internationalism failed to take its opportunity
   –Allies imposed heavy reparations debts on defeated powers – some
     represented feelings not facts.

–Two schools of opinion as to actual clearing up of the debts
1. Leave them alone, to dwindle out of importance – pocket veto
2. Lower figures, to meet actual facts
    –America took this second view
    –Felt peace could only be imposed by real financial power – not by even
        such a treaty as the Versailles
–Failure of Rhine expedition, and French and English, to get money out of
    Germany led to Dawes agreement
–American international scheme for payment [based] upon reason
–Does not affect industry
–Young plan went a step further
–International Bank [for Settlements, Basel, Switzerland] a further step
–Sees that payments are made without disturbance to international exchange
–Economic internationalism is one of the best results of the war
International [Unions] of Labor
–From Right to Left
–Social Democratic Parties
    Labor in England, Social Democrat in Germany
–Socialist proper, Parties
–Social Revolutionary Parties
    –Practically extinct
–Communists
    a. Constitutional
    b. Revolutionary
1. (Political) The Right represented in the Second International – supported
    by British, Germans, French
2. (Political) The Left represented in the Third International
    –The Comintern
    –Eastern Europe and South America
3. (Economic) Amsterdam Trades Union International – corresponds to
    Second International
4. (Economic) Moscow Trades Union International
    –Red
    –Penetrates trade unions for purposes of Communism
    Weakness of labor as an international factor is that 1 and 3 are constantly
        fighting 2 and 4
    Are capable of international action, under certain circumstances, which
        are quite important
    –Helped to stop invasion of Russia
    –British coal strikers given over a million sterling by Moscow,

  –Tried to stop the beginning of the Great War – but feebly
  –Could probably do so in the event of another Great European War
  3. Ethical [incomplete]

[On page 35-A:

  Labor Internationals – after the Great War
    White – exiled soldiers – wandering
    Black – [indecipherable word; possibly English for kulaks (successful farm-
    ers)]
    Green – peasants
    Red – were revolutionary – have disappeared
  Americans apt to rely too much on legalism.]
  4. League of Nations
          –A series of concentric circles
      a. International Labor Office
          –A condescension to the revolutionary international movements – all
          that is left of the four revolutionary labor movements [Single verti-
          cal line in margin alongside this line.]
          –Is not revolutionary, but reform-atory
          –Is working against great odds – capitalistic opposition to social
          legislation
          –Is trying to regulate production in backward countries, to put them on
          par with forward countries
          –Has gotten over a [proposed] general convention for limitation of
          work to eight hours – British have at last promised to sign
          –Is trying to regulate dangerous trades
          –Here is the embryo of international social codes and international factory
          inspectors
      b. International Court – World Court
          –Principle of compulsory arbitration was pushed in the 1890s
          –First Hague court set up in 1899
          –A panel of judges from which countries could draw men to settle
          disputes
          –Were eleven recourses to it before the War [World War I] – a diplomatic
          settlement with judicial authority and sanctions
          –Prize Court
          –Prize law the most contentious before the War
          –Declaration of London
          –Broke down, in short time
          –Conciliation Councils
          –An idea in abeyance

[On page 36-A:

International Inspectorate
International policing
International Judgment]

–<u>Present court</u> set up by Article 14 [establishing League of Nations]
–Competent to <u>determine</u> international disputes, when asked by countries
   – to give advisory decisions when asked by the Councils
–Set up in 1921
–Sixteen powers made jurisdiction obligatory
   –But big powers did not
   –Until 1929 – with reservations
–Several special obligatory rules
–Has been used sixteen times
   –Advisory opinions were more frequent at first
   –In last three years this has been repressed
   –Slowing development from diplomatic to judicial relationship
   –Same place in international affairs we passed through centuries ago,
      internally
–Has been the cause of peaceful settlements of many more

c. Advisory Commissions
   –Semi-independent, international organizations for special functions –
      closely linked to special international associations we dealt with
      before.
   –Non-League members are frequent in some – such as Opium
      Commission – or Permanent Military Commissiion
   –Outer ring are tending to become more and more independent
   –Carry on work where it is dropped by the International Labor Office
   –A form of international police authority
   –One of these commissions has taken up the recodifying of international
      law
   –One commission is trying to recodify international law – which <u>has</u>
      been neither law nor internationalism
   –Another is discussing territoriality in the seas – three mile limit, etc.
   –Another is seeking to standardize nationality.

Internationalism behind the league is <u>not</u> merely negative
  <u>Policy</u> – organization for consultation, conference, and conduct of policy –
  concert of Europe – before the Great War

Peace – restoration of peace and retainment of peace – Holy Roman Empire
Progress – Utopias

Three men most important in giving these three qualities to the League
–Robert Cecil
Woodrow Wilson
Jan Christian Smuts
–These were not all, the idea had been inherent in people's thoughts and minds
    for long ages.
Forces in the people's minds behind the organization
–Internationalism – putting bounds to Nationalism
–Socialism – ethical, not economic

Made an organization with three great functions
(1) Executive authority – super-national
(2) Ethical authority – for promotion of peace
(3) Economic authority – for promotion of prosperity
    –All this business of dividing up into political divisions is foolish
    –Divisions should be made on basis of economic unity
    –Is idea in back of the United States of Europe

[On page 38-A:

Bank for International Settlements
–Comes under Executive authority (1)
–May in time come under Economic authority (3)
[Arrow from second line to:] Is unattractive

Idea that Germany had – that Russia has – was to organize the state along
    economic lines – this will do away with the need for a political organiza-
    tion]

Actual Organization of the League
    1. Inner [Circle], Council (Executive authority)
        –For the penalization and prosecution of the postwar
        –Execution of peace – the peace treaties, status quo, etc.
        [In margin: League, within the League, improper]
    2. Outer [Circle], Assembly (Ethical authority)
        –Has been watered down from original idea
        –Is for prevention of war (not however the promotion of peace)
        [In margin: League proper]
    3. Outermost [Circle], Commissions (Economic authority)
        –Has been greatly watered down

–Relegated to an <u>advisory</u> position
[In margin: League, without the League]

1. Is at best unattractive and unworthy of original idea
2. Is a utopia
3. Comes nearer to original idea (though most overlooked by public)

The Council
–A body of eight until 1922, then raised to ten, in 1926 raised to 14
–Increases were purely diplomatic
–Original eight was to secure a majority for the five victorious Allies – but America did not come in

[On page 39-A: Tripartite character of the League]

–Thus there was a majority of one
–But Germany came in, no longer a majority for Allies
–Thus no longer a pure machinery for enforcement of peace
–Five permanent countries (Germany, Italy, France, United Kingdom, Japan)
–Has taken in several South American delegates – becoming world wide
–Is not a democracy
  –No majority vote rule
  –Is supposed to rule on principle of unanimity
–But these changes have not had the apparent effect
  –The Council – except for the acceptance of Germany – is even stronger and more in the hands of the [Big] Four
–The Presidium
–Small countries are grouping together for getting representation on the Council.
  –Central Europe – Little Entante – A satellite of France – Allied
  –Nordic Group
  –Neutrals
  –Norway, Denmark, Sweden
  –Holland, the Baltic States
  –Doing some of the best work of the League
  –Latin America – actually neutrals
  –Asiatic – neutrals – least important
If the League is ever to become world wide it must have a <u>regional</u> separation
  –Only way to get in the U.S.
  –Is growing up naturally
  –The Council is slowly getting away from its character as a prosecution, and tending toward a character as enforcer of future peace

–The character of the men represented is gradually improving – is becoming a Council of Prime Ministers, and Foreign Secretaries.

The Assembly
–Is nominally the supreme body
–Composed of official representatives – not from people (not democratic)
–Admits new States by two-thirds vote
–One session every September of two or three weeks
–Contrary to general assumption, the U.S. did not try to make it a democratic body, and the Europeans try to make it diplomatic
  –Wilson had no such idea
  –Smuts was the only one to attempt giving it a democratic form
–First thing it did was to set up an annual session
–Doesn't fall under wither legislative or executive class
–Has come to be a sort of World Forum
  –Giving representation to the various public opinions
  –In spite of the poor machinery for it
  –Through different character of governments the delegates represent
–Has forced the hands of the Council several times – especially in disarmament.
–Doesn't conduct its business by diplomatic dickering – as Council

[On page 41-A:
There are three delegates

Monroe Doctrine is already incorporated in the Covenant – absurd – an anomaly

Organization of the Secretariat
–A head – Secretary General (Sir Eric Drummond)] [Jean Monnet was appointed Deputy Secretary General in 1919 at age 31.]
–But conducts itself openly by debate and discussion
–Hasn't yet gotten control of election of new members to the Council
–Delegations are appointed by governments in power in the respective countries
–Future of the League depends on how much the Assembly can go on becoming more and more democratic
–In so far as there is any vitality in the League today – it is the democratic part of the Assembly

The Secretariat
–A British contribution
  –Idea of creating an international Civil Service

–Men should drop their national character, become international
–But the idea went abroad that it should be composed of nationals
–A conflict between British and Germans, against the Latins on this point
–Drummond (Secretary General) followed the British ideal, successfully –
 though for about five years its "nationals" [British] had control
–Civil Service is most important in an organization with a poor executive and
 legislative – as the League
–Did all the technical work
–Kept the rest of the League from breaking down, during first few years – did
 the work for Council and Assembly

[On page 42-A:
 We do find a constant, steady growth, through all the history of the League
 Theocracy – State in which the organization is definitely based on the
 church.
 Blood of the martyrs is the seat of the church. – Fraser]

–Of late years, the work of this body has shifted, and it is returning now to its
 original purpose, as a Civil Service
–Summons the automatic machinery into war – keeps the whole machine
 working
Many people are glad that the U.S. is out of the League, for they can use its
 absence as a club in getting through several much needed reforms
–Regionalization
–Proportional Representation of Home Parties
–Democracy
Results – improving in character as time goes on
–Some of the early ones [the League's actions] were poor
–But new ones are becoming sounder
–As it gets away from the World War

Theory of the State
 I. Historic
 II. Philosophic

I. Historic Theory of the State
 –An a posteriori theory
 –Most theories represent an evolution from the simple to the complex
 –But archeology in the Nile valley shows that the state there was extremely
  more complex than the state structure of the present Hudson or Thames
  valleys.

–Old organization of the five nations [Iroquois?] was also very complex
–Language also evolves from a complex to a simple form

[On page 43-D

    Matriarchy – based on the woman
    Patriarchy – based on the man
    Fratriarchy – based on equals

Theory of the State
  I. Historic
    Clan
    Cult
    Conscious
  II. Philosophic
    Covenant
    Contract (Social)
    Coercion
  Sovereignty
    Attributes
  Constitution – Concession, or Creation

Government
  I. Classifications
    1. Monarchy
    2. Popular Government
      a. Parliamentary, Party
      b. Presidential, personal
      c. Professional
      d. Judicial
    3. Social Democracy – Pluralist governments
      –Class dictatorship
      –Council Government, Corporative Government]

Factors in the Growth of the State
a. Kinship – Clan
b. Cults or religions
c. Conscious

a. Kinship – Clan
  –Blood relationship
  –It is now generally thought that matriarchy was the first form of social
    organization – coupled with polygamy (several husbands)

–<u>Patriarchy</u> has been taken as the basis for most of our modern states, and political theory
  –Philosophy from Aristotle down to H. Maine
  –Has affected all our institutions – primogeniture
  –In the orthodox theory of the State, the first organization was attributed to the head of a family, then the head of a group, then a tribe, then modern state
  –German Constitution, 1919, starts, "The German Reich is an association of the German tribes."
  –<u>Fratriarchy</u>, the political theory of the future – is present today in the newer forms of government
b. Cult – Religion – sentiment
  –This was formerly much more in evidence than it is today
  –All power was supernatural
  –All activity had is own deity – polytheism
  –Led to divine right

[On page 44-A:

Bluntschli – leading Swiss internationalist of the 19th century
Were states formed by Napoleon real states or only states formed by a sort of Caesarian operation?]

c. Conscious Cooperation
  –Association for protection, production, etc.
  –This form of the modern State requires regulation of the <u>equal</u> members
  –Gives rise to Law – first record found in Domesday Books

The Modern State
  1. Direct formation
  2. Indirect formation
  3. Derived formation

1. Direct formation
  –The birth of a State by <u>conscious effort</u> of people coming together for cooperation
  –Greece, California
  –Usually are not long lasting
2. Indirect formation by combination
  –Two states coming together, or two being formed by separation
  –Somewhat like federation

3. Derived formation
   –By <u>concession</u> of an old [state]
   –Colonial state
   –Chartered company
   –Distinguish what are new states and what are merely divisions of old states
II. Philosophic Theory of the State
   –Distinctly <u>a priori</u>
   –Three schools of philosophic political thought
      –About a century of dominance to each
   1. Covenant – the princely state – up to 1600 A.D.
   2. Contract
   3. Coercion – the Police State
   –These, during their dominance, did influence the political philosophy and
   actual organization of the state very greatly

[On page 45-A:

"Render unto Caesar, those things which are Caesar's"
   –Original Christian political philosophy
St. Paul was the propagandist of the Christian theory
   –Changed the original political theory of Christianity, Romans 10:1,2
      –It is one's duty to follow the powers that be
   –Pope Gregory amplified this
      –If the powers that be, are bad, it is a punishment sent by God to bad people,
      they <u>must</u> not resist them.
Democracy – the tyranny of the odd man.]

1. Covenant
   –Tended to a <u>theocracy</u>, exercised by a Prince or Priest.
   –Still colors all our attitudes towards the State
      –Especially in the expected attitude towards the structure of the State
         –Flag, president, etc.
         –A form of patriotism
      –Early Greeks had everything in the State paralleled by Divine organization
      –Later Greeks became secular
      –Romans were secular, but thought the State required the approval of a
         divinity for sanction
      –The present organization is an outgrowth of St. Paul's theory
      –Religion's respect for the State is much stronger in the democracy than in
         the autocracy [Single vertical line in margin alongside this line.]
         –We still feel that there is divine right
         –The divine right of the majority

–Only real theocracies left are Arabia, Abyssinia, <u>Tibet</u>
–Declined because of great susceptibility to corruption
–And because of conflict between autocracy and theocracy
  –Feeling of superiority is backed up by military force
2. Contract (Social)
  –Treated as a theory of the origin of the state
  –There was in every community a definite assumption of mutual responsi-
    bility

[On page 46-A:

Schools that were out of fashion took on an unfavorable aspect
–Spoken of in a derogatory way
–As a result of centuries of opposition – in posterity

Present day international law – is just beginning to have a basis on contract
–We are waiting to build up an international State, based on contract]
  –Old Testament is full of this sort of thing
  –Contract between the King and the people – constitutional kingship
  –In Greece – expression by the <u>Sophists</u>
    –State a necessary evil
    –Must be restricted as far as possible, in the interests of freedom.
    Plato and Aristotle repudiated this
    Epicurean
    –State based on justice
    –Just not found in nature, only in human form – contract
  –In Rome
    –Roman law
    –Both law and liberty were original in themselves
    –Contract is reduced to the tacit consent of the ruled
    –State based not on contract but on consent – Cicero
    –Ulpian
    –The will of the Emperor is law – because the people confer upon him the
      law
  –In Christianity
    –State a necessary evil
      –A result of Adam's fall from a state of nature
      –All citizens had to do was to consent to a good government, or conform
        to a bad government – not unlike Sophists
    –Was being revived in the old Teutonic tribal law
      –Tribal chiefs were elected
      –Oath

[On page 47-A:

Manegold [?]

Princely Rule
Popular Rule
  We are now in the time of conflict between the church and the state – the
  priest and the prince
  The more clerical a priest was the more likely he is to oppose autocracy –
  opposite to today]
–Feudalism
  –A practical application of social contract
  –Described the <u>responsibilities</u> of a feudal lord for his vassals – protection,
    economic
  –Based on a contract – between Lord and Vassal
  –A loss to society, when lord became a landowner
–The Church – supplied statesmen and politicians of the times
–Manegold– [?]
  –God was the remote origin of the state
  –The immediate origin was social contract
  –People could morally revolt from a ruler who was violating his right by
    being corrupt
  –Social Contract was the sanction
–Althusium (1610)
  –Distinction between state as an institution, and government – accepted the
    Social Contract
  –Ecclesiastical-anatomical principle
  George Buchanan, 1559 – Scotch
  Marianna, 1599 – "Kingship" – Spanish
  –Justification for assassination of kings
  Hooker – English
  –Supported the Anglican church as against the crown
–All early exponents of the theory of Social Contract
–In time the pendulum swung back, the theory of Social Contract was either
    watered down, or used to uphold the princely rule
–Grotius, 1625
–New character and color to the theory by Hobbes, 1661 – "Leviathan"
  –Strong attitude in favor of authority
    –Because of prevailing reaction against civil wars
  –Formula for formation of states – "I give up my right of government to
    this authority <u>or</u> assembly, on the condition that you do likewise."

–Attributes legal sovereignty to a personal political sovereign whose will
was law in regard to all conditions
–Locke, 1690
–Writing in a reaction to the conditions of his day – after Revolution which
ended the Stuarts
–Stress is laid on parliamentary rule, as opposed to kingly
–State of nature wasn't so bad
  –Was a law of nature
  –Origin of the state was to have some authority which would interpret and
    enforce this law of nature – interpretation was necessary
  –Social contract was basis of the State
  –State conducted its government on the basis of consent
  –Legal sovereignty was permanently vested in State
  –Political sovereignty was permanently vested in people
  –Sovereign may be politically deposed

[On page 49-A:

Man is born free – and everywhere he is enchained.

Gresham's law in respect to government]

–Montesquieu adopted this same principle
–Rousseau, "Social Contract"
  –Collectivist theory of the State
  –Bases it on climatic conditions
  –Finally bases it on contract
  –State of nature was idyllic – we ought to get back to it
  –Have come to a basis of the State in popular arrangements
3. Coercion – The Police State
  –Highest expression in Germany
  –Based on biological theory of society
  –The rule of the strong
    –In respect to the State, is older than Darwin
  –Came to the top in the middle of the last century
  –Soon began to hedge a little
    –Huxley, Marshall
    –The fittest doesn't do most good to all but usually the one who does the
      most good to himself
  –Inferior will tend to come to the top and suppress the superior.
  –Might is right
  –God is on our side

–When people fight, their God fights
–Fallacy in this theory
Competition on which society is constructed isn't one of force – but one
of persuasion – if any force, it is the force of ideas
–An idea cannot be instilled by force
–It doesn't really matter whether the coercive force is one man, an organ-
ized minority, or the majority – the idea cannot be put across by force.

Sovereignty – orthodox view

–Has only to do with the State (not government)
Aristotle – speaks of supreme power resident in the State
Romans – spoke of plenary powers of the state
Technical sovereignty has nothing to do with titular sovereignty
Bodin – writing in an attempt to strengthen the state
–Gave the State a peculiar moral authority
–Sovereignty is something permanent and inherent in the State
–Sovereign is free from his own laws – bound by laws of God, nature and
nations
–Sovereignty can reside in a person or body – more powerful if in the person
Hobbes – writing in reaction to Civil Wars – trying to strengthen the State
by strengthening the Crown
            –Put sovereignty on a basis of Social Contract
                –A complete and continuous surrender of power by people to the
                Prince
                –Was source of all legislative, executive, and judicial authority
Locke – 1690 – after a change in dynasty – the old idea was rather weak
–Dropped "sovereignty" – took Supreme Right – meant same thing
–Assigned a supreme power – fiduciary – to Parliament
–People are superior to Parliament but in abeyance while Parliament
is sitting
Rousseau
–Sovereignty was assigned wholly to the people – delegation of that to
Parliament, etc.
–A simpler idea of it – followed on the continent, since then

[On page 51-A:

India – neither legal nor political sovereignty (slight political)
Ireland – both political and legal sovereignty (slight legal)
Legal sovereignty is completely unlimited
The concentrated powers of public opinion – focus to a point]

<u>Austin</u> – 1832
–Wrote under influence of the Reform Riots of 1830
–Sovereign must be a determinate person or body – cannot be the people
–Legal right came from sovereign
<u>Maine</u> – attacked the above – pointed out that there was a fallacy in statement
  that all law must emanate from king
Present sovereignty lies in the King-in-Parliament
–Member of Parliament – was a repository of mandate in a man – he was not
  a delegate
<u>Austin</u> [Arrow to above discussion of Austin]
–King-in-Parliament is Sovereign
–King and Peers and Electors are sovereign
–Supposing the King dead – Parliament dissolved, the Electors alone are
  sovereign
–The Commons are sovereign – but secondarily so – as they are merely trustees
A distinction began to be made between legal and political sovereignty
–[Legal] residing in or represented by the authority which <u>lays down</u> the law
  [In margin: is the final law giving authority]
–Political [sovereignty] resides in and represented by the authority which <u>lies</u>
  <u>in back</u> of the law [In margin: is the foremost law-making authority]
Democracy – the people are <u>politically</u> sovereign. Popular and political
  sovereignty are different

<u>Attributes of Sovereignty</u>
  Absoluteness
  Universality
  Inalienation
  Permanence
  Indivisibility

[On page 52-A:
Dominion constitutions, formerly by concession, have become constitutions of
  creation (possibility of amendment and revision).
  Post-war constitutions of Europe are shifting from purely political to economic]

<u>Absoluteness</u> is not possible – things have to be worked out by negotiation
  There are constitutional and unconstitutional limits to absolute sovereignty
  – debt to other nations – to its citizens
  Absolute legal sovereignty doesn't hold much water
Universality – Sovereignty applies to all people
–Sovereign cannot be brought before his own courts – nor his servants

–Extra-territoriality
–The Church usually had immunity
Inalienability – can be defined
Permanence – can be defined
Indivisibility – can be defined
–by the distinction between government and state
Definition of sovereignty
–Has been a concentration of supreme authority of one particular body or person
–Is becoming a coordination of supreme authority – covering future pluralist
    state

Constitution
    –A statute of the structure of the supreme government – Austin
    –Regulation of the relationship of the citizens – Aristotle – wider than
        present-day interpretation
    May be a written charter – or an "unwritten cosmos"
    –But harder to change an unwritten, than a written constitution
    –This rigid and flexible classification is poor
    Sir Henry Maine's classification:
    1. {Historic or evolutionary
    2. {Philosophic or recorded
    The difference between common law or legal law, etc.,
    The unwritten is usually more permanent than the written, which is a
        temptation to [the] dissatisfied
    Constitutions of Conversion or Creation
    Constitutions consist of
    Fundamental principles
    Organic principles
    Rules of procedure
    Constitutions are essential – but are apt to become hindrances – subject to
        superstitious worship – then in reaction are swept away – a cycle
    Amendment provisions are almost all the same
    –Two-thirds vote – of both houses
    –Some form of local or personal referendum

[On page 53-A:

    In Political Science we have the difficulty of terms which remain the same
        – while changing meaning.
    –We are inclined to use the word "Democracy" to represent all that is good.

We are inclined to classify everything as good or bad according to its similarity or dissimilarity to our own customs and ideas.

We are having some difficulty in getting away from these old-fashioned – clumsy – ideas of government.]

Government
Socratic classification
1. Monarchy
2. Aristocracy
3. Democracy

Greek idea
–Government almost identified with knowledge
  1. Perfect knowledge – ideal – no sanctions
  2. Imperfect knowledge – necessity of laws – observed through loyalty
  3. Ignorant government – enforced by laws – no loyalty
    Tyranny – oligarchy, demagogy

Aristotle's classification
–First, on a basis of function
1. Monarchy
2. Aristocracy
3. Polity
–A conservative – believed in aristocracy
 –Thought monarchy represented oriental despotism
 –Thought oligarchy (rule of many) and democracy were bad

Separation of Powers
–Aristotle's division
 –Deliberative
 –Magisterial (executive)
 –Judicial
Middle Ages
 –Had lost idea of advantages of separation until we come to Bodin
Cromwellian Protectorate made a definite separation between judicial and legislative

[On page 54-A:

Separation of powers was a result of need to divide the powers of an autocrat – then to found a principle on which to justify that
 "In my own country."

1. In practice, clear-cut divisions are almost impossible.
2. Even if carried out, they are <u>not</u> guarantees of liberties.
3. Possibility of so <u>balancing</u> the divided powers that the necessary <u>drive</u>, directing power, is lacking
   –as might be said to be true in U.S.]

Separation between judicial and legislative
Blackstone
–There can be no private <u>liberty</u> where all powers are vested in one man or body
Given fullest expression in French and American constitutions
–Massachusetts Constitution, 1780
  –No "law" without separation
–French Declaration of Rights
  –No Constitution without separation
This principle, when examined, is found not to be so effective as these statements would lead us to believe
–President of U.S. – has veto power over legislative
–Senate of U.S. – has power over President in treaty and appointments
–All manner of conventions, etc.
–In England
  –The administrative departments are issuing legislative enactments – true in U.S. also [Double vertical lines in margin alongside first phrase.]
There are no clear-cut divisions in existence
  –Tendency to break down the existing divisions
  –In interest of <u>efficiency</u>
Plato's classification – by function
–A growth of government
–Rule of Reason – ideocracy
–Rule of war – timocracy
–Rule of wealth – plutocracy
–Rule of all – democracy
–Rule of one – autocracy
<u>Epicurean</u> classification
–Under influence of new atomic and astronomic theories – a <u>cycle</u> of government – closed
<u>Stoics</u>
–Didn't like the closed cycle
–Went back to the <u>growth</u> theory
Here the history of the growth of the idea of government stops – a break which lasts until modern times

–Not until <u>Locke</u>, do we find the distinction again made between state and
  government
–[Locke] – many, few, or one
–Rousseau
–Aristocracy
  –Natural
  –Hereditary
  –Elected (preferred this)
1. (Monarchy) princely or priestly government – theocracy – belongs to the past
2. Popular government
   a. Parliamentary and Party government
   b. Presidential or Personal government
   c. Professional government
–Present governments
3. Pluralist governments
   a. Class dictatorship
   b. Council government, or corporate government
–Belong to the future

Functions of government
1. Legislative
2. Executive
3. Judicial
4. Economic

[On page 56-A:

Popular government – <u>counting</u> heads instead of <u>breaking</u> them.
Gierke – popular government developed out of recognition of right of
  sovereignty and right of self-government in any functional or local organism.]
2. Popular Government
   –Has grown from two causes
   (a) Revolt or rebellion – against princely or priestly rule
   (b) Racial characteristics – indigenous in racial history
   a. Two schools of thought about government
      –One, that government is a good thing
        –Includes the bigger men in political philosophy
        –Hobbes, Mill, Bentham, Locke, Laski
      –Another school – that government is a bad thing
        –Interesting, but not as important

–Plato (very like modern Russian Communists)
–Bunyon – St. Simon, Louis Blanc
–Anarchists – extreme form of individualists
–Bakunin
–Are mainly idealistic rebels

b. In Anglo-Saxon history there is a strong tradition of popular government
  –Tendency to ignore principles, concentrate entirely on practice or proce-
  dure
    –We imprison socialist philosophers while leading the world in eco-
    nomic–evolutionary–socialism
  –Capacity for compromise – absolutely necessary for popular government
  –Americans are more anxious for conformity or uniformity than Britons
  –British stress liberty – Americans stress equality
  –Fraternity is weak in both cases
–Gierke – right of self-government
  Wycliff – Christian socialist 1250–
  –"Government of the people, for the people, by the people"
  [In margin: root of the theory/Wycliff]
–Dewey – popular government not an alternative, is an idea of community
  life; itselt – an ideal, clear consciousness of community life in all its
  complications
–Forms a connecting definition between early German theories and future
  pluralist theories

[On page 57-A:

  Rousseau – romantic sentiment – cynical realism
  French Revolution – not a revolt against property – but against privilege
  When is public opinion, public – and when merely opinion
  [Diagram: four concentric circles; labeled, from center outward: control,
  cooperating body, consenting body, conflict]

  Rousseau – popularized popular government
  –Was considered very radical
  –Social Contract
  –Based on a deficient interpretation of history, and faulty psychology
  –Succeeded in impressing on the mind of Europe that the Republic was the
    only form of logical government
  –Was not original – like Marx
  –Social Contract from Locke
  –General Will from Diderot

–Separation of power from Montesquieu

–Political economy from Physiocrats

–Believed in rights of property as most important right in the civil state

–Representative government is not popular government – still a surrender

   –Accepted representative government, as a necessary means toward developing full popular government

   –Was for decentralization, devolution, small states, local government [In margin alongside this line: reactions against his time]

–Distinguished between state and government – reserved sovereignty for the state

Popular government today – made up of four elements

1. Control
2. Cooperation, public opinion, active
3. Consent
4. Conflict – unconstitutional bodies

[See diagram with four concentric circles, above.]

Criticism of Democracy

   Liberty, Equality and Fraternity

Equality – "all men are created equal – endowed by their creator with certain inalienable rights – life, liberty and pursuit of happiness"

   Criticism

–Life needs food, warmth, security

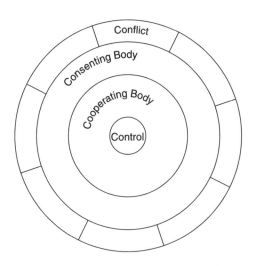

–Happiness – no possibility of equality of this

–All men are not created equal

–Race, color, circumstances of birth

Even in the first wave of enthusiasm for democracy – equality – it was not very well established

–Little suffrage

–Not incorporated into U.S. Constitution

–All our societies are founded on recognition of inequality – in varying degrees

–An equality of opportunity

–Only logical definition

–Right to relationship between service and satisfaction

Liberty – traditional view is pretty negative – an absence of restraint – Habeas Corpus

–Post-war writing defines it otherwise

–As protection

–As something positive and progressive – not fixed

–No positive liberty possible without equality

–Liberty must be looked for, not in terms of individuals but in terms of groups

[Single vertical line in margin alongside preceding line.]

–Manual laborer cannot be put on same plane as manager

–But the laborer's group can be put on a plane with the manager's group

–Relative equality

[On page 59-A:

Fraternity – a certain form of communism of food and lodging – expediency

–Takes on a form of ethical love

(Probably took place the other way round)]

–By giving groups equality, we have given the individual equality

–He can express himself through his group very effectively

–Liberty is the positive power of doing and enjoying something worthwhile in common with others. – Green

–Liberty is capacity for continuous initiative, an approach open to all to have the use of creative activity.

The region in which liberty is sought has changed.

–In the last century we were seeking it in politics – a revolt against privilege

–In this century we are seeking it in economics – a revolt against property

–A shift of objective

The pursuit of liberty has become one for economic equality – rather than for political equality

Fraternity
–Seems to have a double origin
a. Expediency – political
b. Ethics – religious
–First appears in Totemism
–Is always cropping up in every institution
–The normal development is to become a ruling caste, then a conservative group – communism?
–Representation based on religion

[On page 60-A:

Religion – whatever is not reason in one's mind [Single vertical line in margin alongside this line.]
Representation of Reason vs Religion]
Religion in Democracy
How far has the church affected representation?
–World ruled by two powers – Church and State – [after] 400 A.D.
–St. Augustine 420 A.D. – theory of double popular government

Celestial State	Earthly State
–Kingdom of God	–Great Brigandage
–Jerusalem	–Babylon

–This dualism survived throughout the Middle Ages
–Is found in many institutions
 –Limited ideas of private property
  –Pure Christianity is against private property
  –As Christian Socialism, today
 –Representation of religion was based on conscience
  –Impossible to base that on coercion
   –Without running into cruelty – then collapse
   –As did happen, and St. Augustus found
–Gregory VII – 1075
 –Asserted authority of church in temporal affairs
 –Got out of his proper sphere, into realm of rule of reason
 –Began century-long dispute between Church and State
 –As this duel developed, the principle of representation disappeared on both sides
 –Because duel of dictatorships – both destroying former evidences of democracy

–St. Thomas Aquinas
–Tried to clean up matters
–Without a combination of Church and State, the church would inevitably
   become tyrannical
–The church accomplished a victory and began its downfall – became divided
   in itself

[On page 61-A:

   Result of a Representation of Reason is an equitable government
   Result of a Representation of Religion is an ethical government]

Phillip Augustus Boniface 800 A.D. – had declared himself Emperor and Pope
   Church failed in its last battle
–Divided between Clericals and Congregationalists
–And divided by the Great Schism
   –Popes in Rome and Athens
   –A wholly repulsive thought
–The Black Death – 1350 – half of population of Europe died
   –Result – democracy of Europe had a new power in its hands – their own
      scarcity
   Conciliatory councils, 15th century
   Breaking up of Europe into national churches
   Papacy stopped democratic tendency – asserting absolute autocracy of the
      Papacy
   Thus the church lost its chance for representation of religion
   –No universality
   –No democracy

Reform churches developed a certain representation of religion combined in
   varying degrees with the representation of reason
Reformation – keynote in <u>Lutheranism</u>
–Which diverted the Reformation from its first democratic form (under
   Wycliff, etc.)
   –To a frankly middle or upper class representation
   –Wide powers of private property
–It is not an essential element in history that the church has always been
      conservative – but a result of faulty representation of religion [Single ver-
      tical line alongside in margin.]
Representation of Reason [versus] Representation of Religion
   Peculiar effect of change between the balance

Illustrated by France
Revolution was anti-religious – was stopped by the church
Up to the [Franco-Prussian] War, 1870, France was rationalist – anti-religious
–After [German] annexation of Alsace-Lorraine – both very Catholic
–Gave the Church another base
–Today the Church is supporting a Home Rule Policy
Great Britain
–A combination and compromise
–A State church and non-conformist
–The Church of England is very nearly in a state of revolution
–Two movements in the Church of England
  –One for unification with outside
    –Occasioned by mutual loss of vitality [?]
    –For putting the democracy it once had back into effect
  –The other for separating the Church from the State
  –Disestablishment is very near
    –Would come about immediately if it were not for the question of endowments
    –Prayer Book controversy has reached the end
Italy
Conflict between Populist Party – Was eliminated by the Fascists
But when they came into power, they found they had to make friends among former enemies
  –Three legs of Fascism today – itself, Syndicalism, Catholicism
  –Made treaty with church – Roman Catholicism became again the State religion with considerable concessions by government
  –Papacy has new status as a sovereign state – on an international basis – not any more, purely Italian

[On page 63-A:

[A] General butcher's bill [is] to be paid in any fighting revolution.
Our word big, comes from Russian word [God] (Bog) – accounting for "bogey"]

Russia
The representation of religion was autocratic and corrupt – as bad as Czarism – very close alliance between church and state
Revolution was directed as much at church as at state – causing the large butcherings at first

The old church set itself definitely against the efforts of the Communists
to sanitize its practices
–Peasant's summer marching – lice
–Kissing the icons
Then (about five years ago) a representation of reason
–But a swing toward Protestantism
–Was attempted to be stopped – any activity today, versus church
Now a curious mixture of representation of reason and religion – for
Communism is becoming a religion – of a low sort – embryonic

A. Parliamentary Government
   Representative government – executive represents the legislature which
      represents the people
   Responsible government – executive is responsible to the legislature which
      is responsible to the people
   –Principle of responsibility developed historically out of the principle of
      representation (which was a result of the struggle between the people
      and the prince
   –Both England and U.S. are tending toward personal government – a result
      of the Great War period
      –Wilson – personal dictatorship
      –Committee dictatorship in England [Single vertical line in margin
         alongside these three lines]
   Parliamentary Government – principle was first established in England in
   1688
   –This principle is of Anglo-Saxon origin
   –Though adopted all over Europe
      –In France it has been upset three times
      –In Spain it has been upset a variety of times
   –It dominates our minds very much, but has always had critics.
   –Suffrage – it has been becoming universal
      –Grew up on principle of no taxation without representation
         –But shifted in early times to no representation without taxation
            –Property qualification
         –No underlying, general principle – but tendency toward one man, one
            vote
      –Parliamentary system now, is always on a basis of regional representation
      –Make this as equitable as possible
      (–Should suffrage be on basis of functional representation?)
      a. Single-number constituency
      b. Several-number (larger) constituency
         –Scrutin de lisle

[On page 65-A:

Single number system – gives a strong government
Multiple number system – gives an equitable government]

a. Principle of pendulum reaction
b. Various systems of multiple
  –Were introduced because public opinion thought it offensive that minorities should be completely unrepresented
  –Various systems of giving minorities representation

(1) <u>Proportional Representation</u>
  –<u>Have system</u> – <u>single transferable vote</u> – regional
  –Must have at least three members
  –Candidates marked in order of preference
  –Quota obtained by dividing total number of votes by number of vacancies
  Basis of second system is the <u>party</u> (recognized by government)
  –Each voter has as many votes as there are vacancies – give them to party lists
  –Same way of getting quota equal to total number of seats for each party
  –The party apportions these seats among the candidates
  –There lies the weakness, too much in hands of party
  –Proportional representation has been widely adopted in Europe – is most efficient in highly educated countries
(2) Limited Vote
  –Fewer votes than there are members [Single vertical line in margin alongside this line]
  –At least three candidates – only two votes (or 5–3)
  –Only gives representation to the larger minorities
(3) Cumulative Vote
  –A certain number of votes
  –May <u>all</u> be given to one candidate
  –This <u>over</u>-represents the minorities, wastes many votes
(4) Second Ballot
  –Devised by English to keep them from thinking too much
  Plural Voting
  –One man, one vote not agreed with
  –Double vote for men of intelligence – one for university
  Waiting Votes
  –One for residence, one for business

Compulsory Voting
–Penalty for not voting
–Has been taken up in Spain, Belgium and Australia
Postal Voting
–Register vote with postman

Criticism of Representative Government (Democratic)

–Democracy by representation
(1) Is not really representative
–Doesn't represent minorities
–Sometimes not even representing majority
–Man may change his Party after his election by a certain one [sic]
–Government may change its policy, after an election of men on another
    policy
–Doesn't represent man on any basis but regional – geographical not func-
    tional
–Representatives are selected by the Party – are professional, not popular
–Tends to become a representation of money – not of men – cost of elec-
    tion – giving up of work – perhaps non-payment – bond, etc.
These tendencies are attempted to be corrected by – Initiative, Referendum,
    Mandate (sending a man to Parliament with specific orders)

[On page 67-A:

Democracy – Progress of all under leadership of best. – Mazzini
Initiative and referendum attempt to revive aristocracy with democratic
machinery.]

(2) Is not Democratic
–Was begun as a way to collect taxes from the rich – autocratic in aim
–First people represented were landowners and rich – first area was shire
–Power of raising taxes became in time power to refuse to pay taxes
–Grew from a fiscal into a political institution
–That Parliament became democratic was, in its origin, almost an accident
 –Small borough knights were not put in same houses as Lords, etc.
–In 1688 – in England – the landed gentry got control of Parliament –
    representation on property
–Now – when the proletariat gets control, the basis must change to a
 –Representation on work
 –It is foolish to have workers represented on basis of property

–In so far as one has representatives, delegates to govern – there is not
democracy, but aristocracy (government of the best)
New Proposals
–Elect representatives by lot – a Jury for each problem
There is undoubted evidence of the decline of representative government
–Because of their incompetence and inefficiency
–Some changes already
–Men represent party only
–Never disagree
–Debate has become obsolete
–Veto of upper house is being taken away
–In England – any change of government means a general election
–Great political upheaval
–Much expense
–A growing up of interior "Closet System" of executive rule

[On page 68-A:
United States
Political System
President – Supreme Court –Senate – House – Constituency – Sovereign People

Economic System
Republican – Democratic Parties
Conservative Capital 6 Majority Representation of wealth
Progressive Labor 2 Minority Representation of Work
[Meaning of Arabic numbers is unclear]

Diagram with four concentric circles and eight spokes from center. Width
of band indicated by A, B, C, and D on vertical spoke. Eight pie-sliced-
shaped areas between spokes numbered clockwise, I through VIII, commencing at 6 pm, with two areas in each quarter. Names of I through IV,
together identified as Parliamentary, are I. Conservatism, II. Coalitionism,
III. Radicalism, and IV. Laborism. Names of V through VIII, together
identified as Social Democracy, are V. Socialism, VI. Communism, VII.
Fascism, and VIII. Dictatorship.

Before War 5 Empires, 17 Monarchies, 3 Republics
After War 1 Empire, 11 Monarchies (no absolute), 16 Republics
Today [1930] – one-third of Republics have become dictatorships]

The Parliamentary system is based on the Party system – group-party government is coming in

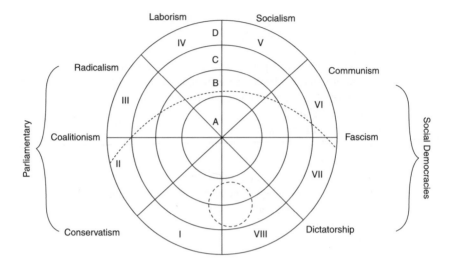

–Real Party government is breaking down
  –Into groups
  –Every real issue cuts right across the party lines
  –Is tending to get a class basis – being replaced by class organizations
  –No party is engaged in Foreign Affairs (?) – at best, a tendency
B. One result is <u>Dictatorship</u> – personal government
       a. Reactionary   b. Revolutionary
       c. Personal   d. Class
    a. A relapse back to old autocratic government
       –Because of failure of democratic government
       –A means of carrying on in a crisis [Single vertical line alongside in
         margin]
       –Romans used to set up a dictator whenever there was something difficult
         to be done
       –Jugo-Slavia
       [In margin: (Machiavelli →?)]
       –Republican
       –Dictatorship of a prince – <u>provisional</u>
    b. Revolutionary
       –Today is only associated with class dictatorship
       –Proclaims itself to be merely provisional – as Russia
       The old idea of a straight line of parties
       Left----------Right

–This is absolute. The circle has come [into being] [see above for
   circle]

[On page 69-A: "True liberalism is radicalism." – George Young]

   Italians leave the whole of the right side organized
   In England – a fighting front between Communists and Fascists
   Russia has V and VI organized
   Germany: II, III, parts of I and IV
The cycle goes inevitably from I through all the others to VIII
–Is this a closed circle?
–No, a spiral, cyclical, but each step higher than that same step the timebefore
[Single vertical line in margin alongside preceding three lines. Beyond it, a
   double-lined rising spiral.]
Always one circle of control – A
Then a circle of interested citizens – B
–Cooperation
Then a circle of uninterested citizens – C
–Individualists
 –Consent
 –Conflict with them necessary to the Party
Then a circle of factions of opposition –D
–Conflict
If the circle of control is not in the center, everything is askew
–As Russia was, under Czar, with control in dictatorship, near rim.
–A great section of conflict – Revolution bound to come
 C. Judicial Government
–Government spreads its authority through the justices
–In England the Justices of the Peace were the first men to administrate
   locally on a grant from the central government
–The Judiciary still retains some of its original representative character
 –Its method of appointment reflects the "mood" of the government of the
   country [Single vertical line alongside in margin]
Three methods of election of Judges
 1. Popular election –democratic
   –Has become party election
   –Short term, possibility of reelection
    –Close to people [arrow pointing to "short term"], responsible [arrow
       pointing to "reelection"]
   –Has been greatly attacked
   –Is American principle, also Russian

2. Parliamentary election
   –A compromise
   –Followed in Switzerland
   –A break in the principle of separation of power
   –Government selects judges – thus controls the interpretation as well
      as the passage of laws
3. Professional appointment
   –Best for getting legal competence
   –Tends to make the judicial chair lose all social contact with the
      community
   –Term of appointment for life or with age limit

Administrative justice
–Regulates relationship between the state and the individual citizen – special
   courts and special body of law
–Tends to favor the state – but is better than the alternative of having <u>no</u> way
   to get justice from the state
–As in U.S., England

The tendency toward judicial Government is growing
–Along with growing power of interpretation of the Supreme Courts
–Building up law by judicial decision and interpretation
–It is pretty true that judicial law is bad law, judicial government, bad law.
–Throws the weight on the side of Conservatism

[On page 71-A:

India – real sovereignty in Indian Civil Service
         nominal sovereignty in King-in-England
–Judicial official combines Judicial, Legislative, Executive functions
–Tendency is to establish a Civil Service responsible to an Indian democracy
   –Principle of representation was already recognized before the War – but
      not responsibility
   –Police and justice still [word indecipherable]
[Diagram two outer concentric circles, similar to above; but now on north-
west to southeast axis are three close small circles, the central one being at
the central point of the two outer concentric circles. Horizontal line drawn
through mid-point of entire diagram (also the mid-point of central of three
close circles). Area above horizontal line labeled Progressive, that below,
Conservative. Three small circles labeled, from NW to SE, Civil Service
Ruling Class, Ideal, and Old Ruling Class]

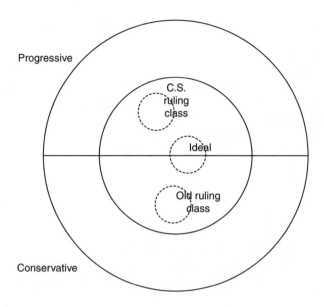

D. Professional Government
  –Government by a civil service
  –Developed out of feudal and ecclesiastic systems
    –Private secretary in England
    –Departments
      –Inclined to be conservative with age
      –Make their own policy
      –A means for contact between people and government
  French Civil Service
  –Partial origin in Revolution
  –Conservative
  –Collectively rebellious
  German Civil Service
  –Bismarckian
  –One cause of breakdown of Revolution (1919)
  American Civil Service
  –Partisan in origin
  –Professional, as a later origin
    –[Theodore] Roosevelt
    –Developing along this line today

–Partisan Civil Service
Boosts partisan pendulum
Professional Civil Service
  –At first retains the pendulum and gives a continuity of policy
  –But soon comes to <u>control</u> the party policy
a. Covenanted Civil Service   b. Uncovenanted
  –Irresponsible
    –Governing without being directly responsibility to any other authority –
      as India [In margin: Security of tenure, etc.]
  –Responsible
    –As in all Western countries
    –Tendency is to increase the importance and power of this form of
      govrnment
    –Represents the modern ruling class
    –Recruited from the ranks by examination
    –Its power depends on its competence and incorruptibility
    –British Civil Service has gone about as far as it can safely – in power
      –America can progress one hundred years yet
      –In Germany it is the principal power in the country, still

[On page 72-A:

During London Navel Conference – the professional government of navel
chiefs prevented any suggestion of "disarming by example" – though public opinion would have backed it –Professional government invading the
realm of Cabinet Government.
Democracy does not come by recruiting only from the ranks.]

b. Uncovenanted Civil Service
  –Definitely employed by the State
  –State has become largest employer of labor in many countries
  –What position do such employees have?
    –A middle region between private employers and Civil Servants half way
      between contracted and covenanted employee
c. Future of Civil Service
  There has always been an opposition to bureaucracy – by democracy
  –Came to a partial end in 1848 (England)
  –Tradition still survived
  –Transition from Professional Bureaucracy to Professional Democracy
    –Representation in Professional Government to replace power lost by
      Parliament – as in Foreign Office in England

–Becoming responsible, autonomous, closer to public opinion [Single
  vertical line alongside in margin]
–If it can be done for covenanted employees – it can be done for the
  uncovenanted
–Leads to guild socialism and pluralism
Strike in Civil Service is very important [In margin: In Egypt, in France]
–Prohibited by Adamson Act in U.S.
–Police strike also effective – usually treated by discharging strikers –
  hiring new men – undermines efficient discipline – change from a civil
  police to a military police
Postal workers have struck.
Line between covenanted and uncovenanted civil service is disappearing

[On page 73-A:

New forms of government – Personal, Professional, Social
Trade Unionism in U.S. is still on craft union basis.
Trade Unionism in Europe is on an industrial union basis.
In the police state, the shadow of the executioner is still the sanction of the
  executive.
Ideas are stronger than institutions
–There are no real facts, there are only forces.
State as policeman is giving way to the state as producer.
                    Walter Lippmann]

Social Democracy – being developed in all states.
–As larger than political democracies of last century
–Deal with groups, rather than individuals
–New self-interest is not an aggregate of private interests, but an association of
  public interests
[Single vertical line in margin alongside preceding two lines.]
–Machinery of our present democracy is out of date.
–Present-day society is organized on a class-war basis for the protection of
  class interests – proletariat versus property
–Instead of on a basis of the propagation of social interests
  –Organization of each camp on its own interest – both are awake and armed
  –Employers using present political system
  –Workers becoming more and more centralized, have given up hope for
    political action, have take up syndicalism
  –Class consciousness-military
  –Claims to be working for the community, also – moral

–Balance of power must either end in civil war and ruin, or in <u>cooperation</u>
–Has been achieved in Russia and Italy by <u>revolution</u>
–Is being achieved in other countries through <u>evolution</u> and devolution
  –State becoming a producer – public utilities
  –Industry acquiring political power
–Proletariat had to fight for
  1. <u>Recognition</u>
    –Of trade unions
    –Through legal decision
    –As government organs – immunities
  2. Representation
  3. Reconstruction
    –Regulation, nationalization, reconstruction

[On page 74-A:

J.D.R. – a trustee of the Lord
[Henry] Ford – a trustee for his employed producers
  –Responsible to the consumer
–Benevolent despotism – not to be relied on for positive reconstruction
Private shareholder is becoming little more than a bondholder with mere money claim – no other right.]

Regulation of evils of capitalism
  Regulation
  –Of industry by the State – police inspection
  –Making the industry responsible for regulating itself
  –Will restore complete public control over production – goal
  Rationalization [British term for "efficiency"]
  –Originates in a change of point of view as to production
    –Once looked on as a search for profit
    –Coming to be looked on as a public service
    –Progress is going slow in political lines, fast in economic – in U.S. – opposite in Europe
  –Change in attitude of public mind – profiteer, etc., looked down on, now
  Reconstruction
  –Three forces are building up this new system – not yet named permanently
  –Equity
    –Built up by discussion as to rate of tax on social groups
  –Efficiency
    –Confederation of efficiency under force of international competition

–For self-protection
–Private enterprise is <u>Wasteful</u>
–Manpower – unemployment – reservoir of labor
–Resources, etc.
–Exigency
–Progress and prosperity depend on consumption
–Not on the profits of a few, but on the purchasing power of the community as a whole
–Must be reckoned in terms of work not wealth

[On page 75:

Dualism between capital and labor – property versus proletariat
Pragmatism – a mental procedure, based on deduction, experience, and facts. – William James
Democracy – government by the corrupt few of the incompetent many. – G. B. Shaw]

Socialism is a reaction, a swinging back to the pendulum to the collectivist state which existed a few centuries ago.
–A reaction to the individualist liberalism of a century ago (England) – 50–25 years ago (U.S.)
–Various schools of the new movement are all socialistic
1. – Marx – Holy War
2. – Owen, communist, but began cooperative movement
3. – <u>Christian Socialists</u> – Morris, Kingsley, Tawney, Landsbury
4. – Aesthetic Socialists – Ruskin, Crane
5. – <u>Pragmatic Schools</u> – <u>modern</u>
   a. – Fabian collectivism
   b. – Conservatist
   c. – Constructionist
   d. – Fascist corporations
a. Fabian Collectivism
   –Transfer to state of control of all politics, production and society
   (1) – G. B. Shaw (Protestant)
     –Redistribution of property – power – equal wages – large taxes
   (2) – Sidney and Beatrice Webb
     –Philanthropic movement
     –Said economic democracy must go through the same development as political democracy had gone through [In margin: <u>Radical</u> and <u>reconstructive</u>]

–Fourfold path
   –Public control, over capital, land, exploitation
   –Against ownership
   –Government supervision
   –Care of dependants of society
   –Redistribution of wealth by taxation
–Were first Utilitarians, then Utopists, then Universalists
      "Proposed Constitution for the Socialist British Republic"
   –Social and political parliaments – supreme court
      "Searchlight of science is going to be the cornerstone of society"
–Army of officials was a bad element of Fabian suggestions
b. Conservatist – British Labor Party – German Social Democratic Part
   –A contradiction between various schools
      –Very British in the illogicality of its theory
      –Based on Darwin and Spencer [In margin: "Socialism in its own time"
         – normal growth]
   –Regulation and socialism as inevitable organic growth of society –
      pendulum
   –Three periods – Macdonald
      –Socialism and society – biological [In margin: – Free Trade]
      –Socialism and government – biological
      –Socialism – cultural and constructive
   –Have no use for dualism of Webbs
      –Single political parliament
         –Reformed but not reconstructed
   Socialism is a growth of society not an uprising of a class [Single vertical
      line in margin alongside this line]
   –Possibility of a National Economic Council
   –Liberal and laissez-faire
c. Constructionist-Active
      [In margin: "Socialism in our own time" – living it]
   –Independent Socialist Party in Germany
   –Comes into conflict with Conservatist school on question of Pace
   –A definite program – propaganda
   –Not for class war – but want conflict rather than cooperation
   –Definite action for their party
   –Put capitalism out of business – control passed to public organization
   –Opposed to tariff – but favors commerce by state trading, protecting
      national industry

d. Corporative Fascist School

All these schools are trying to <u>reconstruct</u> the <u>unitary sovereign state</u> – by cooperation, etc., between capital and labor

–This tendency, in its extreme form, is found in Fascist State

–Has pragmatism in common to all

–But is as far in advance of British schools as they are of conservatism

–Mussolini found Italy in same state as Machiavelli saw it

–Unitary State – the objective

   –Based on Fascism

   –Based on Syndicalism

–Fascists are now a middle class dictatorship

   –But started as proletariat uprising

   –Became so, almost by accident

–Corporative state is not a political democracy

   –Italy now a middle class dictatorship maintaining a truce between property and proletariat until a new social democracy develops

[On page78-A:

Fascism is Nietzschean, nationalist

"We have left imbecilic democracy – come to Fascism."]

Pluralist Schools

–Pluralism a polity and a philosophy

–As philosophy – an attempt to give to each <u>group</u> in society that is capable of crowd psychology or group will, a proportionate share in the system of state sovereignty [Single vertical line in margin alongside this statement]

–Trying to create a corporative state composed of citizens incorporated in respect of their corporation in the community.

–A philosophic reaction against unitary sovereignty or monist state

–Sovereignty centers in King-in-Parliament – unitary

–Distribute sovereignty politically through Federalism

–N.B. <u>The Unitary State</u> – Austin

–There can be no rights except the right of the state

–It is the source of all liberty and superior of all law

–A convenient working theory for statesmen and jurists

–But being attacked by various men

   –Gierke and Maitland – no historical foundation for it in Anglo-Saxon history

   –Economic criticism – Hobhouse and Hobson

   –Philosophic – Dewey

–Psychologic – Graham Wallas
–They are all to that extent pluralist
–Political side of pluralism
–Concessions by state to such bodies as the A. F. of L. [American Federation
    of Labor] – Chamber of Commerce (National), Anti-Saloon League, etc.
    – are evidence of pluralism
–Theories of pluralism
  –Most prominent – Harold <u>Laski</u>
  –Pluralism has a good historical descent
    –Althusius – Locke
  –Thus pluralism is sought [as] a solution of political and social problems
    by federation and redistribution of sovereignty on a basis of function
    [Single vertical line in margin alongside second half of this sentence.]
  –"Pluralist world is like a federal republic"
  –Hope to revitalize the political and economic life of society
  –No political democracy can be real that is not a reflection of an economic
    democracy
    –Attacks unitary state
    –Over-concentration of power in an organ causes disease
   –Pluralism becomes a natural reform to redistribute political power of
    the state in proportion to the economic power of each organization
  –Corporate bodies on a national scope should each be given a real
    responsibility to the state in respect to their own national function
  –Development of such redistribution of power approaches real democ-
    racy
  –Aims at social democracy by devolution of power [Single vertical line in
    margin alongside this line.]
 –Laski's philosophy has had two periods
  –First period, he is dogmatic and destructive, extreme
   –"Theory of legal sovereignty is worthless"
  –Second period, constructive, compromises between his theory and state
    of affairs
  –[Laski,] Grammar of Politics, 1925
   –Departs from early extremism
   –Becomes a friend of parliamentary institutions
   –Shifts objective – from distribution downwards – to devolution (of
    sovereignty) upwards – to a super state – League of Nations
   –Leaves pure pluralism and returns to Fabianism (reliance on central
    control, and civic conscience)

–Can accept a sovereign state on new basis (quotation opposite [On page 80-A: "If the state speaks not for some but for all, it will decide not for a few but for the whole." [Locke]])

–Tends to <u>reject</u> vocational and proportional representation, dual parliaments, or Guild Socialism

–State structure elaborate – an economic democracy coordinates in a central state, with a super-state over it [Single vertical line in margin alongside this line.]

–Left group will, and came to a general will – as Rousseau

–Pluralism also set forth, in another form, by G.D.H. Cole – wild, corporate

–Guild Socialism

–Starts on a different basis than Laski who has workers organized on a syndicalist basis

–Guild Socialism has them organized on a basis of craftsmanship

–Gives value to worker's necessity of self-expression

–A more mediaeval complexion

–Closely connected with Dewey's instrumentalism

–Sets up democracy on a basis of occupational representation – through self-governing organs of production [Single vertical line alongside in margin.]

–Went through development also-

(1) – Began with a dogmatic, destructive doctrine, went to a constructive, compromising one

–Drew near Laski and Webbs in their last periods

–Was a dualist – divided power between a consumers' parliament, and a Guild Congress of producers

–Central control in a supreme council.

–Condemned Fabian state property – thought collectivism overstressed consumption rather than production – the other basis of community

[On page 81-A:

Syndicalism – dualism based on labor organized as a whole, and capital organized as a whole

–Labor <u>power</u> in threat of a general strike – a fighting faith

–Establish a balance of power – ultimately give syndicalists supreme power]

(2) – Began to view Parliament as a great commune, with vocational representation

–It allows man as many votes as he has interests

–Production organized in national guilds
–Consumption organized in classes, with council
–Like Russian Communist theory in its foundations
(3) – A moving back from pluralism to a unitary state
–Coming back to pragmatic solutions
–Objections (to Guild Socialism)
–Over-elaborate – expects too much of voter
–Represents rivalries rather than relationships
–Too revolutionary – wouldn't work in competition with other, simpler
systems
–Practical application is found in Russian Communism
–Made an effort to represent every relationship and every group will
–Pluralism maintained in constitutional state structure – Central authority
maintained by the class dictatorship through Communist Party –
outside constitutional structure
–A pragmatic result of the War, not in original theory
General Notes on Pluralism – application, etc.
–Great Britain
–Money power has been in conflict with manpower since 1906
–Policy is defined and determined by an interplay of economic groups
–Education controlled by ecclesiastics, credit and currency by banking
interests
–Their various associations must be organized – represented in and
controlled by the government
–Extra-constitutional organizations have wide power, politically – Lloyds
[of London]
–Tendency for pluralist schools to compromise and become more dem-
ocratic
–United States
–More extra-constitutional organization with wide powers – influence
–Prohibition groups
–Parties have been given definite constitutional status – by primaries
–Chambers of Commerce
–Development of pluralism is economic
–Two tendencies in pluralist movement – evolutionary and revolutionary
[Single vertical line in margin alongside this line.]
–Also a tendency to personal government – Walter Lippmann
–Present system of government is a mechanism – the constitution a
mechanism which prevents motion
–Not a vital organ

–Democracies have become machines, are dead

–The only life in present-day government is in lobbies, business rings, etc.

–Which cut across and ignore the government machinery.

–Evil, because out of sight and supervision

–Becoming corrupt – leading to revolution

–But, "you can't mechanize a benevolent despotism"

–We are going through an evolution rather than a revolution

–Old constitutions are thrown in melting pot to <u>re</u>-crystallize in new forms

[On page 83-A: Distinction between men and moral persons (corporations).]

–Pluralism from the legal point of view

   –Unity of sovereign state goes back to Bodin, gets full expression in Austin, philosophical expression in Hegel

      –Can all be traced to political conditions of the day, and reactions

   –Sovereign state was justified on utilitarian lines

   –Now it is questioned – represents control of a minority, so can't work for greatest good of <u>all</u>

–Hobbes' and Austin's philosophy connected

   –All legal organs and associations live <u>only within</u> the limits of the license conferred by the state

      –Corporations exist as a figment only

   –Were this true, there could be no plural state, one of only legal fiction

   –But legal principle that corporations couldn't commit torts was idiotic – they can

   –Modern jurisprudence recognizes this – corporations are real entities

   –<u>Ultra vires</u> doctrine is source

      –Corporations are responsible for their share in political and economic developments acted <u>outside</u> their charters.

      –Cannot be limited to their charters – physiologically

      –British chartered companies created empires outside their charters

      –Group life and will of corporations are a form of popular sovereignty

   –"The parts of society are self-sufficient parts, real" – Laski

   –"It is a destructive trait of mediaeval doctrine that within every human group is to be recognized an aboriginal right of the group taken as a whole" – Gierke

–Conflict between unitary sovereign state and pluralist theories

   –So far as our Anglo-Saxon growth is concerned, we seem to have been pluralist until very recent times

   –Our recent unitarianism is from the mechanistic point of view of the Latins

–Arguments against Pluralism

1. Revolutionary in aspect, tending toward an upset of the principal foundations of our democratic system
   –Anarchy with autocracy may be the direction of these revolutions
2. Because sources and sanctions of sovereignty are outside and beneath the law, it does not follow that doctrine of legal sovereignty has no value
3. Pluralism will not lead to Social Democracy, but to industrial feudalism
   –Bases of feudalism
   –Revival of states
     –Organization of classes
   –Russian society is a feudal-like organization
   –But, this is not definitely valuable as a condemnation

Italy – a revolutionized State
   –As [in] Russia – started along same lines
   –1920 – a Communist Revolution
   –Seizing farms and factories
   –[Had] No authority – a reaction

1922, March on Rome under Mussolini – middle class dictatorship
   –1924 – Murder of Mariatti (Workers Opposition to Fascism)
   –Seriously discredited Fascism
   –Was a turning point, Fascism tried to establish itself as more than a class dictatorship
   –1927 – Construction of the new Corporative State begun, is still going on
–Philosophy of Fascism
   –Attacked by enemies as Marxianism
     –Is based on doctrine of [blank space: Marx?], on class war
     –Is revolutionary and radical in motives and methods
       –Government by a minority
       –Proceeding by compromises with old forces
       –Costing Italy much less than the Revolution in Russia
         –Has had easier job
         –Not destroying one class
         –Not been invaded
   –Praised by friends as Mazzini-ism
   –Civic-conscience, religious
   –By impartial observers – Machiavellianism
     –Public opinion does not control government – government develops public opinion
   –Corporative state for social control
   –Pragmatism is also very important

Mussolini is not to be given too much emphasis – anyone who had taken the leadership would have followed same course.

Existence based on three concordats
–One with capitalism
–One with Catholicism
–One with collectivists (workers)

a. Capitalism
    –Strong nationalistic appeal
    –Very imperialistic
      –First shown in Roman Empire
      –Then in Church of Rome
      –Then Italian Renaissance
      –Now Fascism
    –Some look to make world conquest, others merely look to conquest of an idea
    –A certain inferiority complex may be traced in the loud proclamations of egoism
    –Weakness of a nation often shown in chauvinism
    –Has had an effect on the world already – Estonia, Spain, Germany 1923, England 1926

b. Catholicism
    –A strong Catholic party, was finally crushed by Fascism – but a link with Catholicism was needed
    –Concordat is a very fair deal
      –Roman Catholicism reestablished as State religion
      –Papacy a sovereign State – in full possession of the Vatican
      –Church reacquired property it had lost
      –Catholic religious education compulsory in schools
      –Gives up any organized part in politics
        –Renounces claim of temporal sovereignty over Papal States
        –Large payment of money by Fascists

c. Collectivism – Labor
    –Middle class dictatorship realized it could not continue supreme over laborers without a compromise
    –Built up the corporative system – eliminates the democratic Parliament practically
      –Candidates selected by Fascists, elected by the economic organizations

–Economic Corporative state
  –Strikes have been eliminated
  –Labor is being put under pressure to produce – successfully – has been
    partly bullied, partly bribed
  –Extra-constitutional, Fascist organization
    8,500,000 members
    1,000,000 active
    250,000 Fascist army – equals in size the regular army – which does not
      like Fascism
 –Actual Services of Fascism
  –Cutting off of immigration to U.S. leaves a surplus of ½ million yearly –
    putting new land under cultivation

[On page 87-A: Diagram

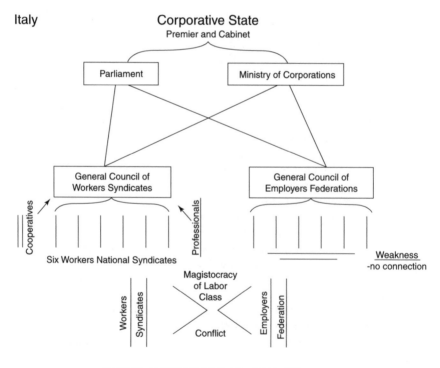

Magistocracy of labor to remove the class conflict

Application of Pluralism to Russia
–Russification given up at Revolution
–Federation was taken up
  –A federal system, surrounded by a ring of independent nations
  –<u>Home rule</u> to peoples in each federated country within the U.S.S.R.
  –While the Communist system puts more and more power in hands of central
    government – yet no conflict
–Central government controls the whole economic life – has right of amending
  constitutional acts – greater power of federal control
–Moscow is the capital of both USSR and RSFSR [Russian Socialist
  Federation of Soviet Republics]
–The U.S.S.R. – <u>claims</u> to be international – any country may join it
–The Red Army is an international army (though officered by Russians)

[On page 88-A: Diagrams]
  –A combination of an imperial system with an international system
  –The federal system <u>is</u> a propagandist system
    –An organ of self-growth
    –As Moldavia, an example to the Moldavians in Bessarabia

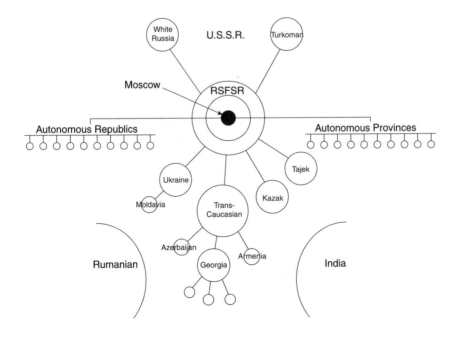

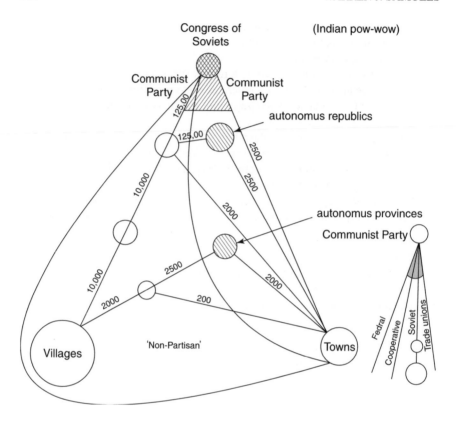

–As Kazak and Tajek – near Afghanistan, and influencial
–Two great imperial systems exist in world today
  –One the Russians
    –Built up in ten months
    –Pragmatic method
  –One the British
    –Built up in two centuries
    –Trial and error method
  –What the Russians have done in setting up the Trans-Caucasian unit –
    artificial, the British are going to have to do with India
Internal System
–Based on balance between town worker and village worker
–No balance between capital and labor (capital wiped out)

–Agricultural population about ten times as much as town population

–System of indirect representation

–People from villages are <u>filtered</u> through several congresses

–While town workers have <u>direct</u> representation in <u>each</u> congress

–Stands on four legs – federal, trade unions, Soviets, cooperatives

–Have tried to represent <u>every function</u> of the citizen – pluralism

    Culture

    Race

    Religion

–Countrymen represented through Federal legislature, consumer through cooperative legislature, region through Soviet, producer through trade-union

–There is a <u>one</u>-party system

–No authorized opposition

–Though this is promised as soon as threat of foreign war is removed

–Indirect election – frowned upon in all democratic systems – but seems to work perfectly all right when people are working together

[On page 89-A:

    Great Britain – Diagram of the real constitutional forces]

    Summary of Pluralism

    –Application of it to the actual constitutional structures of the various countries

     –Remarkable similarities

     –Of actual governing forces and factors

     –Though not of paper constitutions [Single vertical line in margin alongside preceding three lines.]

    –Great Britain

    –Federalism very nearly broke down in Canada 1840

    –Industrialism very nearly broke down with Chartists, 1848

    –Federalism again very nearly broke down with Civil War in Ireland, 1922

    –Industrialism again almost broken with <u>threatened</u> industrial civil war – 1926 – General Strike

    –Representative system is shown in ideal form – and as it really is – crumbling under the modern pressure

    –A federal system is slowly being built up, with a system of cooperation between capital and labor – within industry – which become two additional legs to the whole

    –Ruling class is necessary to hold the whole together – but must not become top-heavy

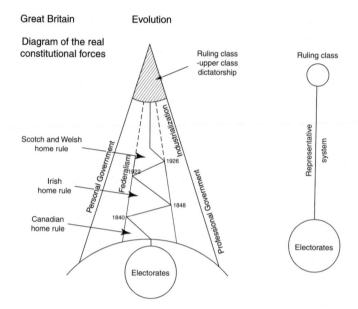

Great Britain   Evolution

Diagram of the real
constitutional forces

Ruling class
-upper class
dictatorship

Ruling class

Scotch and Welsh
home rule

Irish
home rule

Canadian
home rule

Personal Government

Federalism

Industrialization

1926

1922

1848

1840

Professional Government

Electorates

Representative
system

Electorates

[On page 90-A:

Diagram: Germany – Evolution

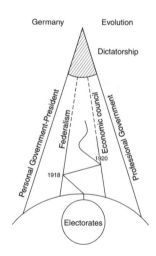

Germany   Evolution

Dictatorship

Personal Government-President

Federalism

Economic council

Professional Government

1920

1918

Electorates

Diagram: Italy – Revolution]

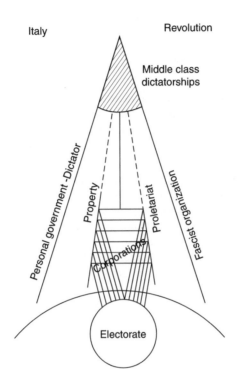

Germany

–New constitution 1918 – with all new gadgets – referendum – initiative – broke down

–1920 – collapse, rebuilt by the Economic Council in their Constitution – but not yet put into practice

–Personal government by very strong Hindenburg

–Professional government-civil service prevented Revolution of 1928 from going too far towards socialism

–A complete system of federalism built up

–And a complete industrial system on paper – at best

Italy

–System standing almost entirely on personal and Fascist legs

–Old representative system still exists at the top, but has lost all connection with the electorate

–Neo-Federal system – is a unitary state
–Two legs – property and proletariat
–Are unified by corporations or syndicates – on which the representative system
    stands

[On page 91-A: Diagram: Russia]

Russia
–Ruling class is so small it is a weakness
–Personal government involved is quite small – and very weak
–One leg very strong, other very weak – but any attempt to push over the system
    – onto its weak leg – would result in an immediate strengthening of that leg
    – to a dictatorship of a Napoleon
–Industrial leg represents citizen as a <u>producer</u>
–Federal leg – represents him according to his <u>culture</u>
–Soviet system represents <u>regional</u> interests
–Cooperative representative system is growing – will represent the citizen as a
    <u>consumer</u>
–Two outer legs are provisional in terms of years
–Four inner legs are provisional in terms of generations

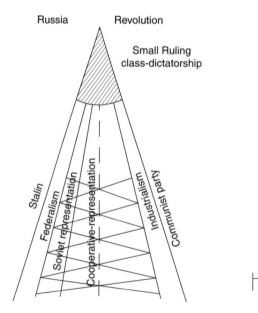

–Thus a new system for posterity is slowly being evolved – on an economic
   basis – only

Progress
–Nothing definite or absolute
–Is something entirely relative
–Early Greeks had no idea of progress – religious idea – idea of Golden Age
   in past
–Pythagoras – theory of a cycle,
   –Vulgar form of progress
   –History repeats itself
   –Same in Virgil – Eclogues
   –Marcus Aurelius – melancholy

[On page 92-A: Golden Age long delayed a conception of progress – giving idea
that all change was further corruption. French Revolution was born of French
exposition and American example.]

Stoics – straight line of progress – knowledge – discovery
Epicureans – came very near the closed cycle
Early Christians – Golden Age in past – and future
–Man was traveling between the two
Middle Ages – Machiavelli – revived the cycle idea – in from of the life cycle
of states
–Renaissance – poets
Freedom of science from religion
Bacon, Roger
–All his science had to conform to religion
–Progress was an escape from Anti-Christ
Bacon, Francis
–Progress was a betterment of the world
Then came the Utopias – following Francis Bacon
–Progress began to be brought down to the political field
Montesquieu
–Defined reason – set it against religion
–A doctrine of progress – heaven on earth
–A form of humanism
Voltaire – progress was substituted for providence
[In far margin alongside preceding line: Natural law/reason]
A later development – principles based not on utopias but on utilities
French Revolution

The Latest Development:
–The cycle theory develops into the spiral theory
–First discovered by an Italian – <u>Vico</u>
  –A cycle of four forms of government, but each turn was higher than the
    previous – didn't enable him to make practicable applications
–Historians of 19th century based their outlook on history on progress –
  Guizot
–Philosophers of 19th century based their theorizing on progress – Hegel
  –Comte – progress by unequal oscillations in a determined direction – pace
    varied
  –Idea of progress dominated all lines of later 19th century life
  –Poets – Tennyson
  –etc.
  –To have idea of progress – it is necessary to have idea of free will (the bus,
    not the train)
  –Each person individually and each nation collectively – must have an idea of
    progress

TWO SUMMARY OUTLINES OF YOUNG'S COURSE PREPARED BY F. TAYLOR OSTRANDER

THEORY OF THE STATE
  I. Historic
    Clan
    Cult
    Conscience
  II. Philosophic
    Covenant
    Contract (Social)
    Coercion
  Sovereignty
    Legal–Political
    Attributes
    Definition
        Past–Future
  Constitution
    Concession
    Creation
  Government

Classifications
Separation of Powers
1. Monarchy
2. Popular Government
      Rebellion or Revolt
      Racial characteristics
  Analysis
    Control
    Cooperation
    Consent
    Conflict
  Criticism of Democracy
    Liberty
    Equality
    Fraternity
  Representation of Reason <u>vs</u> Representation of Religion
  A. Parliamentary Government
    {Representative
    {Responsible
    Suffrage
    Criticism of Representative Government
    Breakdown of Party system
  B. Personal Government
    Reactionary, revolutionary, personal, class
  C. Judicial Government
    Popular, parliamentary, professional-election
  D. Professional Government
    Covenanted
    Uncovenanted
3. Social Democracy
  Regulation
  Rationalization
  Reconstruction
      Equity
      Economic
      Expediency
    Socialism – pragmatic
      Fabian collectivism
      Conservatist
      Constructivist

        Corporative Fascist
      Pluralism – philosophy
        Laski
        G.D.H. Cole (Guild Socialism)
        Evolutionary
        Revolutionary
          Legal aspects
          Application to Italy, Russia, Great Britain, Germany
Progress
        Spiral cycles
EMPIRE
  Nationalism
    Race
      Fertility
      Forcefulness
      Fluidity
        Ethnic
        Economic
        Emancipation
    Region
      Climate
      Shape
    Religion
      Nationalism
    Règime
  Imperialism
      Conquest
        Corruption
        Cruelty
        Collapse
      Commerce
      Colonization
      Confederation
      (British Empire)
  Internationalism
    Executive
      Federation
      Confederation
      Real and personal unions

International associations
Economic
    Internationals of wealth and work
Ethical
(League of Nations – Policy, Peace, Progress)

OTHER MATERIALS

TWO LETTERS ON FRANKLIN D. ROOSEVELT FROM F. TAYLOR OSTRANDER

(1) 24 JUNE 1933

From: F. Taylor Ostrander
To: Warren Samuels
Tuesday, October 09, 2001 3:37 PM

. . .

The News-Letter piece was my first published writing. An Attachment to this message explains it. Like a considerable part of the British public, I admired Ramsay MacDonald and thought he was a commendable Prime Minister, but I had no other contact with the National Labour-ites than this article. I have never been pro-Labour Party, not even under Tony Blair – except for his extraordinary performance now and when he supported NATO in Kosovo.

At Oxford I took one term of lectures by G.D.H. Cole, and have my lecture notes which will be coming to you. He was terribly boring – and my only attempt to read *Das Kapital*, under Cole's tutelage, was worse! (But I underlined in my two-volume edition from covers to covers.)

. . .

Further Documents From F. Taylor Ostrander
Research in the History of Economic Thought and Methodology, Volume 24-B, 315–321
Copyright © 2006 by Elsevier Ltd.
All rights of reproduction in any form reserved
ISSN: 0743-4154/doi:10.1016/S0743-4154(06)24026-4

A NOTE ON MY ARTICLE IN *THE NEWS-LETTER*, LONDON, JUNE 1933: "PRESIDENT ROOSEVELT'S SOCIALIST LEGISLATION"

F. Taylor Ostrander
October 1999
(Revised September 2001)

I held a Henry Fellowship at Oxford University in the academic year 1932–33. My "moral tutor" (advisor) at The Queen's College was Godfrey Elton, a Fellow of the College and an historian. Elton was also editor of *The News-Letter*, the National Labour Fortnightly. This was the political journal of the dozen or so Labour MPs who followed Ramsay MacDonald, also a former Labour MP, into a National government with the Conservatives, when MacDonald became Prime Minister in 1931. These "renegade" Labour MPs continued to call themselves "socialists."

Though I had supported Roosevelt in the presidential campaign of 1932, I could not vote that November as I was already overseas at Oxford. FDR was not inaugurated until March 4, 1933. During the brief period from then until the end of my Oxford year in June, I was only able to follow the exciting events of the early New Deal in Washington in the London Economist and in British and Continental newspapers.

In early June, probably after my farewell call on Godfrey Elton, he asked me to write something about FDR and the New Deal for *The Newsletter*. My brief article was published in the issue dated June 24. I do not recall whether the title of my piece was mine or Elton's. Of course it was he who wrote the three-line introduction: the National Labour MPs were not the "dogmatic Socialist Opposition." The rest of the article is as I wrote it.

It was hard to know what to write after so short a time at so long a distance with so limited knowledge of events in Washington, but I believe my text was not badly off track.

Elton wrote me a note of thanks on June 23, and suggested that I continue writing occasional articles about American events after I returned home. I have long regretted that I did not take up Elton's offer.

For his support of Ramsay MacDonald, Godfrey Elton was later awarded a Lordship.

[Editor's note: The following is from *The News-Letter*, The National Labour Fortnightly, vol. 3, no. 7, 24 June 1933, p. 11.]

PRESIDENT ROOSEVELT'S SOCIALIST LEGISLATION

By F. TAYLOR OSTRANDER

[Mr. Ostrander, a young American economist, briefly explains the novel nature of President Roosevelt's legislative programme and its non-Party origins. Socialist in character, it has been facilitated in the U.S.A. by the absence of a dogmatic Socialist Opposition.]

THE introduction of radically new legislation by the Roosevelt administration provides an interesting basis of comparison between the political situation in England and in the United States. New banking legislation, a Railroad Emergency Bill, a Farm Relief Act, have been preliminary to a National Industrial Recovery Bill. This Bill, which will expire in two years, provides for a "partnership" of government and business acting through a Federal Control Board and industrial trade associations; ownership, management and initiative will be left to private interests, but by means of Federal licensing of all corporations the Government will have the power of compulsion, if private initiative does not respond to what it considers the public interest as regards rationing production, fixing prices, setting working hours, establishing a fair wage scale and eliminating cut-throat competition. It is evident that radical changes in the direction of Socialism are being enacted. Contrary to what might be expected, these steps have not been preceded by the widespread success of any party movement demanding Socialism. Indeed had a formidable Socialist Party existed to terrify the public with Marxian propaganda, it is highly improbable that the present legislation would have been proposed. But the American public has scarcely heard of Socialism. The American Socialist Party is so small (it polled less than three per cent of the votes cast in 1932), its doctrines are so old-fashioned or visionary, so seldom based on knowledge or practical administration, that the influence of doctrinaire Socialism is slight indeed.

The present crisis has called forth the best minds of the country, regardless of party, not dictated by the *dogma* of Conservatism or by the *dogma* of Radicalism. These radical innovations in political structure are being proposed by politicians of both parties, by leaders of industry, by academic economists and by practical financiers. At least for the present, while the shadow of complete chaos still hangs over the country and while support of the new administration is still at high pitch, having practically destroyed the existence of any opposition based on party lines, the efforts of every thinking person are directed towards the passage of whatever legislation is best designed to meet the requirements of present and future economic conditions. As an example of all this, the philosophy of change and of Government control that lies behind the new legislation has been set forth, not in any Party programme, but by two men who, although they are essentially non-party men, are members of the Roosevelt administration: Professor Rexford Tugwell, Assistant Secretary of Agriculture, and Professor Berle, special assistant on railway credit to the directors of the Reconstruction Finance Corporation.[1]

People of left wing inclinations who, however, realise the extreme danger to the efficient operation of any modem democracy that is inherent in Party dogma, cannot but welcome a situation – however temporary it may be – in which Party dogma has had so little, and public intelligence so much, influence as in the radical innovations of President Roosevelt's legislation. For political observers are agreed that, whatever the time limits stated in these Bills, this legislation prefaces a new order requiring the energies of a whole future generation for its perfection.

NOTES

1. *The Modern Corporation and Private Property*. Berle and Means. Macmillan. 1932. *The Industrial Discipline and the Governmental Arts*. Tugwell. Columbia University Press. 1933.

(2) MAY 3, 1945

[Editor's note: The original stationary has black borders. The envelope is addressed to Mrs. Lionel Ostrander, 1560 East West Highway, Silver Spring, Maryland, USA. At the time, Taylor Ostrander was an Intelligence Officer.]

THE FOREIGN SERVICE
OF THE
UNITED STATES OF AMERICA

American Embassy
APO 413
May 3, 1945

Dear Family,

We are in official mourning for the President for the month, as is all too dismally obvious with this example of what we use for official letters. All male members of the Embassy staff have been asked to wear black ties for the month; this I do for the first time in my life, with dull feeling of slight relief, though I know its so infinitesimally inadequate. Thanks for your letters of the 14–15th which arrived Tuesday, just before I rushed down to see Fran. I know that as a family, in three separate places, we must have felt much the same on that first long stark weekend, and for that I'm more than grateful.

It's now nearly three weeks and I haven't been able to bring myself to put anything down on paper. For one thing, what more is there to say? Just the dull sense of intimate personal loss, of gratitude for all he did, of helpless hopelessness, and foreboding future. So much has been said, some of it – like the New Yorker piece – so very poignant; all of it true. About all I can think of adding, and it was my first reaction, is to hope that Roosevelt realized – in the midst of all the turmoil and incredible abuse in which he lived, at home at least – that he realized, humility granted and all that, <u>some</u> concept of what the world would feel and say if he went. That might have given him some reward in his lifetime for all that he <u>gave</u> to his country and the world. It was this concern for whether <u>he</u> realized some of the reward that was his, that dominated my reactions for several days.

Another reason that I haven't written is because I have felt so cut off from the reality of his death; two weeks in a new civilization, without any sense of feel for the sources of news, and without our radio, and just generally divorced from our civilization, have left me emotionally high and dry, so to speak. I think this is true of most of us: we didn't share in the intensity of the mass reaction of our own kind, and we take longer to realize that it all really has happened. It's an odd thing that I was in England and similarly cut off from my civilization when Roosevelt took over in the midst of crisis, and was elected too, for that matter.

I don't want to imply that the British have not had an incredibly sincere and intense reaction. Even though the great moment of Roosevelt's visit to England had not come, the reaction of people here was nearly the same sense of personal loss that we had. That is an incredible tribute to his power. Someone has said that the British will never forget the close confidence of his voice speaking to the world in the dark days when England stood on the brink of invasion. It has been said a thousand times in the press that there has never been so great a friend of England; but it has been my personal experience that the mass of the British felt a much more unselfish reaction. Those who have talked to me, and that is quite a few, for one of the strange things about the British reaction was that they said what they felt to anyone whom they found to he an American, always stressed rather what a great man he was in his own right, and what a loss to the peace it is to lose him now; the specific gratitude for his help to Britain was always a third rank point – and even that was really over-politeness, for I think most Englishmen realize that our aid was <u>entirely</u> selfish, though they would to a man rather have their tongues pulled out than to say so.

About the most impressive public ceremony I've ever seen, was the big memorial service at St. Paul's on Tuesday (April 17th). Practically the entire American colony must have been there, plus everyone in London "who is anybody." The whole hierarchy of the Church of England, most of the Houses of Parliament, the entire top Admiralty and Army, the Royal Family, the heads of all the Governments in Exile, Churchill, Winant, etc.. I was about half way back in the nave, only five feet from the aisle where all these "great" came in, and walked out after the service. As Andy Kerr said, he didn't ever expect to see as much Royalty in one place again – it was quite a sight. The King and Queen, then the Princess in **ATS** private uniform, then a group consisting of Queen Wilhelmina, King Haakon, King George of Greece, King Peter and consorts, etc. As a London newspaper headline put it: "Four Kings and Two Queens Mourn President." It wasn't the pomp or "royalty" (some of it of doubtful or at least precarious stature), but the solemnity that was impressive. It was after all just a bunch of human beings trying miserably to show some sense of what they felt. One of the high points of the service was the reading of the Lesson by Ambassador Winant, looking more Lincolnesque than ever. Another high point was the trumpet calls from a high balcony, overpowering in their loudness and clarity, playing Reveille, and The Last Post. What should have been the third high point – the singing of The Battle Hymn of the Republic as the last thing – didn't quite come off as it should, for the words were perfect; but the organ dragged the unfamiliar (to St. Paul's) tune, and didn't let the Americans take it away. Most Americans felt that the Anglican service had about ten times too much about God, and ten times too little about F.D.R. – but I suppose that was inevitable in St. Paul's.

How incredible, that within three weeks Roosevelt on the one hand, and Mussolini and Hitler on the other, should have died. Truly the end of an age. And nothing could have more fitly shown their respective places in the world's accounting than the contrast of the world's mourning for Roosevelt, the dog-like end of Mussolini, body lying in a gutter and spat upon by his people, and the propaganda death (and total apathy of a beaten people) of Hitler. Roosevelt and Hitler: March 1953 to April 1945. What an unbelievable coincidence, and what a pure essay in black and white, good and bad.

The only reason I was glad to be here, rather than in the States when this happened, was to miss the disgusting sight and words of the orgy of joy and relief that must have swept over the H*Y*P Club and such places. I would have gone quite out of control, if I'd been there to listen to the pygmies. Here, at least, there was no <u>class</u> separation in the mourning. In spite of all the mess and confusion of Europe, now that Italy and Germany are done in, the greatest danger to the world is probably the American rich – "the most irresponsible upper class in the world" – as John or Alex, or both, called them last week.

It will take months before the real loss of Roosevelt is felt. I can't say I look forward with much enthusiasm. If Wilkie were alive, it would be more hopeful.

Truman has done well, and will continue to strive hard, but it will be a poor substitute. I must say, I am more than glad it's he instead of Dewey. To have turned our backs on the Roosevelt course at this point would have been an unremitted disaster. And the end did not <u>have</u> to come at this time – that was chance. It was the thing I have feared for several years, so much I wasn't able to admit or express it in words; but it could have been another way, there was <u>as much</u> chance.

Well, you're right. My greatest relief at this time is that I <u>was</u> a loyal follower and admirer of the President's, for over 15 years. From Albany on. And Walter Lippmann is right, the greatest thing about Roosevelt is that he did see the issues and ask the questions; just as the worst thing I have always said about the management crowd in Pittsburgh is that they don't recognize the issues or know that the issues exist.

F. TAYLOR OSTRANDER'S MEMOIR ON THE FOUNDING OF THE WILLIAMS COLLEGE LIBERAL CLUB

Warren J. Samuels (Editor)

The undergraduate and graduate training of economics majors is certainly part of the history of economics. This should include more than course content and over-all curricula. F. Taylor Ostrander was a student at Williams College, a prestigious conservative liberal-arts college, during four momentous years. Part of his experience was participation in the formation of the Williams College Liberal Club. That this Club was founded in a conservative college tells us something of the mood of that period. Although "liberal" was apparently not "officially" defined by Club members, for most, if not all, it did not equate with either "socialism" or "activism" – other amorphous words.

The self-explanatory memoir published below will be indicative, for the close reader, of a number of things, including:

- The desire that change during the period of evident transition be "peaceful and rational" – certainly indicative of an antipathy toward violence and of the relevance of such sentiments to social order and Hayekian spontaneous order. Comparison may be made with Frank H. Knight's depression during this period.
- The influence, discussed elsewhere in this volume, of Peter Odegard: candor, sharpness and toughness without being "radical."

Further Documents From F. Taylor Ostrander
Research in the History of Economic Thought and Methodology, Volume 24-B, 323–340
Copyright © 2006 by Elsevier Ltd.
All rights of reproduction in any form reserved
ISSN: 0743-4154/doi:10.1016/S0743-4154(06)24027-6

- Notice of membership on the Williams College faculty, at one time or another during the 1930s, of Paul Birdsall, Telford Taylor, Frederick Schuman and Max Lerner.
- A founding group that included James Willard Hurst (Wisconsin law school) and Werner A. Wick (Chicago philosophy department).
- The club brought to campus Harold J. Laski and Bertrand Russell as well as, to a "Inter-Collegiate Conference on 'Capitalism and its Alternatives,'" a group which included Jacob Viner – presenting the case for "Progressive Capitalism" – and William Z. Foster. Viner also debated Norman Thomas on the pros and cons of economic planning. The conference was partly funded by the Economics Department. Apropos of Viner, Ostrander's letter to his parents about the Conference includes the following: "I didn't like Viner – he has practically no philosophy except pessimism and nihilism. Perhaps that is the logical end of Capitalist philosophy!"

June 12, 1997

THE WILLIAMS COLLEGE LIBERAL CLUB
ITS FOUNDING AND EARLY DAYS, 1930-1932

By F. TAYLOR OSTRANDER

The Liberal Club of Williams College was created in the Spring of 1930 by a small group of friends in the Class of 1932. We were Sophomores at the time.

Public announcement of its formation was made some months later, early in our Junior year, in an article in the Williams Record of October 25, 1930. Here is the formal "statement of purpose," as published in the Record:

> Believing that the world is now passing through a period of transition in its social organization and that an intelligent understanding of the forces involved is needed if the change is to be a peaceful and rational one, the Liberal Club of Williams College proposes to promote disinterested consideration of social, economic and political questions in an effort to determine the wisest course of action.

The Record article, probably written by one of our members, concluded:

> The founders of this Club sincerely hope that the organization will stimulate thought about social questions and that it will be a nucleus of liberal thought in this College which has been conservative ever since its founding.

The Club's statement of purpose seems today remarkably low-key for a group of college Sophomores about nineteen years of age who were setting out to add a new dimension to what they saw as the College's long conservative tradition. Its commitment to "disinterested consideration," "peaceful and rational" change, azznd the "wisest course of action" also seems curiously unimpassioned. We did appear to have something fairly specific in mind as the "liberal thought" we proposed to introduce to the campus, but we did not anywhere define it.

Nearly two years later, just after our graduation, the Williams Alumni Review in its July 1932 issue published an article about the Liberal Club, including an illuminating Letter to the Editor from the Club's founding President, Wallace Parks. (See Annex I) He repeated the Club's Statement of Purpose, as quoted above, unchanged from the original text.

The Liberal Club was a unique development on the Williams Campus, and it had some remarkable achievements during its first two years. This Memoir describes the Club's background, its founders, its activities and its success.

Background in the World Outside the College

The stock market crash in October 1929, early in our Sophomore year, had signaled the end of an era and the beginning of what came to be called the Great Depression. There was growing uncertainty and concern about the future. Mature students everywhere began to seek a better understanding of the outside world.

It was also a time of growing concern about international political issues: the problems of German reparations and inter-Allied debts from the 1914–1918 war persisted, disarmament continued to occupy the League of Nations but without progress, Fascist Italy showed a new form of totalitarianism, and the rise of the Nazi Party in Germany carried more worrisome portents. On the other hand, novel developments in Soviet Russia, though little understood, seemed to many to offer new horizons of hope.

Both at home and abroad the situation worsened rapidly during our later years at college. The Depression deepened; public confidence plummeted. The Japanese began to make war in Asia, and the growing Nazi Party promised to do the same in Europe.

Though hard to imagine today, we spent all four of our college years *before* Franklin Roosevelt was even *nominated* to run for President. Hoover was our President throughout our college days. It was a time when there seemed to be no new policies that promised any improvement. No one seemed to know how to stop the rot. Socialists, Communists, and soon Nazis became increasingly vocal in the United States itself; and all across the nation new "isms" of every variety mushroomed. There were even fears of aspiring home-grown dictators. All this was a potent stimulus to student thinking about new alternatives to the status quo.

Background Within the College

We students were not isolated from these outside events. The Class of 1932 lost about 25% (61) of its original 242 members before graduation! The losses were especially heavy in the summer of 1930, between our Sophomore and Junior years, when many of our class had to drop out because their families were having financial difficulties. Undoubtedly, the families of all those who stayed on were also feeling the financial pinch of the Depression. (Nevertheless, with 181 remaining, we were the largest graduating class in Williams history up to then.)

Prior to the founding of the Liberal Club there had been no political clubs on the campus, and no organized expression of either "conservative" or "liberal" or other opinion on the part of either students or faculty.

A few faculty and students may have supported the Democratic candidate, Al Smith, in the national election of 1928, at the beginning of our Freshman year, but they were not many, and certainly not "noisy" about it. The Senior head of my Sigma Phi House in my Freshman year, Bob Healy, was the only student I recall who supported Al Smith; I suspect others in the fraternity were as shocked by his stand as I was!

In general, our impression of the faculty was that many of them not only "looked like Calvin Coolidge," but no doubt mostly voted like him. Students, to the extent they had political views, were overwhelmingly Republican, as were our middle class parents.

Origins of the Liberal Club

The Williams <u>Record</u> article quoted above reporting our Club's formation mentioned that Liberal Clubs had sprung up during 1930 at over 100 colleges, including Amherst, Dartmouth, Brown, Vassar and Smith. Obviously, we must have been somewhat influenced by that trend.

But at Least two individuals played major roles in creating our Liberal Club: Rev. Gardiner Day and Professor Peter Odegard.

Rev. Gardiner Day, a young, very liberal minister interested in social action, came to St. John's Episcopal church in Williamstown in September 1929. As curate, he was "to work with the College students." He began inviting groups of students to meet with him for discussions of current economic and social problems. We met in the large living room of the old Rectory where Rev. Franklin Carter had lived during his long service at St. John's.

I believe none in our group belonged to the Episcopal church, but we were attracted to Gardiner Day and we met with him several times during our Sophomore year. These early discussions led to the formation of a "Liberal Group" sponsored by Rev. Day, with Wallace Parks its leader. In the Spring of 1930, as announced in the <u>Record</u> article, this group became the Liberal Club of Williams College. We were an independent group from then on. Gardiner Day was clearly very influential in our founding the Club, but I do not recall that he thenceforth played any major role in the Club's activities.

One year after coming to Williamstown, Rev. Gardiner Day became Rector of St. John's, and had less time for students. He remained there for only six years before leaving for another post. In 1941 he became Rector of Christ Church in Cambridge, MA where he served for twenty-five years. No doubt he continued his work with groups of students in that larger urban college town.

The other person who had a very strong influence on the creation of our Liberal Club was a new faculty member, Professor Peter Odegard, who came to Williams in the Fall of 1928, just as our Freshmen year began, to teach Political Science.

Odegard had recently published his Columbia Ph.D. thesis, <u>Power and Politics: The Story of the Anti-Saloon League.</u> It was a devastating analysis of the personalities, methods of operation and successes of that organization in the drive for Prohibition ten years earlier. The book was influential at that time in bringing a new sharpness and toughness to academic analysis of the American political scene.

Most of our group had taken Odegard's Freshman course in "Comparative Government" and some of us also took his second year course in "American Government and Politics." These were demanding courses, filled with new information, requiring much outside reading. For Freshmen, they were an exciting quantum leap into college-level work. Odegard's teaching style was highly provocative and iconoclastic. He was a "radical" but only in his tough-minded realism, his way of seeing and saying things that were not usual in those days. He awakened, fascinated and often shocked his students.

I was one of those most shocked by Odegard's starkly realistic analysis of men, motives and events. After a few weeks of his course, I called on Professor Agard, Dean of Freshmen, and asked to be transferred from Odegard to another section of "Poly Sci 1-2." Dean Agard told me: "Taylor, these may be some of the ideas you came to Williams to hear," and urged me not to shift. About six weeks later, I was one of Odegard's principal admirers!

Odegard had perhaps even greater influence on Wallace Parks than on me. Two years after Odegard had left Williams, at the end of Senior year, answering the question, "What Williams Needs Most?," Parks wrote in our yearbook: "More Odegards."

Alas, Odegard did not stay at Williams beyond those two years. He went on to a brilliant career elsewhere. He taught at Ohio State, then five years at Amhurst, was President of Reed College, President of the American Political Science Association in 1957, and settled at University of California at Berkeley for the rest of his career. Obviously, Williams missed the boat badly in not convincing this extraordinary teacher to stay. Perhaps his "style" was too strong for Prexy Garfield or the Political Science Department; or perhaps Odegard's rising reputation in his profession required more rapid career advancement than Williams could find its way to offer. Those of us who benefited from his two years at Williams were always grateful for the experience.

Another newcomer to the College, starting with us in the Fall of 1928, was Professor Paul Birdsall, who taught the history of pre- and post-war Europe. His courses were very popular with the group that formed the Liberal Club. I was close to Birdsall, but I do not recollect his having any direct influence on the forming of the Liberal Club, though he was the main influence in the creation of the student International Affairs Club and served as its faculty advisor.

There was also Telford Taylor, a brilliant young instructor in History and Political Science who taught us for only our Freshman year, between his graduation here and Harvard Law School. These four men, as well as Professor Newhall and others of William's grand teachers whom we encountered, all awakened our interest in world events and therefore influenced our group's decision to organize our interest by forming a Club.

(I should note that five years after Odegard left Williams, a new President, Tyler Dennett, brought to Williams two new professors, Frederick Schuman and Max Lerner, and announced that his purpose was to shake up the College's conservative mold.)

The Founding Members of the Liberal Club

Our founding group included six members of our class: James Willard Hurst, Wallace Judson Parks, Robert Frederick Reeves, Harry Acheson Sellery, Warner Arms Wick, and the author of this reminiscence, F. Taylor Ostrander. Robert Lawther, Class of 1933, was also with us. We were the Executive Committee of the Club. We have photographs of this group, taken in Senior year.

Wally Parks was President of the Club; Tay Ostrander was Vice-president; Bob Lawther was Secretary and Treasurer. Parks was certainly the leader in pushing to create the Club and played a large role in its success in our Senior year. He was the "activist" in our group, with great zeal for liberal causes, including some that were fated to become lost causes.

Parks and I studied abroad in the summer of 1931, and that experience came to play a major role in our Liberal Club's Inter-Collegiate Conference in February of Senior year.

I went to the Geneva School of International Studies. Its excellent lecturers covered all aspects of international problems, and its lively graduate students from many nations and universities gave me new understanding of other countries' problems. I was one of the group of students and seminar leaders who founded a Socialist Club that met many evenings at a café near the University for discussion and to hear a different type of speakers: Roger Baldwin, the noted American Socialist, French, Belgian and German socialists, students from Ruskin College, the working men's school at Oxford. It was a stimulating summer: an international *graduate* experience before Senior year at Williams!

Parks too studied that summer at Lausanne, and he visited me in Geneva for a few days; he met my new friends and attended a few of our lectures, including one at the Socialist Club. He also saw the opening of the League of Nations in Geneva before returning to college for his Senior year.

Other Members of the Liberal Club

In addition to the Executive Committee members mentioned above, there were seven other members from the Class of 1932 were: Jim Carter, Jim Gordon, Roger Kent, Tony Miller, Sam Herrick, Asher Schwartz and Reg Zalles. All had interesting later careers. There were a dozen members each from the Classes of 1933 and 1934. All who took part in the Club's discussions and activities were dues-paying members.

Only one complete list of all the Club's members exists, that published in the above mentioned <u>Alumni Review</u> article in July 1932, presumably a part of Wally Parks' Letter to the Editor (see Annex I). That list also gives the names of our Faculty members. It was not surprising that the Club attracted a number of active members from our Faculty friends. This was another unique feature of our Liberal Club. These members were:

Willis J. Ballinger	Economics
W. Edwards Beach	Economics
Paul Birdsall	History
Donald Blaisdell	Political Science
Stuart Chapin	English
John Comer	Political Science
Charles Keller	History and Political Science
Allan Latham	Economics
John William Miller	Philosophy
Richard Newhall	History
Donald Richmond	Mathematics

The Club's Statement of Purpose was undoubtedly a consensus text agreed by all of our founding members, but I believe it strongly reflects the maturity and writing skill of two of our members, J. Willard Hurst who was soon to become Editor-in-Chief of the <u>Williams Record</u> and Warner A. Wick who was to be another top Editor of the <u>Record</u>.

Hurst was Valedictorian of our Class and of his Harvard Law School class. He was for 40 years Professor of Law at University of Wisconsin, noted for his writings on the history of American jurisprudence. He studied at Cambridge, England and later was a visiting Professor of American History and Institutions there. Recently, the Wisconsin Law School established in his honor the J. Willard Hurst Professorship in Legal History. Williams awarded him an Honorary LLD in 1974.

Wick was Class Salutatorian at graduation and was awarded the College's Moody Scholarship for two years at Exeter College, Oxford. He later was a distinguished Professor of Philosophy and Dean of Humanities at University of Chicago.

Parks won a College Fellowship for a year at University of Lyon, France. He became a lawyer and also earned a Ph.D. in Political Science at Columbia University. He worked in several government and Congressional posts, but died early, aged only 47.

Ostrander held a Henry Fellowship at The Queen's College, Oxford and also studied at University of Chicago. After teaching economics at Williams, he served as a government economist in the New Deal, in the Occupation of Germany and the Marshall Plan, then had long overlapping careers in MBA teaching and in public affairs work for an international mining company.

Reeves became a Presbyterian minister and served for many years as Chaplain at Cornell-Presbyterian Hospital in New York. Sellery became a lawyer and had a long career in the Office of the Chief Counsel of the Department of Justice.

Reeves and Ostrander belonged to fraternities; the other four founders were of the remarkable Commons Club group of our class. (I joined the Commons Club in Senior year while continuing to live and be steward at the Sigma Phi House.) Only Hurst, Ostrander and Reeves survive at this writing.

The Liberal Club did not receive any financial support from the College or from the student Non-athletic Council. It was not included in the "Gul." All its founding members were also leaders of other campus organizations, none of which had the same area of interest as the Liberal Club.

The newly founded International Affairs Club, of which Hurst was President and Ostrander Vice-president in our Senior year, was active, but its interest was chiefly in following and understanding developments in foreign relations. The long-established Philosophical Union, of which Wick became President that year, had its own essentially non-political interests. The Adelphic Society, of which Reeves became President, debated with other colleges on Resolutions that were often economic or political, but these were formal competitions, not discussions. Sellery became President of the Little Theater, which also conducted a campaign against "block booking" which prevented the local movie house from obtaining the foreign films we all wanted so much to see.

Our new Liberal Club group obviously thought something else was needed on campus. None of those existing organizations pursued a purpose such as introducing "liberal thought" to the campus or *discussing* seriously with the intent to seek solutions to the major economic and social problems facing the nation, and the world.

What we Wanted the Liberal Club to Be and Do

The Club's Statement of Purpose was certainly a far cry from what falls under the heading of "liberal" in the 1990s!

We did not think of ourselves as a "Socialist Club," as was the case with many of the other Liberal Clubs that were being formed at other colleges and universities at that time. We were eager to discuss Socialism and the Soviet experiment, but none of us became "fellow travelers" or committed Communists, as was so often the case in so many of the student groups in New York City or at some other colleges at that time.

I keenly recall the visit our Liberal Club made to meet with the Vassar Liberal Club, probably sometime early in our Senior year. As we walked into the big hall at Main Building on the Vassar campus, the President of their club, Charlotte Tuttle, came forward to greet us, saying "I trust you are all true Socialists." Harry Sellery, who happened to be at the front of our group, replied, jokingly, but meaning it, "Oh No, not me, I'm just parlor pink." We all laughed; I don't think she did.

Another indication of our kind of "liberalism" was when one of the factories in North Adams had a strike. We had quite a debate in the Club as to what we should do about it. Wally Parks wanted us to go as a group to join the picket line. The consensus was not to do that: such activism was not the majority's concept of "liberalism." We preferred to limit ourselves to analyzing the facts behind the strike and the positions of the two sides to the dispute.

I was surprised to find a reference to the League of Industrial Democracy (LID) in the above mentioned Record article about the Club's founding:

> [The Club] is affiliated with the national League of Industrial Democracy, although this connection is not to imply any commitment of the Liberal Club to the policies and views of the League.

LID published an inexpensive Newsletter on national affairs that had wide circulation among college students. Its motto, "From each according to ability; to each according to need," came straight from Engels' Communist Manifesto, but Norman Thomas, no Communist, was its Executive Director. Apparently, some of our members wanted to claim a connection with LID, others to disavow one. In that sentence both sides appear to have had their way!

How the Club Would Operate

The Record article announcing formation of the Liberal Club described how the Club would operate:

> . . . it is still in the experimental stage and does not wish to publish too much about its future activities. . . . The Club is chiefly a discussion group whose membership is limited to a small number of students and faculty members in order to make the discussions as intelligent and as comprehensive as possible.

From today's perspective this seems a rather exclusive, even possibly arrogant, outline of how we would operate! Of course, in those "good old days" students were able to band together in any private way they wanted to. We did not have any members from outside the College community. I can't believe that we ever excluded any student who wanted to participate.

The Club's Activities, 1930–1932

Some of the Liberal Club's activities during those two years are indelibly inscribed in memory. We brought, or helped bring, to Williams two of that era's outstanding intellectuals, Bertrand Russell and Harold J. Laski. And in February 1932 we staged a successful Inter-collegiate Conference in Williamstown that was certainly the Liberal Club's single greatest achievement.

The Club kept no records of its discussions, and we have been unable to find any Club records in the College Archives or in my otherwise extensive personal files of notes on courses or other things from my college days. So the full story of the Club's many activities can only be found in the events recorded in the Williams Record.

Immediately after its formation, the Club launched its active program of bi-weekly discussion meetings, many of them with outside speakers. Only ten days after our formation in late October 1930, the Club sponsored a public lecture to hear Henry Raymond Mussey, the noted Editor of the Nation. He criticized the lack of interest of so many college students in political and international events, and called for a reversal, as our Club was doing. In December a dinner meeting at Rev. Day's home heard Astronomy Professor Milham and a Rev. Hall '21, describe their recent visit to Russia

In March 1931 the Liberal Club sponsored a lecture by University of London Political Scientist, Harold J. Laski, then a visiting professor at Harvard. He was noted as a brilliant speaker, and he enchanted a full audience in Chapin Hall. Prexy Garfield hosted a reception afterwards for faculty and students.

In December the Liberal Club co-sponsored, in collaboration with the Williams Forum and the student lecture bureau, a speech by Lord Bertrand Russell, the famous British philosopher and scientist, who outlined to a capacity Chapin Hall audience his proposal "for the establishment of world peace." I remember my excitement at being able to speak to this great man at a reception after this lecture at President Garfield's home.

And so our program continued, for month after month, with growing participation of our Faculty members.

Inter-Collegiate Conference on "Capitalism and its Alternatives"

This Conference was certainly the Liberal Club's greatest events. I wrote to my parents just after it ended:

> *The Conference was a spectacular success. Williamstown has never seen such a performance before. And Pres. Garfield has said that it was the biggest and best thing done by any undergraduate group in his 30 years as President. The stock of the Liberal Club is very high, at present.*

Attached Annex II gives the full text of that letter to my parents with my detailed and vivid account of the proceedings. Two issues of the Williams <u>Record</u> reported the Conference in full, with summaries of the speeches and Round Table discussions.

(See attached Williams <u>Record</u> pages on the Conference.)

The three-day Conference was held on February 12–14, 1932. Over 200 visiting delegates came from some 17 Eastern Colleges. Speakers "presented the case" for various alternatives: Professor Jacob Viner, University of Chicago, for "Progressive Capitalism;" Maynard Krueger, University of Pennsylvania, for Socialism; William Z. Foster, President of the Communist Party of America for Communism and Carlo Flumiani, a businessman from New York, for Italian Fascism. Why did we omit Nazism? This question is an intriguing one since, exactly one year later, Hitler would take power in Germany. Was that considered too improbable?

The final Conference event, on Saturday evening in Chapin Hall, was a debate between Jacob Viner and Norman Thomas, who was to become perennial Socialist candidate for the Presidency, on the *pros* and *cons* of Economic Planning.

A number of friends from the 1931 Geneva Summer School were the Rapporteurs for the six Round Table discussion groups, open only to delegates, that met Saturday afternoon. We even crowded in a short Soviet documentary, "The Five Year Plan." Delegates paid a registration fee of $3.50, covering all sessions, meals and room for one night, second night, $1.00 additional! The Commons Club provided all meals. The lectures and debate were open to the public, but they had to pay 50 cents for the Soviet film at the Walden Theater (which had 500 seats then). There was so much interest in this documentary that the Club earned $200. The Soviets charged us $70 for their propaganda film.

Parks was Chairman of the Conference; Hurst and Ostrander had responsibility for program, Richard Kent for finance, Reeves and John Ohly '33 for publicity, Lawther '33 for registration and Sellery and Wick for entertainment. Dick Kent of our class was a valued new associate for a key post, as was Jack Ohly of the class of 1933. Kent became a leading physician in Indianapolis. Ohly had a notable career in the Federal government.

The Conference's Program had a modernistic cover drawn by our Executive Committee member, Warner Wick. See Annex III.

A Note on the back cover of this Program explained how the Conference was financed; the Club's Faculty members had obviously helped a lot, as had some friendly Trustees of the College:

The financing of the Conference has been made possible through cooperation of the Economics Department, the Political Science Department, the Alumni Office, the Non-Athletic Council, and five members of the Board of Trustees.

The Conference must have taken months to prepare, all done by our student members. The logistics alone must have been an innovation for the College: to house for two nights over 200 visiting delegates, many of them from women's colleges, while Williams was in regular session, must have required great ingenuity and substantial assistance from the whole community.

Even today, after all these years, I keenly recall the lively excitement, and the success, of that Conference.

ANNEX I. EXCERPT FROM THE WILLIAMS ALUMNI REVIEW, JULY 1932

AIMS AND OBJECTS OF THE WILLIAMS LIBERAL CLUB

Some members of the Liberal Club, an undergraduate organization, have protested to the Editor of the Alumni Review that a recent editorial did not discriminate between the acts of certain individuals and the activities of the Club as an organization. They call attention to the fact that the "Gargoyle Issue" of the Williams Record and the protest against Class Day were not activities of the Club, although some Club members may have been involved.

We are pleased to make this point clear, and have asked Mr. Parks, the retiring president of the Liberal Club, to prepare a statement of the aims and objects of the group, its accomplishments, and its membership. The Editor of the Alumni Review takes the attitude that when the undergraduates cease to think for themselves, the campus becomes dead to the living issues of the day. Better give up attempting to educate youth if they must be turned out according to a pre-arranged pattern. Nor does this mean that we are ready to take a rubber stamp and mark many undergraduate acts and attitudes as "approved."

Letter to the Editor,
   Williams Alumni Review

   From Wallace J. Parks,
      Retiring President, Williams Liberal Club

Some of us who read the June issue of the Alumni Review gathered the impression that the Editor was preferring charges against the Liberal Club for a long list of "crimes" ranging from the anti-Class Day agitation to the "Gargoyle Issue" of the Williams Record. One might think from these charges that the Liberal Club was the most formidable and powerful organization on the campus, yet that is far from being true. Besides, we have had no connection with these "stirrings" which the Editor proclaimed to have been distinctly lacking in a "sense of proportion."

Our Statement of Purpose reads: Believing that the world is now passing through a period of transition in its social organization and that an intelligent understanding of the forces involved is needed if the change is to be a peaceful and rational one, the Liberal Club of Williams College proposes to promote disinterested consideration of social, economic and political questions in an effort to determine the wisest course of action.

Thus, in characteristic "liberal" fashion, we have drafted a statement which might mean anything you choose and which has proved offensive only to Communists and certain Trustees. Yet our aims are not so shilly-shally as they might appear. To be sure, we have no particular creeds or panaceas – unless one calls a creed the conviction that decisions arrived at after impartial investigation are more likely to be sound and to lead to well-directed activity than those reached after prejudiced treatment, whether conservative or radical.

Generally speaking, we have opposed united action on the part of the Liberal Club on the grounds that it is the primary aim of students of college age to explore the political, economic, and social panoramas of the world rather than to preach poorly-thought-out cure-alls. We recognize, however, that the present era demands immediate and courageous action. We are not liberals of the futilitarian or pussy-footing brand who place themselves in academic aloofness from the world and criticize all those who are striving for any program whatsoever.

Due to the tolerance with which we approach all points of view, we have members of both capitalistic and socialistic inclinations. We have been accused of being unduly socialistic, yet the majority of Williams' Socialists are not members of the Liberal Club. Rather than to classify ourselves, we prefer to be liberal in the sense that we are continuously ready to reconsider even our most basic assumptions.

I think that the Liberal Club has an important part to play in Williams College. If the younger generation is going to take up the challenge presented to it by the incredible morass into which society has plunged itself, then the recruiting station for leadership must locate itself in colleges and universities. Chancellor Brown, of New York University, says that the colleges are being blamed for the present ailments of civilization, and surely it is true that American colleges have become too much like country clubs in their over-emphasis on social life and athletics and too much like monasteries in their isolation from the mainstream of life.

The future of democratic civilization is a race between education and catastrophe, and the responsibility of the colleges for the outcome of this race is great. I would suggest, therefore, that organizations such as the Liberal Club are a vital factor in the life of any college of twentieth century America.

Now, a word as to achievements. In such matters our shafts always fall short of their mark. Yet, perhaps we have had some effect during the two and a half years of our existence. Large numbers of students have been given a chance to do some original thinking by being "exposed" to people such as Harold J. Laski, Bertrand Russell, Jennie Lee, and Norman Thomas. Most important of all have been the regular bi-weekly meetings, limited to our own members for the purpose of achieving fruitful discussion, and at which there have been no taboos – each idea put forward having only its intrinsic merit to recommend it.

Perhaps we have served to some extent as a thorn in the side of the spirit of academic quietus and soporific complacency which has been Williams' prevailing ideology. Maybe we have fostered a more active and realistic interest in American and world affairs. All this is problematic. At least, however, by our presence on the Williams campus we afford an opportunity for all those interested in liberal politics to express and develop themselves.

A problem arises over our relation to the campus. Should we take any active part in undergraduate affairs? On the whole we have been opposed to such an orientation of our policy, yet some of us have felt that certain shortcomings (if there be such) in our own little society in Williamstown should not be disregarded. Little has been done. However, plans for committee reports on the curriculum, prices on Spring Street and the feasibility of the establishment of a student cooperative store for certain lines of merchandise, the industrial conditions in the environs of Williamstown, and the athletic tax have been discussed and are awaiting next year for further development. We have never considered, however, engaging in any of the activities which the Editor of the <u>Review</u> declares to be lacking in proportion." On the whole we, like fools, "have our eyes on the ends of the earth."

Williams Liberal Club Membership List <u>Spring 1932</u>
(From <u>Williams</u> Alumni Review, <u>July 1932)</u>

<u>Seniors:</u>	W. J. Parks	President
	F. T. Ostrander	Vice President
	J. W. Hurst	Executive Committee
	H. A. Sellery, Jr.	" "
	R. B. Reeves	" "
	W. A. Wick	" "
	J. B. Gordon	
	S. Herrick, Jr.	
	R. N. Kent	
	A. F. Miller	
	A. Schwartz	
	R. H. Zalles	

<u>Juniors:</u>	R. E. Lawther	Executive Committee
	B. D. Causey	
	M. E. Dakin	
	S. D. Fisher	
	G. Ford, Jr.	
	A. B. Gilfillan, Jr.	
	C. F. Hamilton	
	J. H. Ohly	
	C. Rudd	
	J. B. Snowden	
	R. Webster	
	A. M. Woodruff, Jr.	
	W. H. von Elm	

<u>Sophomores:</u>	R. D. Baum	
	A. M. Collens, Jr.	
	R. F. Ebinger	
	J. P. Elder	
	A. Gomez	
	G. W. Hawkins	
	O. Jameson	
	J. G. Pinkham	
	A. R. Phipps	
	E. T. Ray	
	J. H. Rhoades, III	

Faculty:

	Mr. A. Latham
Mr. W. J. Ballinger	Mr. J. Comer
Mr. W. E. Beach	Mr. C. Keller
Mr. P. Birdsall	Mr. J. W. Miller
Mr. D. Blaisdell	Mr. R. A. Newhall
Mr. S. Chapin	Mr. D. Richmond

ANNEX II. FTO COMMENTS ON THE LIBERAL CLUB CONFERENCE IN A LETTER TO HIS PARENTS FEBRUARY 15, 1932

We left [Wellesley on Friday] at 4:45 pm and before we had reached Worcester we were in fog worse than the one I came down in. I was glad I had someone along to talk to – as we pursued our blind and guessing and crawling way. We had a small supper at Northampton, and the fog lifted as we left the city; from there on it was grand driving.

We got to Williams about 10:00 pm for the last part of the William Z. Foster [President of the U.S. Communist Party] lecture and questions.

It was a very odd sensation, leaving town on Thursday, everything normal, not much rush having started, even among those of us who were working for the Conference, and arriving home again the next day to find almost 200 visitors from other colleges, and the whole atmosphere of Williamstown a different thing. Also it was a rare experience to meet Arthur Fletcher [U/Penn] and Harriet Fleischl [Vassar] and Florence Smith and Mary Losey [Wellesley] and Margaret Scott [Smith] and a few other Geneva [summer 1931] people – all in the lobby of Chapin Hall.

The Commons Club held a reception after the lecture. Will Hurst and Warner Wick and Wally Parks and Harry Sellery met the 3 Wellesley girls I had under my wing [Florence and the two Marys], we all talked until midnight, then went downtown to eat until 1:00 am. Mary and I had a "late date," then I came home and talked with Arthur Fletcher for over an hour – he stayed in my study [in the Sig House].

Saturday morning, I was in charge of the session from 9:00–10:00 am. Maynard Krueger, Arthur's idol, friend, teacher and roommate [U/Penn] – was presenting the case for Socialism. I introduced him. The Hall – Jessup this time – was packed and overflowing. Krueger gave a very good speech – proved Socialism to be an economic necessity – not by going back to Marx or anything like that, but by analyzing economic theory. It was the most scholarly lecture of the program.

Then our North Adams Communist [Spitzer] gave his usual <u>speech-question</u>, taking 12 minutes to rebut the lecture. It was interesting, so I let him go on – but had to ask him to "bring his 'question' to a head" which silenced him amid chuckles.

After a few more questions, I spied Norman Thomas in the back – who had arrived, late, from Providence. I saw he had a question to ask, so stood up and, instead of letting Krueger acknowledge the [Spitzer] question, said "Mr. Norman Thomas" – it was a dramatic gesture – and worked – for no-one knew he was in town yet; you could fairly feel the thrill that ran thru the audience. He spoke for 5 or 10 minutes, was answered by Spitzer – the Communist – and a 3-cornered debate developed among them and Krueger. It was very exciting. I never felt such intense interest or high excitement in that Hall, everyone in the balcony was standing up, crowding to the front, etc. I had my hands full quieting Spitzer at times, and bringing the thing to a close.

At 11:00 am, Flumiani spoke [for Italian Fascism]. Harry Sellery was Chairman. Flumiani was a marvelous orator, fiery, positive, etc. – but in contrast his speech was not profound; however, it fit into the general atmosphere of the session. Then to lunch for all delegates, at the Commons Club. At 2:00 pm the various Round-tables began. Mary Losey was in Jacob Viner's, with Arthur Fletcher as Chairman and Will Hurst as Secretary. Florence Smith was Chairman of Krueger's. Mary Lyman was in Spitzer's Round-table which met in the Chi Psi Lodge. I was Secretary of Norman Thomas's Round-table – and took notes furiously for 2 hours. Harriet Fleischl was Chairman of another.

Then came the Russian movie – "The Five Year Plan." We had allowed for the cost of it in our budget – $70 – and decided to allow outsiders to attend for 50 cents. It was outstanding, every seat in Walden Theatre was full (500 seats) and 15 standing; we made about $200, by complete surprise. The Conference atmosphere was beginning to pervade Williamstown.

Then a banquet dinner at the Commons Club for all delegates. I presided – with Norman Thomas sitting on my right, Flumiani across from me, and Mary Losey on my left. Thomas is the most inspiring and stimulating person I've ever met. It was thrilling at one point, when Flumiani asked: "Mr. Thomas, who do you think will run for Socialist candidate for the Presidency this year" and Thomas replied: "we haven't had our Convention yet, but I probably will run." Of course we all knew that – but it's different to sit next to a man who calmly announces that he will probably run for the Presidency of the U.S.

Then the debate between Thomas and Viner, in Chapin, with about 600–700 people present. Thomas gave his first public speech – for an hour – and practically had the roof jumping off when he finished; then a half-hour rebuttal [by Viner], and then 2 short rebuttals by each man. I didn't like Viner – he has practically no philosophy except pessimism and nihilism. Perhaps that is the logical end of Capitalist philosophy!

Afterwards there was a Victrola dance at the Commons Club, and we talked; and Harriet and Arthur and Mary and I talked, over here at the Sig House till very late, then Arthur and I talked till later.

I had breakfast with the 3 [Wellesley] girls before they left Sunday morning – then slept thru the Chapel service.

The Conference was a spectacular success. Williamstown has never seen such a performance before.

And Pres. Garfield has said that it was the biggest and best thing done by any undergraduate group in his 30 years as President.

The stock of the Liberal Club is very high, at present.

Last night [Sunday], Sir Norman Angell spoke on <u>Disarmament</u> – giving the most <u>brilliant</u> lecture the Williams Forum has had in way over a year. It was a fitting climax to the week. To-night [Monday] is The Beggar's Opera [done by an English company, sponsored by the Williams Little Theater].